ROUTLEDGE LIBRARY EDITIONS:
DISCOURSE ANALYSIS

Volume 4

DISCOURSE-PRAGMATICS AND THE VERB

DISCOURSE-PRAGMATICS AND THE VERB

The Evidence from Romance

Edited by
SUZANNE FLEISCHMAN AND
LINDA R. WAUGH

LONDON AND NEW YORK

First published in 1991 by Routledge

This edition first published in 2017
by Routledge
2 Park Square, Milton Park, Abingdon, Oxon OX14 4RN

and by Routledge
711 Third Avenue, New York, NY 10017

Routledge is an imprint of the Taylor & Francis Group, an informa business

© 1991 Suzanne Fleischman and Linda R. Waugh

All rights reserved. No part of this book may be reprinted or reproduced or utilised in any form or by any electronic, mechanical, or other means, now known or hereafter invented, including photocopying and recording, or in any information storage or retrieval system, without permission in writing from the publishers.

Trademark notice: Product or corporate names may be trademarks or registered trademarks, and are used only for identification and explanation without intent to infringe.

British Library Cataloguing in Publication Data
A catalogue record for this book is available from the British Library

ISBN: 978-1-138-22094-2 (Set)
ISBN: 978-1-315-40146-1 (Set) (ebk)
ISBN: 978-1-138-22378-3 (Volume 4) (hbk)
ISBN: 978-1-138-22390-5 (Volume 4) (pbk)
ISBN: 978-1-315-40358-8 (Volume 4) (ebk)

Publisher's Note
The publisher has gone to great lengths to ensure the quality of this reprint but points out that some imperfections in the original copies may be apparent.

Disclaimer
The publisher has made every effort to trace copyright holders and would welcome correspondence from those they have been unable to trace.

Discourse-Pragmatics and the Verb

The Evidence from Romance

Edited by Suzanne Fleischman and Linda R. Waugh

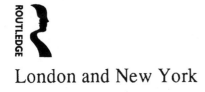

London and New York

First published 1991
by Routledge
11 New Fetter Lane, London EC4P 4EE

Simultaneously published in the USA and Canada
by Routledge
a division of Routledge, Chapman and Hall, Inc.
29 West 35th Street, New York, NY 10001

© 1991 Suzanne Fleischman and Linda R. Waugh

Typeset in 10/12pt Times by
Ponting-Green Publishing Services, London
Printed in Great Britain by
T J Press (Padstow) Ltd, Padstow, Cornwall

All rights reserved. No part of this book may be reprinted or reproduced or utilized in any form or by any electronic, mechanical, or other means, now known or hereafter invented, including photocopying and recording, or in any information storage or retrieval system, without permission in writing from the publishers.

British Library Cataloguing in Publication Data
Discourse-pragmatics and the verb : the evidence
   from Romance. – (Romance linguistics).
   1. Romance languages. Verbs
   I. Fleischman, Suzanne II. Waugh, Linda R. III. Series
   445

Library of Congress Cataloging in Publication Data
Discourse-pragmatica and the verb : the evidence from
   romance/ edited by Suzanne Fleischman and Linda R. Waugh.
          p.   cm. – (Romance linguistics)
   Includes bibliographical references and index.
      1. Romance languages–Verb. 2. Romance languages–
Discourse analysis. 3. Pragmatics. I. Fleischman, Suzanne. II. Waugh,
Linda R. III. Series.
PC145.D57 1991
440–dc20   90-47903

ISBN 0-415-05720-5

Contents

1 Introduction   1
  Suzanne Fleischman and Linda R. Waugh

2 The temporal structure of discourse: setting, change, and perspective   7
  Co Vet

3 Verb tense and point of view in narrative   26
  Suzanne Fleischman

4 Tense switching in Italian: the alternation between *passato prossimo* and *passato remoto* in oral narratives   55
  Giulia Centineo

5 Multivalency: the French historical present in journalistic discourse   86
  Monique Monville-Burston and Linda R. Waugh

6 The status of imperatives as discourse signals   120
  Béatrice Lamiroy and Pierre Swiggers

7 A contextual reconsideration of the Spanish *-ra* "indicative"   147
  Patricia V. Lunn and Thomas D. Cravens

8 Losing ground: a discourse-pragmatic solution to the history of *-ra* in Spanish   164
  Flora Klein-Andreu

9 The pragmatics of Spanish mood in complements of knowledge and acquisition-of-knowledge predicates   179
  Jorge M. Guitart

10 Verbs of cognition in spoken Spanish: A discourse profile   194
    Elizabeth G. Weber and Paola Bentivoglio

    Index of subjects   214
    Index of names   218

1 Introduction

Suzanne Fleischman and Linda R. Waugh

Over the last two decades a growing number of linguists have come to acknowledge the need to look at various linguistic phenomena, particularly morphological and syntactic phenomena, from the viewpoint of their functional motivation in actual human communication, in real discourses and texts – in preference, that is, to concentrating exclusively on the formal algorithmic properties of syntax, and considering in isolation often implausible sentences that can be contextualized only with great difficulty. In particular, there is increasing recognition that whatever intrinsic meaning grammatical categories may have, pragmatic factors and discourse context play a crucial role in the interpretation of their meaning. We understand pragmatics here, as most linguists and philosophers of language do, to refer to the use of language in actual contexts of communication, that is to the ways in which speakers – or writers – manipulate the resources of their language to accomplish particular communicative objectives. This view of discourse-pragmatics subsumes a variety of different notions having to do with structuring information (e.g. the encoding of topic-focus relations, foreground-background, assertion, and presupposition), creating textual cohesion and connectivity, establishing discoursal point of view, expressing speaker attitudes in discourse, and conveying information pertinent to the relations between speech-act participants and the text. Such a view implies, then, that grammatical categories, properties of the text, and characteristics of the context (in particular the speech-act context) are inextricably interwoven, and thus collectively provide the appropriate foundation for a general and explanatory functional analysis of the categories in question.

Grammatical categories associated with the verb, such as tense, aspect, mood, or voice, have served as an important arena for demonstrating the relevance of discourse-pragmatic approaches to grammar (see, for example, the pertinent contributions in Givón 1979; Hopper

1982; Hopper and Thompson 1982; Klein-Andreu 1983.) Though the Romance languages have been a significant testing ground (e.g. as evidenced in several papers in Vincent and Harris 1982), they have also been used to demonstrate more formal approaches to categories of the verb (see the Romance-based studies in Tedeschi and Zaenen 1981 and Lo Cascio and Vet 1986). The present volume is intended as a further contribution to the ongoing dialogue on the verb and its grammar, and one which seeks specifically to underscore, with reference to the major Romance languages (French, Spanish, Italian), the extent to which discourse-pragmatic considerations are crucial in the process of our coming to understand the work that verbal categories do in actual language use, work that clearly transcends what we normally think of as their basic grammatical functions.

The studies in this volume have been grouped according to their focus – in terms of the particular verbal category they treat and the language(s) at issue.

The first four chapters each deal with questions involving the interpretation of tense-aspect categories in relation to their discourse-pragmatic contextualization.

Co Vet examines problems in the interpretation of texts involving the perfective (*passé simple*) and imperfective (*imparfait*) past tenses in French. He argues that an analysis of tense which makes use of the notions of "setting" (a period in the past or an object or event located therein which functions to provide temporal reference), "change" (of setting), and "perspective" (consideration of the point of view from which the setting or change of setting is perceived), is capable of solving certain problems that cannot be resolved by positing an anaphoric relation between sentences in which the perfective and imperfective occur. Analyses of the latter type assume that sentences in the simple past introduce temporal antecedents or a temporal reference point for states of affairs reported by sentences in the imperfect. Vet shows that the "overt" tense markers and adverbials of a text must be supplemented by information conveyed by the *Aktionsart* of the sentence and/or by purely pragmatic factors. His analysis also provides a fine-grained semantic base for research on the discourse functions of tense/aspect which posits a continuum from foreground to background.

The next two chapters, by Suzanne Fleischman and Giulia Centineo, both deal with pragmatic functions of tense – and specifically of tense alternation – in several varieties of Romance narrative discourse. Fleischman's chapter looks at tense as a marker of point of view, and at how tense alternations operate to discriminate the different "focalizations" or perspectival filters through which a story-world is presented. Using data drawn from French, Spanish, and Italian narrative fiction, she considers such phenomena as free indirect discourse and interior monologue in terms of the tenses that mark these varieties of discourse off from the narrations into which they are embedded, the tense shifts enabling subtle transitions into and out of the minds of story participants. Though the focus of this chapter is on literary narration, Fleischman points to the existence of similar discourse strategies in natural narration in an attempt to narrow the gap many investigators perceive between poetic discourse and natural language.

Giulia Centineo's chapter takes as its point of departure the failure of extant grammatical descriptions of Italian to account adequately for the contrast in narrative discourse between the two perfective tenses of the past system: the compound past (*passato prossimo*) and the simple past (*passato remoto*). The explanations traditionally offered – dialect differences or speech vs. writing – fail in particular to account for the contrast in discourse forms where both past tenses can occur and at times co-occur. One such discourse form is "natural" narration. Through this investigation into tense selection – and specifically tense switching – in Italian natural narratives, Centineo seeks to provide a more compelling analysis of the functions of these two past tense categories, and of the historical present, based on a number of grammatical and pragmatic factors involved in the structuring of narrative discourse: clause type, foregrounding, evaluation, and subjectivity vs. objectivity of representation. The various patterns of tense usage identified in Italian narration today are then shown to correlate with diachronic shifts in meaning observed in several varieties of Romance with respect to simple and compound pasts.

In their contribution, Monique Monville-Burston and Linda Waugh study the French present tense, which they characterize as a rich communicative device having the potential for two or more simultaneous meanings, given the appropriate context. This semantic multivalency is linked on the one hand to the possibilities inherent in the present as the unmarked tense of the French system and on the other hand to the types of contexts in which it may be used. The authors focus on the historical present in journalistic discourse, which supports and perhaps even favors the proposed multisemanticity, and show that in certain contexts there may be oscillation for a given present tense form between a historical present interpretation and one or more of the other interpretations of present, producing temporal multivalency. Moreover, there are also cases of aspectual multivalency. This coexistence of two (or more) meanings is linked to the nature of journalistic discourse and to specific characteristics of the local context: temporal adverbs, date of the newspaper, nature of titles/leads, lexical meaning of the verb, and the presence of other tenses.

The chapter by Béatrice Lamiroy and Pierre Swiggers claims that some imperative forms of the verb in French, Spanish, and Italian function as discourse signals, since they are connectors rather than commands, and thus serve as linkers between different segments of an utterance and/or between the participants in a communicative exchange. In terms of the authors' typology of discourse signals, these forms are morphologically analyzable and undergo some of the paradigmatic alternation characteristic of the general class of imperatives (e.g. alternation between singular and plural), but they exhibit few of the normal discourse-pragmatic properties of true imperatives. Rather, they have basically a pragmatic function, subsuming a number of morphological, syntactic, and semantic properties which are related to that function. Thus, the authors argue, these verbal forms have undergone functional displacement.

The next two chapters deal with the Spanish verb form in -*ra* (*amara, tuviera*), currently classified as an imperfect subjunctive, but formerly in Spanish, and etymologically in Latin, a pluperfect indicative.

Patricia Lunn and Thomas Cravens' examination of the use of -*ra* in journalistic texts provides motivation for the current classification of the -*ra* form as a bona fide subjunctive within a unified description of mood choice in Spanish centered on the notion of "discourse relevance." Departing from the traditional view linking the use of the subjunctive with the reality status of events (i.e. correlation with irrealis), they argue that the subjunctive marks information that a speaker takes to be of lesser relevance to the addressee, i.e. information that has lower priority, or is backgrounded, in the discourse. This characterization then provides the descriptive framework for a reappraisal of the traditional understanding of the -*ra* form's functions in the earliest Spanish texts, and demonstrates that the usage condemned by the Real Academia is solidly motivated on pragmatic grounds and in fact has a long history.

Flora Klein-Andreu looks at the -*ra* form along similar lines of discourse saliency, focusing on its development from pluperfect indicative to imperfect subjunctive. Taking issue with accounts which give primary importance to the -*ra* form's early role in the apodosis of conditional sentences, which led eventually to its usage in the protasis and thence to its current function for non-assertive reference, she claims that the shift in meaning was motivated by the competition between it and the new periphrastic pluperfect (*habia amado*). By examining examples from the period when the new and old pluperfect indicatives were both still used, she contrasts their functions in terms of the relative "focus of attention" the speaker wishes to place on an event (high vs. low focus).

The last two chapters in this volume treat complementation in Spanish, one continuing the discussion of mood, the other focused in particular on transitivity.

Jorge Guitart presents a pragmatic analysis of the selection of indicative vs. subjunctive mood in Spanish in the complements of two predicate types: "knowledge" and "acquisition-of-knowledge" predicates (e.g. *saber, darse cuenta*, and *notar, descubrir* respectively). His treatment differs significantly from both traditional accounts and from certain current analyses, particularly from the theory of mood selection based on semantically grounded notions of assertion and presupposition. Arguing that there are no invariable correlations between semantic notions like presupposition and the use of one or the other mood, he distinguishes semantic presupposition, which is independent of speaker and hearer relationships, from pragmatic presupposition, which is equivalent to an assumption on the part of the speaker that the information in the sentential complement is shared by the hearer – and uses the latter as a crucial basis for his analysis. Moreover, he provides a pragmatic explanation for certain phenomena observed in the syntax of Spanish negation.

The chapter by Elizabeth Weber and Paola Bentivoglio presents a discourse profile of two verbs of cognition in Spanish, *creer* "believe" and *pensar* "think," through an examination of the syntactic variation exhibited by clauses in which these verbs occur. The syntactic properties characteristic of the class of cognition verbs (transitivity, complement type, tense-aspect, lexical choice, intonation contours, and relative ordering of main and subordinate clauses) are specifically related to the syntagmatic patterns associated with these verbs in actual discourse. Inspired by recent work arguing for the discourse origins of grammatical phenomena, this chapter seeks to explain the emergence of the syntactic patterns identified in terms of the demands which discourse use places on these verbs.

While the chapters in this volume have in common a general commitment to a more contextualized treatment of grammatical meaning, as may be inferred from the characterizations just given, they do not all operate with a uniform approach to discourse-pragmatics. Nevertheless, there are various notions that recur in several of the chapters, such as: the pragmatic functions of tense switching (Fleischman, Centineo, Monville-Burston and Waugh); the use of verbal categories for signaling discourse saliency, i.e. the marking of textual foreground and background (Vet, Centineo, Lunn and Cravens, Klein-Andreu), for showing point of view (Fleischman, Vet), and for conveying irony (Guitart, Lunn and Cravens); the pragmatic determinants of language change (Lamiroy and Swiggers, Lunn and Cravens, Klein-Andreu, Weber and Bentivoglio); the interrelation of system, i.e. paradigmatic comparison, and use, i.e. contextualization (Monville-Burston and Waugh, Lamiroy and Swiggers, Klein-Andreu); and the pragmatic functions of the lexical meanings of verbs (Vet, Monville-Burston and Waugh, Lamiroy and Swiggers, Weber and Bentivoglio).

It is the recurrence of these and other themes, as well as the insights they offer into the functions and uses of grammatical categories associated with the verb, which will, we hope, induce those interested in the analysis of verbal categories – from whatever perspective – to explore further the contribution of discourse-pragmatic approaches.

We would like to thank the editors of this series, Nigel Vincent and Martin Harris, for their support of this project.

(Copyright information: A revised version of Suzanne Fleischman's chapter appears in chapter 7 of her book *Tense and Narrativity*, London: Routledge, 1990.)

REFERENCES

Givón, Talmy (ed.) (1979) *Syntax and Semantics*, vol. 12 *Discourse and Syntax*, New York: Academic Press.

Hopper, Paul (ed.) (1982) *Tense-Aspect: Between Semantics and Pragmatics*, Amsterdam: John Benjamins.

Hopper, Paul and Thompson, Sandra (eds) (1982) *Syntax and Semantics*, vol. 15 *Studies in Transitivity*, New York: Academic Press.

Klein-Andreu, Flora (ed.) (1983) *Discourse Perspectives on Syntax*, New York: Academic Press.

Lo Cascio, Vincenzo and Vet, Co (eds) (1986) *Temporal Structure in Sentence and Discourse*, Dordrecht: Foris.

Tedeschi, Philip and Zaenen, Annie (eds) (1981) *Syntax and Semantics*, vol. 14 *Tense and Aspect*, New York: Academic Press.

Vincent, Nigel and Harris, Martin (eds) (1982) *Studies in the Romance Verb*, London: Croom Helm.

2 The temporal structure of discourse: setting, change, and perspective

Co Vet

1. INTRODUCTION[1]

The function of tense and aspect in narrative texts has given rise to an extensive literature in which two main lines of thought can be distinguished. The first makes use of a spatial metaphor to describe the temporal structure of (narrative) texts: "foreground" versus "background" or "figure" versus "ground" (Weinrich 1973; Hopper 1982; Fleischman 1985; and, for a survey of the question, Waugh and Monville-Burston 1986). In this approach the discourse function of the perfective aspect, the simple past in Romance languages, is to indicate which events belong to the main plot-line of the story (the foreground or figure). Sentences with imperfective aspect, the imperfective past, serve to describe states of affairs which constitute the background of the story (they give information about the setting in which the story takes place, contain comments, etc.).

The second approach sees the relation between the two types of states of affairs described by the sentences of a text as being anaphoric (Partee 1973, 1984; Kamp 1981, 1984; Kamp and Rohrer 1983; Hinrichs 1981; Vet and Molendijk 1986). Roughly speaking, sentences in the simple past (the *passé simple* in French, for example) introduce temporal antecedents for the states of affairs reported by sentences in the *imparfait* (Kamp 1981), or introduce a reference point to which the state of affairs described by the *imparfait* sentence has to be attached (Kamp and Rohrer 1983).

Both the foregrounding/backgrounding and the anaphora approach offer interesting and intuitively satisfactory insights into the way the imperfective and perfective aspects or tenses function in narrative discourse. However, both also meet with serious problems. The foregrounding/backgrounding approach runs the risk of circularity: very often the only formal clue for deciding whether a state of affairs belongs to the foreground or background of the story is precisely the presence in the sentence of one of the two aspect markers or tense forms. It has been shown, too, that the notions of foreground/background are too narrow (Waugh and Monville-Burston 1986) or that there is not a clearcut dichotomy but rather a continuum between the two levels (Fleischman 1985).

The anaphora approach meets with quite different problems. For example, there is no complete parallelism between nominal and temporal anaphora; with nominal anaphora the antecedent and the anaphoric element denote the same individual. This is rather exceptional with temporal anaphora. Most often the "anaphoric element" coincides here only partially with its temporal antecedent, but examples where the anaphoric element is posterior or even anterior to it are also relatively frequent. Criteria which are capable of predicting the right relationships are difficult to formulate in this approach.

In this chapter a proposal will be formulated which is capable of solving the problems encountered by the anaphora approach. It will be shown that the "overt" tense markers and adverbials of a text do not provide the hearer/reader with sufficient information for a correct interpretation and that it has to be completed by information conveyed by the *Aktionsart* of the sentences and/or by purely pragmatic factors. The general idea is that all the temporal and aspectual information (overt and covert) is used for two purposes: either to construct "settings" or to modify these settings.

It will also be shown that it is sometimes necessary to take into account "perspective." In some of the fragments analyzed in this chapter it is important to know who perceives the (modification of the) setting.

The chapter is structured as follows. In section 2 I will give an outline of the anaphora theory proposed by Partee (1973), Kamp (1981, 1984) and Kamp and Rohrer (1983), and discuss some of its main problems. In section 3 the role of the "temporal theme" (Ducrot 1983) and *Aktionsart* will be discussed. In section 4 the distinction between settings and change will be given a more precise formulation and a number of illustrative fragments will be analyzed by means of these notions. In section 5 it will be shown how this approach can solve the problems of the anaphora approach, and in the final section the role of "perspective" will be briefly examined.

2. ANAPHORIC TEMPORAL RELATIONS

To my knowledge Partee (1973) contains the first attempt to draw a parallel between nominal and temporal anaphora. For example, in both (1) and (2), the underlined parts have to be regarded as anaphoric: the event *got drunk* of (2) has to be interpreted as taking place at the time of the party; it refers back to a temporal antecedent in the preceding sentence just as *it* refers back to *the car* (in 1):

(1) Sam took the car yesterday and Sheila took *it* today.
(2) Sheila had a party last night and Sam *got drunk*.

Partee shows that there are parallel cases of deictic and bound temporal anaphora as well.

Kamp (1979, 1981, 1984) offers an elaborate proposal for the treatment of pronouns in the so-called donkey sentences (*If Pedro owns a donkey he beats it*) and of the French *imparfait* [Imp] and *passé simple* [PS]. I will indicate here how the latter two are handled in this framework. Kamp regards the tenses as giving instructions about the way in which the temporal relations between the states of affairs have to be interpreted. These relations are first represented in a discourse representation structure (DRS) of a text and next the DRS is interpreted in a model. The idea is that the Imp and the PS introduce entities of different natures into the DRS, namely "states" and "events." See the following example (from Kamp (1981)):

(3) Pedro entra [PS] dans la cuisine. Marie faisait [Imp] la vaisselle. Il passa [PS] au salon et alluma [PS] sa pipe.
"Pedro entered the kitchen. Marie was washing the dishes. He went to the living room and lit his pipe."

This means that the PS of the first sentence introduces an event into the DRS, $e1$, and establishes the relation $e1 < n$ ($e1$ is anterior to the speech point (n)). The Imp of the second sentence gives the instruction to introduce a state into the DRS, $s1$, and to look in the preceding part of the DRS for an event with which an overlapping relation has to be established. In the fragment of (3) the event to be found is $e1$, so that the relation "$e1$ O $s1$" can be represented in the DRS (where "O" stands for the overlapping relation). The PS of the third sentence introduces a second event into the DRS, $e2$, and the rules prescribe now that a posteriority relation has to be established between this $e2$ and the event which was last introduced into the DRS (in our case $e1$), so that $e2 > e1$ (or, equivalently, $e1 < e2$) (where $>$ stands for "posterior to" and $<$ for "anterior to"). The rules for the PS stipulate further that the relation $e2 < n$ is introduced into the DRS. For the fourth sentence the same rules apply, which gives rise to the introduction of event e3 and the relations: $e2 < e3$ and $e3 < n$. The DRS for (3) now contains the correct representation of the temporal relations holding between the events and the state of that fragment.

The interesting point in Kamp's approach is that his rules are capable of taking into account the context in which a sentence occurs. Moreover, the rules for the treatment of the Imp show a striking parallelism with the rules for the treatment of pronouns, in that in both cases an antecedent has to be looked for in the preceding DRS. The states introduced by Imp sentences always have to be related to a preceding event which functions as its temporal antecedent.

Kamp and Rohrer (1983) offer a slightly different view: the notion of reference point that remains implicit in Kamp (1981, 1984) is now explicitly taken into account in the analysis. The general principle is that, after a sentence is processed and the result is introduced into the DRS, a particular time or event is marked as the reference point. If the sentence is in the PS the event it introduces into the DRS normally becomes the new reference point. For the fragments of (4) and (6) this leads to the representations (5) and (7) respectively.

(4) Pierre entra [PS] (e1). Marie téléphona [PS] (e2).

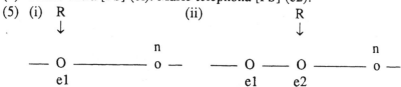

(6) Pierre entra [PS] (e1). Marie téléphonait [Imp] (s1).

(7)
```
        R
        ↓                                    n
─── O ─────────────────────────────── o ───
       e1
        \............../
           s1
```

In the fragment of (5) the introduction of a new event leads to the moving forward of the reference point. This is not the case in (7), where the state is attached to the existing reference point (introduced by the event e1). So, here it is the reference point which serves as the antecedent for the state.

The reference point is particularly important in texts where there is a tense switch of a more complicated character than in the texts that will be considered in this chapter. I refer to Kamp and Rohrer

(1983) for more details about the way in which the reference point is assigned to events or times.

I will now indicate some difficulties of the anaphora approach. The first problem has no direct bearing on the anaphoric relations. It concerns Kamp's thesis that the "*passé simple* indicates that the reported event is to be viewed as punctual, or temporally undivided" (1979: 401), i.e. as an atomic entity which cannot be split up into smaller parts. Kamp and Rohrer (1983: 260–1) recognize that this assumption is probably too strong. They give, among others, the following counter-example:

(8) L'année dernière Jean escalada [PS] le Cervin. Le premier jour il monta [PS] jusqu' à la cabane H. Il y passa [PS] la nuit. Ensuite il attaqua [PS] la face nord. Douze heures plus tard il arriva [PS] au sommet.
"Last year Jean climbed the Cervin. The first day he climbed to cabin H. He spent the night there. Next he attacked the north face. Twelve hours later he arrived at the top."

One could argue that in this example the splitting up of the first event is facilitated by the time adverbials of the subsequent sentences. Molendijk (1987) and Vet and Molendijk (1986), however, give examples without adverbs in which an event turns out to be divisible:

(9) Jean monta [PS] dans sa chambre. Pierre le suivit [PS].
"Jean went up to his room. Pierre followed him."
(10) Nadine s'assit [PS] et lut [PS] la lettre. Elle fut [PS] étonnée de constater que la lettre la touchait [Imp] beaucoup.
"Nadine sat down and read the letter. She was surprised to notice that the letter touched her very much."

In both examples there is an event that lies or starts within the preceding event. In the normal interpretation of (9), Pierre starts following Jean before the latter has reached his room. In (10) Nadine notices her emotion while she is reading the letter, not after she has finished.

This means that Kamp's rules for the treatment of events do not lead automatically to the correct interpretation: events do not always follow each other in time. We will return to this problem in section 5.

The following problems concern the nature of the anaphoric relation itself. As I have just remarked, there are cases in which the state described by an Imp sentence is posterior to the event described by the preceding PS sentence:

(11) Jean alluma [PS] une cigarette (e1). La fièvre donnait [Imp] au

tabac un goût de miel (s1). (Molendijk 1987)
"Jean lit a cigarette. His fever gave the tobacco a taste of honey."

It is evident that Kamp's rules would lead to an incorrect interpretation of this fragment, since they predict that the event e1 and the state s1 overlap.

Hinrichs (1981: 61) tries to solve this problem by formulating the following rule for the English simple past: if the event of the first simple past sentence is an accomplishment or an achievement (in the Vendler (1967) classification), then the reference point is not the event itself but a moment after the event. This leads to a correct interpretation of fragments such as (12):

(12) Jameson entered the room, shut the door carefully and switched off the light. It was pitch dark around him, because the Venetian blinds were closed. (Hinrichs 1981: 66)

Here it is certain that the state "be pitch dark" does not overlap the switching-off event. However, it is not difficult to find counter-examples to this rule:

(13) A midi M. de Villeneuve entra [PS] (e1). Nous étions [Imp] dans la salon (s1) et y formions [Imp] un tableau très agréable (s2).
"At noon Mr de Villeneuve entered. We were in the living room and made a very pretty picture there."

In this example we have an accomplishment in the first sentence but the reference point is not posterior to the event since both s1 and s2 (partially) coincide with the event (e1). It is not evident what kind of criteria may be used in Kamp's or Hinrichs' framework to distinguish between (12) and (13).

A less frequent case is that in which the state precedes the event as in (14):

(14) Je déchirai [PS] l'emballage en plastique qui recouvrait [Imp] le jeu.
"I tore open the plastic wrapper which covered the game."

Although the state is reported by a relative clause, it nevertheless constitutes a difficulty for the anaphora hypothesis since there is no event which can function as its antecedent. If a Hinrichs-style rule were formulated which placed the reference point/antecedent anterior to the event of the main clause, this would lead to the same paradox as that met with in (12) and (13). Such a rule would indeed lead to an incorrect interpretation of sentences such as (15), in which the event of the main clause and the state of the relative clause overlap:

(15) Le général attaqua [PS] l'ennemi qui se retirait [Imp].
"The general attacked the enemy that was withdrawing."

Finally, a fundamental problem for this analysis is that a story normally begins with one or more sentences in the Imp, while the first sentences of the PS occur only later in the text. This is the canonical way of starting fairy-tales, and also other narrative texts; for example:

(16) La petite marquise de Rennedon dormait [Imp] encore, dans sa chambre close et parfumée, dans son grand lit doux et bas ...; elle dormait [Imp] seule, tranquille, de l'heureux et profond sommeil des divorcées. (Beginning of G. de Maupassant, "Le Signe")
"The little Marquise de Rennedon was still sleeping, in her closed, perfumed bedroom, in her big, low, soft bed ...; alone and quiet, she was sleeping the happy and deep sleep of divorced women."

In the anaphoric approach this seems to be an anomaly, since one would not expect that an anaphoric tense would be systematically used before its antecedent shows up, sometimes much later, in the text.[2]

These difficulties suggest that, although the anaphora approach has been a stimulating way of stating the problem, there is nevertheless something fundamentally wrong with it. Considering the nature of the counter-examples mentioned above (see (8)–(15)), one may indeed pose the question whether the term "anaphora," instead of illuminating the problem, might not obscure a more realistic approach. The analogy between temporal and nominal anaphora is indeed far from being regular and it seems necessary to treat the two phenomena in separate ways.

I will attempt to give an alternative analysis of the difficulties posed by the anaphoric approach, but will first define, in the next section, some of the notions which are needed for my analysis, namely "temporal theme" and "transitional" and "non-transitional" events.

3. THEME AND TRANSITION

3.1. Temporal theme

In Ducrot (1983) a description of the Imp is proposed which at first sight has much in common with Kamp's and Kamp and Rohrer's anaphora approach. For his description of the function of the Imp he uses the notions of *theme* (topic), *propos* (comment), and property. According to Ducrot, a sentence in the Imp forms the comment of a temporal topic. This may be a period in the past or an object or an event considered within a past period. The Imp sentence qualifies the whole topic, not just part of it. To illustrate this point he compares sentences such as:

(17) a. L'année dernière à Paris il a fait [PC] chaud (à savoir au mois de mai) [PC: *passé composé*, "perfective past"].
"Last year in Paris it was hot (namely in May)."
b. L'année dernière à Paris il faisait [Imp] chaud (* à savoir au mois de mai).
"Last year it was hot in Paris (* namely in May)."

In (17a) the *passé composé* isolates an interval within the topic indicated by the adverbial (*l'année dernière à Paris*); this is not possible with the Imp, where the topic as a whole is qualified. According to Ducrot the same kind of difference is found in the following examples:

(18) a. Pierre a volé.
"Pierre has stolen/stole."
b. Pierre est un voleur.
"Pierre is a thief."

In (18a) only some stage in Pierre's life is described. In (18b) the person Pierre as a whole is characterized by the predicate.

In the rest of this chapter I will follow Ducrot in his general view of the Imp, and especially the point illustrated by (17a) and (17b), which show clearly that some tenses are capable of breaking into the topic, the PC and the PS, while others are not (the Imp). In order to generalize the description, I will introduce the term "spatio-temporal setting" to designate the entity referred to by Ducrot's topic. It will be shown that sentences can describe such a setting even if there is no overt mention of it. In this sense, the presence of a topic is a marked case. It seems to me that the topic is used if the setting which is talked about is not already known or if one wants to change the setting (this is clearly the case in example (8)).

3.2. The role of *Aktionsart*

In Vet (1980: 62f.), it is argued that states of affairs can be classified according to the feature [± transitional]. Intuitively, there are sentences that report states of affairs in which no change occurs, for example *être malade* in:

(19) Pierre semble être malade.
"Pierre seems to be ill."

Here the state of affairs *être malade* may continue indefinitely without there being a "natural" result to which the state of affairs will lead sooner or later. The sentences referring to this type of state of affairs will be given the feature [− transitional]. One of the tests which can be used to decide whether or not a sentence is [− transitional] is its compatibility with the adverbial *pendant* ("during," "for") [+ duration] (see also Verkuyl 1972):

(20) Pierre a été malade pendant deux jours.
"Pierre was ill for two days."
(21) *Pierre est tombé malade pendant deux jours."
"Pierre fell ill for two days."

The asterisk in (21) means here that the reading in which the sentence refers to only one state of affairs is excluded.

The other category of sentences refers to states of affairs which sooner or later have to arrive at a final point; in other words, if they are not interrupted, they lead to some result which closes the event. For example:

(22) Jeanne a descendu l'escalier.
"Jeanne went down the stairs."

Here, as in (21), the adjunction of the adverbial *pendant* [+ duration] gives rise to an iterative reading. The transitional sentences are, however, compatible with *en* [+ duration] (*en deux heures* "in two hours"), whereas the non-transitional sentences are not. In Vet (1980) it is shown that transitional sentences carry both a presupposition, of a state preceding and overlapping the event, and an implication, of a state posterior to the event. The schema for transitional events (illustrated by the example of (22)) is as shown in example (23).

(23)   presupposition   implication
    ─────────────────────────────/─────────────────────────
                         transition
    ──────────────────── ///////////////// ────────────────
    ¬ *descendue* (J)   *descendre* (J, e)   *descendue* (J)
      "gone down"   "go down"   "gone down"
       (where ¬: negation;   J: *Jeanne*;   e: *l'escalier*)

Before Jeanne starts going down the stairs it is presupposed that she has not yet gone down them, and as long as she is going down the stairs this presupposition holds, until she has reached the bottom;

at that moment the implication takes effect. Non-transitional states of affairs are not accompanied by this kind of presupposition and implication.

The function of the Imp seems to be that it enables the speaker to present a transitional event as being non-transitional. See example (24):

(24) Jeanne descendait l'escalier.
"Jeanne was going down the stairs."

Here only the presupposition holds, the implication does not.

In the opposite case, a non-transitional sentence in the PS may become event-like (see Vikner 1985: 105), for example:

(25) Peu après, il sut [PS] la réponse.
"A little later, he knew (= he found out) the answer."

Here there is a transition from not knowing to knowing the answer. However, not all non-transitional sentences become transitional when they occur in the PS. Consider for example:

(26) Jeanne regarda le tableau.
"Jeanne looked at the painting."

This sentence carries only the implication that Jeanne did not look at the painting immediately before or after the event. There is no change, the situation which follows the event is identical to that which precedes it.

In the next section I will show how the notions of (spatio-temporal) setting and the features [− transitional] and [+ transitional] may be used for the analysis of narration in French.

4. SETTING AND CHANGE

In this section I will propose a more fine-grained analysis of narrative texts with the help of the notions defined in the preceding section. Consider for example the following fragment, which is the beginning of a version of the fairy-tale of Snow White:

(27) Il neigeait [Imp] (s1). Les flocons tourbillonnaient [Imp] comme des papillons blancs (s2). Si joli était [Imp] le spectacle (s3) que la reine, pour mieux le voir, se pencha [PS] à la fenêtre (e1).
"It was snowing. The flakes were swirling like white butterflies. The sight was so beautiful that, in order to see it better, the queen leaned out of the window."

Even without an overt topic adverbial, the first sentence is easily understood as indicating that at a certain place and at a certain time in the past it was snowing. In what follows I will use the term "space-time region" to indicate such a combination of a place and an interval (cf. Bartsch 1986). Thus the first Imp sentence of (27) describes the first space-time region, r1, of this story. The second and third Imp sentences of (27) give more information about the same space-time region. I will use the term "setting" to indicate the space-time region together with the states which hold in it. Thus for (27) the setting (S1) can be represented as follows:

(28) SETTING S1 :<<r1 < n>, <r1, s1>, <r1, s2>, <r1, s2>> where r1 < n: r1 is anterior to the speech point; <r1, s1>: the state s1 (*il neige*) is true in r1, etc.[3]

Let us now examine what happens to S1 once we arrive at the PS sentence of the fragment. The sentence has the feature [+ transitional] so that we have here the structure shown in example (29) (cf. (23)).

(29)
$$
\begin{array}{cc}
s' & s'' \\
\hline
\neg penchée\ (r) \quad\quad\quad \setminus/ \quad\quad penchée\ (r) \\
\text{"leaned out"} \quad\quad e1 \quad\quad \text{"leaned out"} \\
\hline\quad\quad\quad\quad ////////////// \quad\quad\quad\quad \\
(S1) \quad\quad se\ pencher\ (r) \quad (S2) \\
\quad\quad \text{"lean out"}
\end{array}
$$

(where r: *la reine*)

It is easy to see that the PS sentence modifies the setting S1 so that after e1 we have a new setting, S2, in which the queen leans out of the window. In other words S2 contains s" (*penchée* (r)), a state which did not belong to S1. But the PS sentence also gives a posteriori information about S1 in that it adds to that setting the information (s') that the queen was not leaning out of the window at that time. The complete representation of (27) is given in (30).

(30)
$$
\begin{array}{ccc}
S1 & & S2 \\
\cdots\cdots\cdots\cdots\cdots\cdots\cdots\cdots/\cdots\cdots\cdots \\
\hline\quad\quad\quad -////////- \quad\quad\quad \\
s1, s2, s3 & e1 & s1, s2, s3 \\
s' & & s''
\end{array}
$$

This schema shows that only one element of setting S1 is modified by the event e1, that is s' which becomes s". The rest of the states pertaining to S1 are not modified. They belong to both S1 and S2. This continuity in the settings of a text guarantees its coherence on that count. The hearer only modifies a given setting if told to do so.

Note that the setting introduced by an adverbial in topic position is not modified by a PS sentence (or a sentence in the PC). This is the case in (17a), repeated here as (31):

(31) L'année dernière à Paris il a fait [PC] chaud (à savoir au mois de mai).
"Last year in Paris it was hot (namely in May)."

The fact that *il a fait chaud* in this example denotes a non-transitional state of affairs is not important here. If it is replaced by a transitional sentence this does not affect the setting (described by *l'année dernière à Paris*) either. Within this general setting, however, the event *il a fait chaud* brings about a change, first from not being hot to being hot and then from being hot to not being hot (cf. (26), where we had the same non-transitional type of state of affairs). The analysis of (31) is as shown in example (32).

(32)
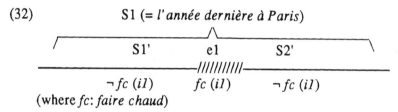
(where *fc*: *faire chaud*)

Here S1', S2' and e1 pertain to the general setting S1. Setting S1' is temporarily modified by e1, which as a non-transitional event does not leave any trace in S2'. Thus S2' is identical to S1'. The fact that the topic introduced by a preposed adverbial is not normally affected by PS sentences implies that more than one event can take place within such a setting. This implies that a topic such as *l'année dernière à Paris* has a wider scope than the sentence in which it occurs. In other words, this kind of adverbial seems to have a discourse function,[4] and the setting it denotes may only be changed by another adverbial with a topical function (cf. (8)).

An interesting point is that an event can also function as a setting. For example:

(33) Jeanne descendit [PS] l'escalier (e1). Elle souriait [Imp] (s1).
"Jeanne went down the stairs. She was smiling."

In this sentence e1 itself constitutes the setting; a part of it is described by the following Imp sentence.

A last point to be mentioned here is that the same analysis can be applied to fragments in which there are no sentences in the Imp at all.

Consider for example the following fragment:

(34) Mon médecin s'essuya [PS] la bouche (e1), se leva [PS] de table (e2) et disparut [PS] dans une autre pièce (e3). Il reparut [PS] avec un short (e4).
"My doctor wiped his mouth, got up from the table and disappeared into another room. He reappeared with (a pair of) shorts on."

The first sentence of this fragment carries the presupposition (prior to e1) that the doctor's mouth was not wiped. This presupposition pertains to the first setting (S1) of this text. The event e1 it describes leads to an implication, namely that his mouth is wiped after e1. This implication belongs to the second setting (S2). In the same way the second sentence carries the presupposition that the doctor was not standing up before e2. This information belongs to both S1 and S2. After e2, we have a new setting (S3) in which his mouth is wiped and the doctor is standing up. The third sentence changes S3 into a new setting S4, in which the doctor has disappeared. The fourth sentence changes S4 into S5, in which the doctor is back again, but his mouth is still wiped and he is still standing up. So this fragment can be represented as follows:

(35)   S1   e1   S2   e2   S3   e3   S4   e4   S5
        ——— /// ——— /// ——— /// ——— /// ———

The coherence of this text is again guaranteed by the continuity in the content of the settings.
In the following section, this analysis will be used to solve the problems encountered by the anaphora approach.

5. A REANALYSIS OF PROBLEMATIC "ANAPHORIC" RELATIONS

In this section I will show how the framework sketched above can be used to solve the problems encountered by the anaphora approach (see section 3). The first sentence I will analyze is (11), repeated here as (36):

(36) Jean alluma [PS] une cigarette (e1). La fièvre donnait [Imp] au tabac un goût de miel (s1).
"Jean lit a cigarette. His fever gave the tobacco a taste of honey."

The first sentence of this fragment refers to a transitional event, which brings about a change from setting S1 in which the cigarette is not lit to a setting in which the cigarette is lit. Since, as we have seen, an event itself can function as a setting (cf. (33)), there are theoretically three settings about which the Imp sentence can give information. These are shown in example (37).

(37)   S1   S1' = e1   S2
    ─────────────────//////////////─────────────────
        ¬ lit (c)   lit (J,c)   lit (c)
    (where c: *cigarette*; J: *Jean*)

State s1 described by the second sentence of (36) cannot belong to S1 since in this setting the cigarette is not yet burning. The same is true for S1', so that the only possible setting to which s1 can belong is S2. S2 contains the information that the cigarette is burning and thus the tobacco can have a taste of honey in that setting. For (12), the analysis is analogous to that given in (37).

The same explanation can be given to (14), repeated here as (38):

(38) Je déchirai [PS] l'emballage en plastique (e1) qui recouvrait [Imp] le jeu (s1).
   "I tore open the plastic wrapper which covered the game."

In this fragment there are again three possible settings about which the Imp sentence of the relative clause can give information. The event e1 is [+ transitional] so that the presupposition it carries (the wrapper has not yet been torn open) pertains to the first setting, S1. The second candidate is e1 itself, and the third setting, which is posterior to e1, is the last, shown in example (39).

(39)   S1   S1' = e1   S2
    ─────────────────///////////////─────────────────
     ¬ *déchiré* (e)   *déchirer* (j,e)   *déchiré* (e)
       "torn open"   "tear open"   "torn open"
    (where j: *je*; e: *l'emballage en plastique*)

This analysis shows that state s1 described by the Imp sentence of (38) is incompatible with both S1' and S2, since as soon as the *je* starts tearing the wrapper off the game, this wrapper does not cover it any longer. The only setting that is compatible with s1 is S1 (more precisely S1 minus e1), since this is the only setting in which the wrapper is still intact. In (15) (*Le général attaqua l'ennemi qui se retirait*) there are no such incompatibilities and in this case the Imp sentence can give information about S1, S1', and S2. And this seems indeed to be the normal interpretation: that the enemy was already withdrawing before the attack (that is in S1), at the moment of the attack itself (in S1' = e1) and in S2 which is subsequent to e1. This is also the interpretation of sentences such as (3). This fragment has as its normal interpretation that Marie was already washing the dishes before Pierre entered the kitchen and most probably after his entering. The "vagueness" as to the precise location of the state described by the Imp sentence of (3) is caused by its compatibility with S1, e1, and S2.

Let us consider now the cases of (9) and (10) repeated here as (40) and (41):

(40) Jean monta [PS] dans sa chambre (e1). Pierre le suivit [PS] (e2).
"Jean went up to his room. Pierre followed him."
(41) Nadine s'assit [PS] et lut [PS] la lettre (e2). Elle fut [PS] étonnée de constater (e3) que la lettre la touchait [Imp] beaucoup (s1).
"Nadine sat down and read the letter. She was surprised to notice that the letter touched her very much."

In (40) the first event is transitional, so that we have again as possible settings S1, in which Jean is not in his room, S1', in which Jean is going to his room, and S2, in which he has reached his room. We have seen that a PS (or a PC) is capable of breaking into a setting (cf. (17a)). The verb *suivre* ("follow") implies that the person or object which is followed is moving too. This gives the clue for the interpretation of (40), since this fact selects e1 as the only possible setting with which e2 is compatible. This setting is broken into by e2 which selects, as in (17a), a subinterval within it. This last point may provide the explanation for the inchoative reading of e2 ("started to follow Jean"), since a PS sentence cannot characterize the whole topic (or setting), but only part of it.

The second sentence of (41) has the same preferred inchoative reading. The event e3 breaks into the setting which is identical to e2, but only occupies a subinterval of this setting. At that subinterval Nadine starts being astonished (and probably will remain astonished for some time, but this is only an implication). The setting of e2 is the most probable candidate as a setting for e3 since the reading of the letter is the only possible cause for the astonishment mentioned in the sentence. Note that in both (40) and (41) it is a non-transitional event (*suivit, fut étonnée*) that breaks into the preceding event. (I do not know if this is a condition for this type of sentence.) If e3 in (41) is replaced by a transitional event (*elle se leva brusquement* "she got up suddenly," for example) it is interpreted as being subsequent to e2, in spite of the fact that this event may also be caused by the reading of the letter.

Example (8) can be analyzed along the same lines. Here the first sentence contains an adverbial which indicates the general setting. Event e1 breaks into this settting of which it occupies a subregion (cf. (17a)). It constitutes the setting of which the second setting, indicated by *le premier jour* "the first day," occupies a subregion. The event e2 occupies a subregion of *le premier jour*. The rest of the fragment can be analyzed in the same way.

6. PERSPECTIVE

In this section I will briefly discuss a factor which can influence the interpretation of narrative texts. Consider for example the following fragment:

(42) Je dus [PS] baisser la tête (e1) pour entrer dans la chapelle (e2). Les murs étaient [Imp] couverts d'armoires (s1).
"I had to lower my head in order to enter the chapel. There were cabinets all along the walls."

The first sentence carries the implication that the *je* effectively entered the chapel, so that it describes two events (e1 and e2). Since both events are [+ transitional] we have six possible settings about which the Imp sentence can give information. The problem is that s1 is compatible with all these settings. It is certainly true before I lower my head, at e1 itself, after e1, and before, during and after e2. Nevertheless, it is the latter that is selected in the preferred reading of this fragment. This can only be explained if the factor of "perspective" (to be understood as the point of view of an observing individual) is taken into account. The Imp sentence describes what is seen by *je* after e2. The fragment would be somewhat strange if it were known from the context that *je* was blind, for example.

Let us finally consider an example in which the acceptability or at least the interpretability of the fragment depends totally on perspective:

(43) La clef tourna [PS] dans la serrure de la porte d'entrée (e1). M. Chabot retirait [Imp] son pardessus (s1) qu'il accrochait [Imp] au portemanteau (s2), pénétrait [Imp] dans la cuisine (s3) et s'installait [Imp] dans son fauteuil d'osier (s4). (G. Simenon, *La Danseuse du Gai Moulin*, discussed by Tasmowski-De Ryck 1985)
"The key turned in the lock of the front door. Mr Chabot took off his coat which he hung on the coat rack, entered the kitchen and sat down in his cane chair."

Normally the states introduced by the Imp sentences following the PS sentence would have to be interpreted as pertaining to one of the three settings which are available in this case (e1 is [+ transitional]). But this would lead to a very strange interpretation because these states cannot all be simultaneous. Tasmowski-De Ryck notes that this fragment becomes interpretable if one knows that it is taken from a context in which a mother and her son are awaiting the home-coming of the father. It is from their point of view that the states are perceived. They have to be interpreted as belonging to the implicit setting in which the mother and son are watching what the father does (they saw that he took off his coat, they saw that he hung his coat on the coat rack, etc.) (note that the complement clause of a perception verb in a past tense has to be in the Imp). Without this context the PS would be obligatory in this fragment. Tasmowski-De Ryck observes that even in this context the use of the Imp is extremely marked.

7. FINAL REMARKS

The framework proposed in this chapter for the analysis of the use of tense in narration has proven to be capable of analyzing and explaining the sometimes puzzling irregularities met with by the anaphora approach developed by Kamp and others. The analysis proposed here provides a fine-grained semantic base for the foreground/background approach, in which "change" corresponds to "foreground" and "setting" to "background." Although the analogy between the latter approach and my proposal is evident, the main difference is that the relations between the temporal entities (settings, states, and events) have turned out to be much more complex than the dichotomy adhered to in the foregrounding and backgrounding analysis. It has been shown, for example, that an event can be temporally embedded in another event and that the settings introduced by adverbials have other properties than those introduced by sentences in the *imparfait*, so that a distinction has to be made between several types of "setting." The complexity of this kind of relations appears to be one of the main causes of the continuum between foreground and background (Fleischman 1985).

NOTES

1. I wish to thank Brigitte Kampers-Manhe and Dolf Hartveldt for their valuable suggestions which have improved the form and content of this chapter.
2. In literary work this pattern is often not followed, which causes an effect of surprise, or gives the reader the impression that the story has already

begun, for example. But these stylistic effects are only possible because of the violation of the canonical way of beginning a narration.

3 This sentence gives more information: for example, that there is a person called "the queen" who is present in the setting and that it is this person who finds the swirling of the flakes beautiful. Since this information is provided by noun phrases it will not be taken into account here, but it is evident that this kind of information is important in a complete description of the text.

4 The following fact confirms this view. Newspaper articles can have as their title a sentence such as (i) from *Le Monde*:

(i) Il y a cent ans naissait [Imp] Franz Kafka.
Hundred years ago was-born Franz Kafka.
"Franz Kafka was born one hundred years ago."

But they could not have (ii), although it is a perfectly acceptable sentence:

(ii) Franz Kafka naquit [PS] il y a cent ans.
"Franz Kafka was born one hundred years ago."

The explanation is that a title indicates the setting for the rest of the article. We have seen that the function of preposed adverbial followed by an Imp sentence is precisely to describe such a setting. The presence of (ii) in the title of an article would, however, be interpreted as constituting the beginning of the story itself (cf. Tasmowski-De Ryck 1985: 65) since the PS of (ii) gives the instruction to change some preceding setting.

REFERENCES

Bartsch, Renate (1986) "On aspectual properties of Dutch and German nominalizations," in Vincenzo Lo Cascio and Co Vet (eds) *Temporal Structure in Sentence and Discourse*, Dordrecht: Foris.

Ducrot, Oswald (1983) "L'imparfait en français," in Franz-Josef Hausmann (ed.) *Études de grammaire française descriptive*, Heidelberg: Julius Groos.

Fleischman, Suzanne (1985) "Discourse functions of tense-aspect oppositions in narrative: toward a theory of grounding," *Linguistics* 23: 851–82.

Hinrichs, Erhard (1981) *Temporale Anaphora im Englischen. Zulassungsarbeit*, University of Tübingen.

Hopper, Paul J. (ed.) (1982) *Tense-Aspect: Between Semantics and Pragmatics*, Amsterdam: John Benjamins.

Kamp, Hans (1979) "Events, instants and temporal reference," in Rainer Bäurle, Urs Egli, and Arnim von Stechow (eds) *Semantics from Different Points of View*, Berlin: Springer.

—— (1981) "Événements, représentations discursives et référence temporelle," *Langages* 64: 39–64.

—— (1984) "A theory of truth and semantic representation," in Jeroen Groenendijk, Theo M.V. Janssen, and Martin Stokhof (eds) *Truth, Interpretation and Information*, Dordrecht: Foris.

Kamp, Hans and Rohrer, Christian (1983) "Tense in texts," in Rainer Bäurle, Christoph Schwarze, and Arnim von Stechow (eds) *Meaning, Use and the Interpretation of Language*, Berlin: de Gruyter.

Molendijk, Arie (1987) "Point référentiel et implication temporelle: le passé simple et l'imparfait du français," in Brigitte Kampers-Manhe and Co Vet (eds) *Études de linguistique française*, Amsterdam: Rodopi.

Partee, Barbara H. (1973) "Some structural analogies between tenses and pronouns in English," *The Journal of Philosophy* 70: 601–9.

—— (1984) "Nominal and temporal anaphora," *Linguistics and Philosophy* 7: 243–86.

Tasmowski-De Ryck (1985) "L'imparfait avec et sans rupture," *Langue Française* 67: 59–77.

Vendler, Zeno (1967) *Linguistics in Philosophy*, Ithaca: Cornell University Press.

Verkuyl, H. J. (1972) *On the Compositional Nature of the Aspects*, Dordrecht: Reidel.

Vet, Co (1980) *Temps, aspects et adverbes de temps*, Geneva: Droz.

Vet, Co and Molendijk, Arie (1986) "The discourse functions of the past tenses of French," in Vincenzo Lo Cascio and Co Vet (eds) *Temporal Structure in Sentence and Discourse*, Dordrecht: Foris.

Vikner, Carl (1985) "L'aspect comme modificateur du mode d'action: à propos de la construction être + participe passé," *Langue Française* 67: 95–113.

Waugh, Linda R. and Monville-Burston, Monique (1986) "Aspect and discourse function: the French simple past in newspaper usage," *Language* 62: 846–77.

Weinrich, Harald (1973) *Le Temps*, Paris: Seuil.

3 Verb tense and point of view in narrative[1]

Suzanne Fleischman

1. INTRODUCTION

In his commentary on Camus' *L'Étranger*, which offered a radical departure from French novelistic protocol by casting narration almost entirely in the *passé composé*, Jean-Paul Sartre (1947) suggested that it is in the tense of a text that the secret of its special strangeness lies. The basic referential (grammatical) function of tense, most linguists would agree, is the establishment of time reference in a sentence or discourse. More specifically, tense involves the deictic location of events relative to the moment at which an utterance is produced or to an intervening reference point whose temporal location is predicated in turn in relation to the moment of utterance. In narrative discourse, time reference is normally established at the outset of the text, and since it tends to be a property of large stretches of discourse, or even of entire texts, it need not in principle be reiterated in each successive clause. However, the grammars of many languages require that tense information be encoded (redundantly) on every finite verb – a state of affairs which linguistic economists might well view as a profligate use of grammatical resources. Fortunately for language consumers, the *laissez-faire* economies of natural languages tend to make more efficient use of available resources than their controlled counterparts in sociopolitical institutions. One result is that in the narrative grammars of many languages tense is in large measure freed from its primary referential function of locating events in time, and the available morphology is pressed into service for other, notably pragmatic, purposes.[2] In this chapter I propose to explore one particular pragmatic function of tense oppositions: their use to mark what is traditionally referred to as "point of view" in narrative.[3]

2. POINT OF VIEW AND "FOCALIZATION"

Discussion of point of view has been carried out largely in the camp of literary criticism, and the majority of examples cited in this chapter will be drawn from literary texts – from various periods and from several Romance languages, with emphasis on French. Also, the theoretical underpinning for the concept comes mainly from the work of literary narratologists.[4] This is not to imply that either the concept of point of view or the linguistic means through which it is realized in actual narrative discourse is exclusive to literature.

2.1.

Most theoretical work on point of view, Gérard Genette has observed, suffers from a confusion between what he refers to as narrative "mood" and narrative "voice,"[5] a confusion between the question "Who is the character whose point of view orients the narrative perspective?" and the very different question "Who is the narrator?" – the question "Who sees?" and the question "Who speaks?" (Genette 1980: 186). Obviously a single individual is capable of both speaking and seeing and even of doing both simultaneously – a state of affairs which has led to the confusion between these two activities as carried out in narrative. But it may also be the case that a narrator undertakes to tell what another person sees or has seen. Thus speaking and seeing, narration and what Genette labeled "focalization," may but need not be associated with the same agent. When focalization changes, what changes is not the narrative "voice," for the angle of vision through which events are filtered in a text will always be verbalized by the narrator.

What changes is rather the consciousness through which these events are projected.[6] The example in (1) from "L'Expiation," Victor Hugo's quasi-epic verse narrative about Napoleon, should serve to illustrate the distinction between the speaker and the focalizer.

At a certain point in the battle of Waterloo, with things still looking up for the French, Bonaparte is gazing across the plain of Waterloo and suddenly discerns in the distance an approaching figure he believes to be his general Grouchy; at this moment the (third-person) narrator utters the two sentences given in (1a):

(1) a. Soudain, joyeux, il *dit* [PS]: Grouchy! – C'ÉTAIT [Imp] Blücher.
"Suddenly, joyful, he *said* [PS]: Grouchy! – It WAS [Imp] Blücher."[7]

$[t_1 \text{ in } W_S]$ $[t_1 \text{ in } W_N]$

Commenting on this example, Ducrot (1979: 13) observes that by using the Imp in the second sentence, Hugo's narrator adopts the omniscient perspective of God or the historian who, at the moment the approaching figure comes into view (t_1), already knows his identity.

Had Hugo used the PS in place of the Imp, as in (1b),

(1) b. Il *dit* [PS]: Grouchy! – Ce *fut* [PS] Blücher.
     [t_1 in W_S]   [t_2 in W_S]

this same narrator would instead be conveying the more limited perspective of Napoleon, who would identify the approaching figure as Blücher only at a later moment (t_2 in "story time," or what French narratologists refer to as the time frame of *énoncé*.[8] In terms of chronology the situations referred to respectively by the two sentences in (1a) are simultaneous; however, they pertain to different worlds. The first sentence refers to the diegetic world of *énoncé* (W_S), the second to the extradiegetic world of *énonciation* (W_N). By contrast, the situations referred to by the two sentences in (1b) are sequential, both referring to the diegetic story world (W_S). In (1a) the narrator can, through a simple shift in tenses, *narrate*, using the PS for the appearance of the person assumed by Napoleon at t_1 to be Grouchy, and at the same time *comment* to his readers via the Imp and from his own panchronic angle of vision on the true identity of this personage.[9] By contrast, the two PS verbs of (1b) impose a sequential reading: *fut* must refer to a later moment t_2 in the story world when the approaching character will be identified as Blücher by Napoleon, through whom the second sentence is focalized. The difference between the (a) and (b) versions of this example is a difference in point of view, or more precisely, in focalization, and this difference is expressed linguistically through a tense contrast.

2.2.

Genette initially proposed a three-way typology of focalization, distinguishing "external," "internal," and "non-focalized" sentences. Subsequently, other theoreticians (Bal 1977, 1983; Vitoux 1982; Rimmon-Kenan 1983) have demonstrated the advantages of a binary contrast – internal vs. external focalization – depending essentially on whether the focalizer is the narrator or a character. Changes in focalization thus imply changes in the agent whose consciousness orients the representation (in so far as focalization is associated with an agent at all and not simply with a textual stance – as is often the case in third-person fiction). Typically focalization shifts involve a change from the narrator to a character, as in the text given below in (2), but they may also involve a shift from the perception of one character to that of another. The shift from an external to an internal focalization has been discussed most often with regard to narrations in which the roles of narrator and focalizer are not associated with the same agent, i.e. in third-person fiction. Consider the passage in (2) below:[10]

(2) Nessuno però la VOLEVA neppure la maestrina, perchè le stanze ERANO grandi e, d'inverno, gelate, e piene di topi e di scarafaggi. La serva non CHIUDEVA OCCHIO quando la signorina DOVEVA USCIRE di notte per il suo mestiere; e Giovanna, a sua volta, sebbene coraggiosa e senza pregiudizi, POSSEDEVA una rivoltella col relativo porto di armi.
   La rivoltella *È* lì, anche quella sera, sulla tavola da pranzo che *SERVE* da scrittoio, come la grande stanza, terrena, *È ADIBITA* a uso di salotto e, occorrendo, da sala e ufficio di consultazioni. Un lume a petrolio *RISCHIARA* la stanza; le finestre *SONO CHIUSE*, sebbene la notte, fuori, *SIA* già un po' CALDA, ricca di luna e di stelle.
   Ma Giovanna AVEVA PAURA più delle stelle e del profumo del tasso e del lamento dell'assiolo sul ciglione, che dei malviventi notturni. (Deledda 1939: 232)[11]
   "No one WANTED it [the house], not even the schoolteacher because the rooms WERE large and freezing in the winter and full of mice and cockroaches. The servant WOULDN'T CLOSE HER EYES when her young mistress HAD TO LEAVE at night for her job; and similarly Giovanna, though normally free from fears or prejudices, OWNED a revolver and a permit to use it.
   That night too the revolver *IS* there, on the dining table that *IS USED* as a writing desk, in the same way as the large room on the ground floor *IS USED* as a sitting room and when necessary, as an office and consultation room. A gas light *ILLUMINATES* the room; the windows *ARE CLOSED*, even though outside the evening IS a bit WARM perhaps, filled with light from the moon and the stars.
   But Giovanna WAS more AFRAID of the stars and the perfume of the yew-tree and the cry of the owl on the embankment than of nocturnal criminals."

We observe that the first paragraph of this text, a description of the sinister atmosphere of an old house, is entirely in the Imp. In the second paragraph (in bold) the tense shifts abruptly into the Pr, though the narrative *voice* remains that of the third-person narrator.

The Imp resumes in the third paragraph as the narrator continues with his description, now of the character of Giovanna herself.

What is signaled by the switches between the Imp and the Pr are changes in focalization – from the external perspective of the third-person narrator to the internal perspective of the character Giovanna, then back again to the perspective of the narrator. The function of the present tense here is clearly not temporal (it does not shift the story into present time) but pragmatic. A demarcative "traffic signal" of the text, the Pr signals a shift into the discourse form known as interior monologue (further discussion and examples in section 5). The bolded paragraph offers a representation of Giovanna's thoughts as they passed through her mind at that "now" in her past at which we see her contemplating the room. It will be observed that the Pr functions here in a fashion similar to so-called free indirect discourse (discussed at various points below), a stylistic device traditionally associated with modern fiction,[12] through which thoughts or comments are injected into a narrative without being attributed directly to the character whose subjectivity they express (see note 30 below).

2.3.

It was noted above that most discussions of focalization concentrate on shifts between the subjectivity of the narrator and that of a character, notably in situations in which these two personae are not associated with the same agent, i.e. situations of third-person narration. Once we enter the domain of first-person, or purportedly experiential, narration, where the grammatical "I" is shared by the narrator and his or her character-self, we are confronted with focalization shifts that involve the same "person" (human and grammatical). In contrast to third-person narration where the contrast between the narrating discourse and the narrated discourse is formally supported by grammatical distinctions of person and tense, in first-person narration this contrast is more concealed, being no longer marked by distinctive personal pronouns. The task of identifying the subject of the grammatical "I," which is split into two (or more) subjectivities, devolves on other linguistic signals, notably tense-aspect. We will have occasion in section 5 to consider several examples in which the point of view of the "I" is split between the narrator's focalization as speaker,[13] narrating from the temporal vantage of his or her own "now" (the "now" of *énonciation*), and the focalization of this same individual as a character in the story – what Banfield calls a "self in the past," reporting events as they were experienced at some past moment (a "now" of *énoncé*).[14]

3. "NARRATING-SELF" VS. "EXPERIENCING-SELF"

Banfield (1982) identifies two sentence types of narrative fiction that contrast according to whether or not they contain a "self" at a moment corresponding to an act of consciousness. Sentence (3a) in the *passé simple* merely reports an activity – gazing at the moon – as a completed past event and does so objectively, independent of an explicitly perceived narrating-self:

(3) a. Elle *vit* [PS] la lune.
  "She saw the moon."
(3) b. Elle VOYAIT [Imp] la lune maintenant.
  "She saw the moon now."[15]

By contrast, (3b) with the *imparfait* implies that this event has been *experienced* at some moment, and reports it by representing an experience of it. Sentences in which a past-tense verb collocates acceptably with "now" (or some other non-past adverb), Banfield argues, represent past events "from within a consciousness" and endowed with the "quality of the experiential" (Banfield 1982: 158). It should be noted that sentences of this type are only possible in, and constitute a distinctive discourse feature of, the marked pragmatic context of narrative; in most languages they are further restricted to fictional narration.[16] In French as in English only imperfective past tenses can normally co-occur with "now"; (3c) with the (perfective) PS is ungrammatical;

(3) c.* Elle *vit* [PS] la lune maintenant.

As I argue elsewhere (Fleischman 1990), what distinguishes the narrative stance of the preterit (the *passé simple* in French) from the narrative stances established by other tense-aspect categories used in narration is that all other categories implicate an experiencing-self at some degree of remove (which varies according to the tense) from the events represented as having been experienced; the preterit by contrast is non-experiential, entirely detached from its speaker.[17] By obliterating all self-reference, an "objective" narrator such as the narrator of sentences (3a) and (3c) cuts deictics loose from their normal connection to an identifiable speaker, leaving them free to gravitate to the here-and-now of the characters, as in (3b) or the bolded sentences of free indirect discourse in (4) from Flaubert's *L'Éducation sentimentale*:

(4) Au coin de la rue Montmartre, il [Frédéric] *se retourna*; il *regarda* les fenêtres du premier étage; et il *rit* intérieurement de pitié sur lui-même, en se rappelant avec quel amour il les **avait**

souvent *contemplées!* **Où donc VIVAIT-elle? Comment la rencontrer maintenant?** La solitude SE ROUVRAIT sur son désir plus immense que jamais! (Flaubert 1954: 41)

"On the corner of the Rue Montmartre he [Frédéric] *turned round;* he *looked* at the first-floor windows; and he *laughed* inwardly, pitying himself, recalling how lovingly he *had* often *gazed at* them. **Where DID she LIVE then? How to find her now?** Solitude OPENED UP once more about his desire, which was vaster than ever!" (Flaubert 1964: 52)[18]

In the (bolded) sentences above, the "now" of the second question is clearly Frédéric's "now," *not*, however, at the point in the current narrative plane at which the narrator is recounting his actions (in the PS), but at a "now" in Frédéric's past when he would routinely gaze at those same windows wondering about the enigmatic Mme Arnoux. It is Frédéric's thoughts at that past "now," represented in the process of their articulating themselves in his mind, that the imperfective past is able to recapture.

3.1.

Among sentences which contain a self, Banfield distinguishes further between those in which "self" and "speaker" coincide temporally, i.e. sentences in which the "now" of the experiencing self is also the "now" of the narrator, and sentences in which the "now" of the experiencing self is in the past, divorced from the moment of narration. The first of these sentence types can only occur in first-person narration (see examples (5a), (6a) below), while the second can occur in either third-person (as in example (4) above) or first-person narration (examples (5b), (6b) below). To illustrate the contrast Banfield (1982) cites the sentences given in examples (5) and (6), from *The Dubliners* and *Jane Eyre* respectively, which differ according to whether the time adverb (the surface linguistic mark of the "now") is past, as in the (a) versions, or present, as in the (b) versions:

(5) a. How my heart *beat*/WAS BEATING **then** as he came toward me!
    b. How my heart *beat/WAS BEATING **now** as he came toward me!
(6) a. How fast I *walked*/WAS WALKING **then**!
    b. How fast I *walked/WAS WALKING **now**!

As these sentences show, the imperfective past progressive can co-

Verb tense and point of view 33

occur with either "now" or "then," while the perfective simple past is excluded from sentences with "now." As Banfield observes (1982: 159 f.), although the expressive force of all the sentences derives from their first-person "self," that self is not located in the same moment in the two instances. Consciousness will always be "now," but it is not always the speaker's present. The co-temporality of past with "now" means that the experiencing self in sentences like (3b), the bolded sentences of (4), or the past progressive versions of (5b) and (6b), is represented as a self in the past. The exclamatory force represents a reaction in the past to a simultaneously past event. What the imperfective aspect of the past progressive (or the French *imparfait*) is able to capture is precisely this simultaneity of the event *qua* event and the character's consciousness of it as it was occurring. The expressivity of examples (5a) and (6a), on the other hand, represents a present reaction to a past event on the part of the narrating-self (speaker).

This focalization split between speaker (= narrating-self) and self (= experiencing-self) emerges with greater clarity if we expand the past progressive versions of (5a) by adding tags anchored to the speaker's present, as in (7):

(7) a. How my heart WAS BEATING then..., I remember now.
   (SELF = Present/SPEAKER = Present/)
 b. How my heart WAS BEATING now..., I realized then.
   (SELF = Past/SPEAKER = Present/)
 c. How my heart WAS BEATING now..., *I realize now.
   (SELF = Past/SPEAKER = Present/)

As these examples make clear, the first-person voice, the grammatical "I," can be split between speaker and self. The temporality of the speaker is always obligatorily present, hence the "now" of all the tags is a present "now." The temporality of the experiencing-self may *also* be present, in which case speaker and self coincide, as in (7a); but the temporality of the experiencing-self may also be past, as in (7b) and (7c), in which case speaker and self do not coincide. (The ungrammaticality of (7c) results from the co-occurrence of two temporally distinct "nows" in the same sentence.) This focalization contrast within the first-person voice between speaker and self, between the narrating-I and the experiencing-I, finds linguistic expression in English, French, and no doubt other languages through a contrast between perfective and imperfective past tenses, a contrast which reveals itself most transparently when these respective tenses are combined with temporal-deictic adverbs.

4. TENSE, ADVERBS, AND "FREE INDIRECT DISCOURSE"

Many languages distinguish two varieties of time adverbs: (a) strictly deictic adverbs anchorable only to the moment of utterance (French *aujourd'hui* "today," *demain* "tomorrow", *tout à l'heure* "in a bit/ just now," *il y a huit jours* "a week ago"), and (b) adverbs whose temporal reference point may be a moment other than the moment of utterance (French *maintenant* "now," *deux heures plus tard* "two hours later," *dans trois jours* "in three days," etc.). These are sometimes referred to as "absolute" and "relative" adverbs respectively. The example in (8) recounts a sequence of past events in the expected tenses of written narration in French – the *passé simple*, the *imparfait*, and the so-called "forme en -*rait*" (future-of-the-past), which are combined alternately with absolute (bold) and relative (italicized) time adverbs:

(8) Le capomafia *alla* tranquillement *au lit* à minuit. Il ne SE DOUTAIT pas qu'il SE COUCHAIT sur une bombe qui exploserait *six heures plus tard/dans six heures/*demain.* (cited in Kamp and Rohrer 1983)
"The Mafia boss *went to bed* peacefully at midnight. He DIDN'T SUSPECT he WAS SLEEPING on a bomb that *would* explode *six hours later/in six hours/*tomorrow.*"

Kamp and Rohrer hypothesize correctly that the unacceptability of "tomorrow" in this context derives from the fact that the Mafia boss could not possess the information contained in the relative clause, which, however, is reported in a way that would approximate the words he would have used at the time. If a past tense is co-temporal with an absolute non-past adverb, then the sentence must be one of free indirect discourse; yet it makes no sense pragmatically to represent the propositional content of the relative clause in this way, since the Mafia boss could not have thought or said these words at that time. Nor is it his perspective we are given; rather, the entire sequence is focalized externally through the narrator.

Consider now the examples in (9)–(12) from Flaubert's *L'Education sentimentale*:

(9) Ensuite, Arnoux *parla* d'une cuisson importante **que l'on DEVAIT FINIR aujourd'hui, à sa fabrique. Il VOULAIT LA VOIR. Le train PARTAIT dans une heure.** (1954: 127)
"After that Arnoux *talked* about an important firing at his factory **that WAS DUE TO BE FINISHED today. He WANTED TO WATCH IT. The train WAS LEAVING in an hour's time.**" (1964: 133)

Verb tense and point of view 35

(10) Jamais Frédéric n'*avait été* plus *loin* du mariage. D'ailleurs, Mlle Roques lui SEMBLAIT une petite personne assez ridicule. **Quelle différence avec une femme comme Mme Dambreuse! Un bien autre avenir lui ÉTAIT RÉSERVÉ! Il en AVAIT LA CERTITUDE aujourd'hui.** (1954: 350)
"Frédéric's thoughts *had* never *been further* from marriage. Besides, Mademoiselle Roques STRUCK him as a somewhat ridiculous little thing. **What a difference between her and a woman like Madame Dambreuse! A very different future WAS AWAITING him! He WAS CERTAIN of that now.**" (1964: 347)

(11) Un jour, en feuilletant un de ses cartons, il *trouva* dans le portrait d'une bohémienne quelque chose de Mlle Vatnaz, et, comme cette personne l'INTÉRESSAIT, il *voulut savoir* sa position.

Elle *avait été*, CROYAIT Pellerin, d'abord institutrice en province; maintenant, elle DONNAIT DES LEÇONS et TÂCHAIT D'ÉCRIRE dans des petites feuilles. (1954: 38)
"One day, looking through one of Pellerin's sketchbooks, he *came across* the portrait of a gypsy [which bore] a certain resemblance to Mlle Vatnaz, and, as that lady INTERESTED him, he *inquired* into her circumstances. **She *had started* as a schoolteacher in the provinces, Pellerin THOUGHT; now she WAS GIVING LESSONS and TRYING TO WRITE for the cheap magazines.**" (1964: 49)

(12) Il *se demanda*, sérieusement, s'il serait un grand peintre ou un grand poète; et il *se décida* pour la peinture, car les exigences de ce métier le rapprocherait de Mme Arnoux. **Il *avait* donc *trouvé* sa vocation! Le but de son existence ÉTAIT CLAIR maintenant, et l'avenir infaillible.**

Quant il *eut refermé la porte*, il *entendit*.... (1954: 50)
"He *wondered* in all seriousness whether he would be a great painter or a great poet; and he *decided* in favor of painting, for the demands of this profession would bring him *closer* to Mme Arnoux. **So he *had found* his vocation! The object of his existence WAS CLEAR now, and his future assured.**

As soon as he *had shut the door*, he *heard*...." (1964: 61)

In contrast to the pragmatic infelicity of the example in (8), the examples from Flaubert are pragmatically felicitous inasmuch as the focalization shifts at the bolded sentences from the external perspective of the narrator to the inner speech and thoughts of the focalizing characters at moments in their past. Here the past tense – more precisely the *imparfait* in its reading as a "past co-temporal with 'now'" (Banfield's term) – is acceptable with absolute deictic adverbs ("today," "now").

5. INTERIOR MONOLOGUE

The preceding examples have illustrated the operation of tense in a discourse-pragmatic capacity to mark focalization shifts, specifically shifts from an external or narrator-focalization to an internal or characterfocalization. With the exception of (5) and (6), these examples have all involved third-person narration. In effect, what free indirect discourse retains from the indirect mode are precisely its third-person pronouns and backshifted tense.[19] However, focalization shifts also occur in first-person narration where transitions between the subjectivity of the narrator, speaking from the "now" of *énonciation*, and that of his or her self in the past are likewise marked by oppositions involving tense. The examples in (13)–(15) are from Proust's monumental *À la recherche du temps perdu* (hereafter referred to as *Recherche*) in which the narrator Marcel – a figure who has been identified with Proust himself but who must be considered above all as a fictional speaker within the text – recounts the experiences of his own life.[20]

5.1.

In the passage given in (13) from the opening paragraphs of the first book of the *Recherche*, segmented here to facilitate analysis, Marcel is describing his childhood ordeal of going to bed. He begins by recalling – in the Imp (see note 23) – certain habitual actions associated with this ritual:

(13)

1	J'APPUYAIS tendrement mes joues contre les	Marcel-narrator
2	belles joues de l'oreiller qui, pleines et	(external
3	fraîches, *SONT* comme les joues de notre enfance.	focalization
4	Je FROTTAIS une allumette pour regarder ma	(foc.))
5	montre.	
6	Bientôt minuit.	Marcel-character (internal foc.)
7	C'*EST* l'instant où le malade qui **a été obligé**	Marcel-narrator
8	**de partir** en voyage et **a dû coucher** dans un	(external foc.)
9	hôtel inconnu, réveillé par une crise, *SE*	COMMENTARY
10	*RÉJOUIT* en apercevant sous sa porte une raie	

11 de jour.

12 Quel bonheur, c'*EST* déjà le matin! Dans un   The invalid
13 moment les domestiques SERONT LEVÉS, il   (internal foc.)
14 POURRA SONNER, on VIENDRA lui porter secours.

15 L'espérance d'être soulagé   Marcel-narrator
16 lui *DONNE* du courage pour souffrir.   (external foc.)
17 Justement il **a cru** entendre des pas;   COMMENTARY

18 les pas *SE RAPPROCHENT*, puis *S'ÉLOIGNENT*. Et   The invalid
19 la raie de jour qui ÉTAIT sous sa porte **a**   (internal foc.)
20 **disparu**.

21 C'*EST* minuit; on *VIENT* d'éteindre le gaz; le   Marcel-character
22 dernier domestique **est parti** et il FAUDRA   (internal foc.)
23 rester toute la nuit à souffrir sans remède.

24 Je ME RENDORMAIS, et parfois je n'AVAIS plus   Marcel-narrator
25 que de courts réveils.... (Proust 1954: I, 4)   (external foc.)

"I WOULD LAY my cheeks gently against the comfortable cheeks of my pillow, which, plump and blooming, *ARE* like the cheeks of babyhood. Or I WOULD STRIKE a match to look at my watch. Nearly midnight. The hour when an invalid, who **has been obliged to embark** on a journey and who **has had to sleep** in a strange hotel, awakened in a moment of illness, *REJOICES* at the sight of a streak of daylight showing under his bedroom door. Oh joy of joys! it *IS* morning. The servants WILL BE ABOUT in a minute; he CAN RING, and someone WILL COME to look after him. The thought of being made comfortable *GIVES* him the strength to endure his pain. Indeed, he thinks he has heard footsteps; they *COME NEARER*, and then *DIE AWAY*. And the ray of light that GLIMMERED underneath his door **has disappeared**. It *IS* midnight; the gas *IS* just now turned off; the last servant **has gone [to bed]**, and he [the invalid] WILL BE OBLIGED to lie awake in agony with no surcease.

I WOULD FALL ASLEEP, and often I WOULD BE AWAKE again for short snatches only...."[21] (Proust 1934: I, 3)

Noteworthy here are the subtle transitions from the external focalization of the first-person narrator, either recounting habitual past activities in the Imp (lines 1–5, 24–25), or offering a flash of omniscient insight into the thoughts of the invalid (lines 15–17),[22] to the internal focalizations: first, of Marcel as a child – "bientôt minuit" (line 6) and its sequel (21–3) are the thoughts that would habitually articulate themselves in the child's mind each time this night-time drama would replay itself[23] – then of the displaced invalid, whose "inner transparency"[24] is appropriately verbalized in the third person (*il*) and reported in three tenses of direct speech, present, future and *passé composé*, all deictically anchored to the midnight "now" of this hypothetical "self" (lines 12–14, 18–20).[25]

5.2.

If Proust's narrator represents the thoughts of the Other in the third person and in direct-speech tenses, how does he render the thoughts of his own self-in-the-past? As Ricoeur (1985: 134) observes, *Recherche* makes us hear at least two narrative voices, that of the hero and that of the narrator, their separation problematized by the shared first person.[26] How are these two perspectives kept apart? Once again tense oppositions come into play to demarcate the interior monologues which "enclose the character in the subjectivity of a 'real experience' without transcendence or communication" (Genette 1980: 179 f.).[27]

5.3.

Interestingly, a number of the critics who have addressed themselves to the question of "inner speech" in fiction reject the idea that interior monologue figures in Proust's arsenal of stylistic devices (Dujardin 1931; Raimond 1966; Genette 1980). "Nothing," writes Genette, "is more foreign to Proustian psychology than the utopia of an authentic Interior Monologue whose inchoateness supposedly guarantees transparency and faithfulness to the deepest eddies of the 'stream of consciousness' – or of unconsciousness" (1980: 180). It was Dujardin who insisted on distinguishing between the "infra-linguistic hodgepodge" of inchoate thoughts found in stream-of-consciousness novels and the more orderly sequences of ideas found in quotations of the mind from more traditional novels, reserving the term interior monologue for the modern "flowing" variety. It is in line with this distinction that he rejects the notion of interior monologue in Proust, who, he observes, has an undeniable penchant for *explanation*: "Ce 'parce que,' à lui seul, nous transporte aux antipodes du monologue intérieur" (Dujardin 1931: 275). Though adherents to Dujardin's distinction have adopted such labels as "traditional monologue" or "silent soliloquy" for thought quotations cast in more ordinary discursive patterns, the term interior monologue will be retained here.[28]

Genette acknowledges but a single instance of interior monologue in all of Proust's *Recherche*. I give this example in (14) below, in context. To facilitate analysis, I have again divided the passage into segments corresponding to narrative functions (narration, commentary, etc.). The sentences I assign to interior monologue appear in the inner rectangle; Genette's sentences of interior monologue remain in bold.

(14)

1	Ces concerts matinaux de Balbec N'ÉTAIENT PAS ANCIENS.	NARRATION
2	Et pourtant, à ce moment relativement	Orientation[29]
3	rapproché, je ME SOUCIAIS peu d'Albertine.	(Marcel-narrator)
4	Même, les tout premiers jours de l'arrivée,	
5	je *n'avais* pas *connu* sa présence à Balbec.	
6	Par qui donc l'*avais*-je *apprise*?	COMMENTARY
7	Ah! oui, par Aimé.	(Marcel-narrator)
8	IL FAISAIT UN BEAU SOLEIL comme celui-ci.	(Orientation to
9	Brave Aimé! Il ÉTAIT CONTENT de me revoir.	the commentary)
10	**Mais il *N'AIME PAS* Albertine.**	Interior monologue
11	**Tout le monde *NE PEUT PAS L'AIMER*.**	(Marcel-character)
12	Oui, c'*EST* lui qui m'a annoncé qu'elle ÉTAIT à Balbec.	
13	Comment le SAVAIT-il donc?	
14	Ah! Il l'*avait rencontrée*,	
15	il lui *avait trouvé mauvais genre*.	
16	A ce moment, abordant le récit d'Aimé par une face autre.... (Proust 1954: III, 84)	NARRATION (Marcel-narrator)

"Those morning concerts at Balbec WERE NOT REMOTE IN TIME. And yet at that comparatively recent moment, I WAS GIVING LITTLE THOUGHT to Albertine. Indeed, on the very first mornings after my arrival, I *had not known* of her presence at Balbec. From whom *had* I *learned* it? Oh, yes, from Aimé. It WAS A FINE SUNNY DAY like this. A fine fellow, Aimé. He WAS GLAD to see me again. **But he *DOES NOT LIKE* Albertine. Not everybody *CAN BE IN LOVE WITH HER*.** Yes, he's the one who told me that she WAS at Balbec. But how DID HE KNOW? Ah! he *had met* her, *had found her undesirable*. At that moment, looking back on Aimé's story from a different perspective...." (Proust 1934: II, 436)

A salient feature of Proust's narrative technique that appears in this passage – also in the passages in examples (13) and (15) – is the interpolation of metanarrative commentary by the narrator (text enclosed in the outer rectangle) into Marcel's narration of the events of his life. Here Marcel ponders aloud, at the "now" of *énonciation*, the source of information which he – as a character – had received in the past concerning Albertine's presence at Balbec. In the midst of this commentative musing, externally focalized through the narrating-self, the text slips very briefly into an interior monologue in which the subjectivity we are confronted with is suddenly the unmediated subjectivity of the experiencing-self in the past, no longer filtered through the voice of the narrator but now internally focalized. The line of demarcation between sentences that are externally and internally focalized is not at all sharply drawn, whence Genette's inclusion of the (bolded) sentence in line 12 as part of the interior monologue. Yet in terms of its focalization this sentence is no different from those in lines 6 and 7 or in 13–15; they all belong to the internal dialogue of Marcel-*narrator* with himself in the "commentative" mode and in the time frame of *énonciation*. What sets apart the internally focalized sentences of the interior monologue is the diacritical use of the present tense. Only in the sentences of lines 10–11 are we given direct access to the thoughts of Marcel-character at a past "now," a moment located in the time frame of *énoncé*, albeit represented here in its erstwhile presentness.[30] It is precisely at line 12 that the text shifts back to past tenses and back once again to the external focalization of the momentarily eclipsed narrator. Had Genette taken his cue from tense usage, he would have recognized that the sentence in 12 lies outside the interior monologue. Finally, at line 16 Marcel-narrator leaves the commentative mode altogether and resumes narration.

5.4.

Another striking example of Proust's use of interior monologue/ internal focalization occurs in the pivotal episode of "the madeleine," which provides the catalyst for Marcel's discovery of the involuntary memory that sets him on his quest, across more than 2,000 pages, for "lost time" and for his vocation as a writer.[31]

Some forty-five pages into his odyssey, Marcel recounts the occasion, many years after his sojourn at Combray, when his mother offered him a cup of tea and a madeleine; the aftertaste produced in him a most exquisite sensation, conjuring up memories from his childhood at Combray which he had assumed were lost. His reflections on this sensation are given in (15) below (sentences of interior monologue are in bold):

(15)

1	**D'où *avait pu* me *venir* cette puissante joie?**	Int. mon.
		(Marcel-character)
2	Je SENTAIS qu'elle ÉTAIT LIÉE au goût du thé et du	NARRATION
3	gâteau, mais qu'elle le DÉPASSAIT infiniment, NE DEVAIT	Orientation
4	PAS ÊTRE de la même nature.	(Marcel-narrator)

Verb tense and point of view 41

5   D'où VENAIT-elle? Que SIGNIFIAIT-elle? Où l'appréhender?   Int. mon.
                                                               (Marcel-character)

6   Je *BOIS* une seconde gorgée où je *NE TROUVE* rien de plus   NARRATION
7   que dans la première, une troisième qui m'*APPORTE* un peu   in the HPr
8   moins que la seconde.

9   Il *EST* temps que je *M'ARRÊTE*, la vertu du breuvage   Int. mon.
10   *SEMBLE DIMINUER*. Il *EST CLAIR* que la vérité   (Marcel-character)
     que je *CHERCHE*
11   *N'EST PAS* en lui, mais en moi. Il l'y a éveillée, mais
12   *NE LA CONNAÎT PAS*, et *NE PEUT QUE RÉPÉTER* indéfiniment,
13   avec de moins en moins de force, ce même témoignage que
14   *je NE SAIS PAS INTERPRÉTER et que je VEUX* au moins
15   *POUVOIR LUI REDEMANDER ET RETROUVER INTACT*, à ma
16   disposition, tout à l'heure, pour un éclaircissement
17   définitif.

18   Je *POSE LA TASSE* et *ME TOURNE* vers mon espirt.   NARRATION
                                                                     in the HPr

19   *C'EST* à lui de trouver la vérité. Mais comment? Grave   Int. mon.
20   incertitude, toutes les fois que l'esprit *SE SENT*   (Marcel-character)
21   *DÉPASSÉ* par lui-même; quand lui, le chercheur *EST* tout
22   ensemble le pays obscur où il *DOIT CHERCHER* et où tout
23   son bagage ne lui <u>SERA</u> de rien. Chercher? pas seulement:
24   créer. Il *EST EN FACE DE* quelque chose qui *N'EST PAS*
25   encore et que seul il *PEUT RÉALISER* puis *FAIRE ENTRER*
26   dans sa lumière.

27   Et je *RECOMMENCE A ME DEMANDER* quel POUVAIT   NARRATION
                                                                     in the HPr
28   ÊTRE cet état inconnu, qui N'APPORTAIT aucune preuve   (Marcel-narrator)
29   logique, mais l'évidence, de sa félicité, de sa réalité devant
30   laquelle les autres S'ÉVANOUISSAIENT. Je *VEUX ESSAYER* de
31   le faire réapparaître. Je *RÉTROGRADE* par la pensée au
32   moment où je *pris* la première cuillerée de thé. Je
33   *RETROUVE* le même état, sans une clarté nouvelle. (Proust 1954: I, 45f.)

"Whence *could it have come* to me, this all-powerful joy?

I SENSED that it WAS CONNECTED to the taste of tea and cake, but that it infinitely TRANSCENDED those savours, COULD NOT, indeed, BE of the same nature as theirs.

Whence DID it COME? What DID it SIGNIFY? How to seize upon and define it?

I *DRINK* a second mouthful, in which I *FIND* nothing more than in the first, a third, which *GIVES* me rather less than the second.

It *IS* time that I *STOP*; the potion *APPEARS TO BE LOSING ITS MAGIC*. It *IS PLAIN* that the truth that I *SEEK LIES*

NOT in the cup but in myself. The tea has called up in me, but *DOES NOT* itself *UNDERSTAND*, and *CAN ONLY REPEAT* indefinitely with a gradual loss of strength, the same testimony; which I too *CANNOT INTERPRET*, though I *HOPE* at least *TO BE ABLE TO CALL UPON [THE TEA] FOR IT AGAIN AND TO FIND IT* there presently, intact and at my disposal, for my final enlightenment.

I *PUT DOWN* my cup and *EXAMINE* my own mind.

It *IS* for it to discover the truth. But how? What an abyss of uncertainty whenever the mind *FEELS SOME PART OF IT TO HAVE STRAYED BEYOND ITS OWN BORDERS*; when it, the seeker, *IS* at once the dark region through which it *MUST GO SEEKING*, where all its equipment <u>WILL AVAIL</u> it nothing. Seek? More than that; create. It *IS FACE TO FACE* with something which *DOES NOT* so far *EXIST*, to which it alone *CAN GIVE REALITY AND SUBSTANCE*, [which it alone *CAN]* BRING INTO* the light of day.

And I *BEGIN TO ASK MYSELF* what it COULD HAVE BEEN, this unremembered state which BROUGHT WITH IT no logical proof of its existence, but only the sense [that it was] happy, [that it was] a real state in whose presence other states of consciousness MELTED AND VANISHED. I *WANT TO TRY* to make it reappear. I *RETRACE* my thoughts to the moment at which I *drank* the first spoonful of tea. I *FIND* again the same state, illumined by no fresh light." (Proust 1934: I, 34f.)

The identification of focalizers and time levels in this passage is more complicated than in the previous passage, given the use of a single tense – the Pr – for both narration in the historical present,[32] where the narrator is both speaker and focalizer, and for sentences of interior monologue, where the Pr – a *présent de la parole* – is that of the focalizing character Marcel; not, however, at the moment when he *first* tasted the tea and madeleine, which I will call t_1, (this point in story time is referred to by the single PS verb *pris* "drank" in line 32), but some years later, at a time t_2 when the same experience of tea and a madeleine would engender the exhilarating sensation which he will then seek to conjure up at will, and which he describes *qua* narrator at t_3, the present of *énonciation*, in the passages marked NARRATION. The bold sentences in lines 1, 5, 9–17, and 19 – 26 represent the thoughts of Marcel-character at t_2; the remainder of the passage (save for the PS clause in line 32 which refers to t_1) is spoken at t_3 by Marcel-

Verb tense and point of view 43

narrator, who uses the historical present to report narrative events, and the imperfect for sentences of orientation (2–4) and restricted (subordinate) clauses within the complicating action (27–30). Within the interior monologue the imperfect (5) and pluperfect (1) function respectively as imperfective and perfective pasts in relation to the character's "now" (= t_2).

Linguistic signs of *discours* (in Benveniste's sense (1959)), notably present-tense verbs and absolute deictic adverbs (*tout à l'heure*, line 16) are among the devices used by Proust to represent the unmediated thoughts of the character Marcel as he ponders – at t_2 evoked here in its presentness – the *recherche* he is about to undertake. It should be noted, however, that in the section in bold, lines 19–26, all present-tense verbs but the first are generic presents referring to habitual activities of the human mind (= the seeker) "toutes les fois que" (cf. note 25). And although the grammatical person switches also in this section from first to third, what we are confronted with are not the thoughts of an *il*, as in (13), but those of a *je* (Marcel-character) reflecting on his own interiority personified as the Other (= *il/le chercheur*).

The pragmatic use of tenses in Proust could easily provide material for a monographic study. The few examples cited here will hopefully give some indication of the linguistic complexities of Proust's narrative style and of some of the ways in which tense comes into play in signaling point of view.

5.5.

One final example of the use of tense to encode the internal focalization of a character's interior monologue is drawn from "En los campos de Alventosa," an anonymous Spanish ballad (*romance*) from the Carolingian cycle, which deals with events from the Roland legend. The ballad presumably circulated for a long time in the oral tradition prior to its first printing in the sixteenth century.[33] This version relates a father's search for his son, the warrior Beltrán, who disappeared as Charlemagne's army was crossing the Pyrenees. The text is entirely in the third person except for passages of direct speech; however, it alternates narration with quasi-lyric meditations by the narrator on the narrated events (a poetic form of commentary). In the section given in (16) below, Beltrán's father rides across the countryside searching for his son, whom he fears he will find dead. As the narrator tells us:

(16)

	NARRATION	
1	...*vido* [PS] todos los franceses	"he *saw* [PS] all the Frenchmen
2	y *no vido* [PS] a don Beltrán.	but *didn't see* [PS] Lord Beltran."

LYRIC MEDITATION

3	MALDICIENDO IBA [P-Prog] el vino,	"He RODE ALONG CURSING [P-Prog] the wine,
4	MALDICIENDO IBA [P-Prog] el pan,	he RODE ALONG CURSING [P-Prog] the bread
5	el que COMIAN [Imp] los moros,	– the bread the Moors ATE [Imp]
6	que no el de la cristiandad:	not that of the Christians –;
7	MALDICIENDO IBA [P-Prog] el árbol	He RODE ALONG CURSING [P-Prog] the tree
8	que solo en el campo *NASCE* [Pr],	that *GROWS* [Pr] only in the country;
9	que todas las aves del cielo	All the birds in the sky
10	alli *SE VIENEN* [Pr] *A ASENTAR*,	*COME* [Pr] *TO ALIGHT THERE*;
11	que de rama ni de hoja	In no branch, in no leaf
12	no la DEJABAN [Imp] GOZAR:	WOULD they TAKE PLEASURE [Imp].
13	MALDICIENDO IBA [P-Prog] el caballero,	He RODE ALONG CURSING [P-Prog] the knight
14	que CABALGABA sin paje;	who RODE [Imp] without a squire."

Interior monologue

15	si *SE* le *CAE* [Pr] la lanza	"If he *DROPS* [Pr] his lance,
16	*NO TIENE* [Pr] quien se la *ALCE*,	he *HAS NO ONE* [Pr] *TO RETRIEVE IT*;
17	y si *SE* le *CAE* [Pr] la espuela	If he *DROPS* [Pr] his spur,
18	*NO TIENE* [Pr] quien se la *CALCE*:	he *HAS NO ONE* [Pr] *TO REPLACE IT*.

19	MALDICIENDO IBA [P-Prog] la mujer	"He RODE ALONG CURSING [P-Prog] the woman
20	que tan solo un hijo PARE [Pr];	who BEARS [Pr] but a single son:"

Interior monologue

21	si enemigos *SE* lo *MATAN* [Pr]	"If his enemies *KILL* [Pr] him
22	*NO TIENE* [Pr] quien lo vengar.	he *HAS NO ONE* [Pr] to avenge him."

NARRATION RESUMES

23	A la entrada de un puerto,	"At the entrance to a pass
24	saliendo de un arenal,	coming out of a sand-pit,
25	*vido* [PS] en esto *estar* un moro	he *spied* [PS] a Moor there, who WAS
26	que VELABA [Imp] en un adarve:	STANDING WATCH [Imp] on a sentry-walk.
27	*habló*le [PS] en algarabía,	In Arabic he *spoke* [PS] to him
28	como aquel que bien la SABE [Pr].	like one who KNOWS [Pr] it well."

The narrator's lyric meditation begins at line 3 with a description of the old man's solitary wandering, represented *as process* by the imperfective past tenses (Imp and P-Prog). The Prs in lines 8, 10, 20, and 28 are all general or timeless Prs.[34] At line 15 we are suddenly admitted, with no formal transition save the switch into the Pr, directly into the private thoughts of the old man as he reflects on his plight, wandering alone with no squire to attend him. The poignancy of both this monologic character-lament (all the sentences beginning with *si* "if") and the narrator's meditation in which it is embedded is underscored by the rhythmic repetition of key formulaic phrases.

5.6.

To conclude this discussion of interior monologue, it should be observed how systematically the present tense is selected as the linguistic mark of this particular discourse form: in both first- and third-person narration, in the "immediate speech" of both first- and third-person subjectivities,[35] in a range of literary genres,[36] and in languages with different tense-aspect systems. In Fleischman (1990) I elaborate on why the present indicative, the sole tense category which in its basic meaning neutralizes all positive time reference (i.e. it is temporally unmarked), lends itself so well to this kind of pragmatic utilization in narrative.

6. CONCLUSION

In the preceding paragraphs I have sought to illustrate one of the striking discourse functions carried out by tense in the linguistic structuration of fictional narrative: that is, the use of tense oppositions to discriminate the different focalizations or perspectival filters through which events in a story are projected in every narrative transaction between an author and a reader. My focus has been primarily on French, in particular on the *passé simple/imparfait* contrast and on the present as used in interior monologue. But other tense contrasts can do the job equally well, the possibilities limited only by the tense-aspect categories available in a given language. French, for example, has two perfective pasts: the *passé simple* and the *passé composé*, assigned respectively to *histoire* and *discours* (Benveniste 1959) or, in the terms of Weinrich (1973), to the "narrative" and "commentative" modes. This contrast may also be pressed into service to signal point of view. Boyer (1979) looks specifically at the PS/PC contrast in a contemporary French novel, *La Dentellière* (*The Lacemaker*), pointing out the author's use of the PS to mark the (external) perspective of the third-person narrator on a particular sequence of events, while in the final chapter these same events are recounted in direct speech and in the PC by the character involved. Additionally, this same character's thoughts, when filtered through the voice of the narrator in free indirect discourse, are – not surprisingly – reported in the Imp.

6.1.

From the examples cited here it should not be inferred that the use of tense-aspect to manipulate point of view is an exclusive prerogative of literary narration. This pragmatic use of tense-aspect morphology is well documented across languages in the spontaneous "natural" narratives that punctuate everyday conversational exchanges. Longacre (1976) reports that in one type of story-telling in Oksapmin, a language of New Guinea, a particular person or group of persons will be singled out as the "vantage point," a concept analogous to what is here referred to as the focalizer; verbs which reflect the perception of this focalizer will exhibit one type of morphology, while verbs which reflect the vantage point of other focalizing agents will exhibit a different type of morphology. As the story unfolds, listeners are continually informed *by the morphology* whose perspective they are privy to.

6.2.

Another pragmatic contrast which might figure under the heading "point of view" is expressed by languages with evidentials or analogous verb-based devices through which a narrator can adjust the *epistemic* modalization of a sentence or larger discourse. A language like Bulgarian uses verb morphology to distinguish different narrative stances according to the narrator's subjective distance from or involvement in events of the story-world. The Bulgarian narrator is obliged to choose between presenting events in one of three ways: as *directly experienced* (what Chvany (1979) labels the "visualizing" mode), as perceived at some remove (the "direct reminiscing" mode), or merely *inferred* (the "indirect reminiscing" mode). These modes are signaled linguistically by combinations of tense, aspect, and mood. In a work of non-fiction, Chvany observes (1979: 299), the writer chooses one of these narrative stances and sticks with it. In fiction the narrator is free to shift from one perspective to another and usually does so. Givón (1982) describes a similar situation in Ute story-telling, whereby narrators can express differing degrees of deictic immediacy or involvement in a story through a choice of aspect markers.

6.3.

One property shared by the literary and non-literary examples is the fact that many of the sentence types at issue, with their particular combinations of tenses and adverbs, would be if not ungrammatical at least pragmatically infelicitous outside a story-telling context: a sentence like D.H. Lawrence's "tomorrow was Monday" (*Women in Love*), with its past tense and future time adverb, is acceptable only in a narrative. From this perspective, then, this chapter may be seen as yet another piece of evidence in favor of the position, not entirely uncontroversial, that narrative discourse constitutes a marked category of linguistic performance, with a grammar that differs in certain crucial respects from that of ordinary interactive language.

NOTES

1 A preliminary version of this chapter was presented at the 1986 Meeting of the Modern Language Association (New York). Sections of the present version have been incorporated into Chapter 7 of my book *Tense and Narrativity* (Fleischman 1990).
2 It is generally recognized that elements of a language operate simultaneously in different functional-semantic capacities. The distinction I am drawing here apropos of tense-aspect categories is one between referential functions (e.g. past or future time reference, perfective or imperfective aspect), which I take to be ontogenetically primary, and pragmatic functions, which develop as secondary extensions of the basic grammatical meanings. Under the heading of pragmatic I am concerned primarily with discourse functions, i.e. the ways in which tense-aspect categories are pressed into service in the structure and organization of the text itself.
3 Throughout this discussion tense should be understood to include aspect, given that in many languages, including all of Romance, tense information and aspect information are packaged synthetically in the same morphology.
4 According to one informed observer (Martin 1986), the most spirited debates about narrative theory today concern precisely point of view. From the extensive literature on this topic with respect to narrative fiction, the reader is referred in particular to Friedemann (1910), Doležel (1967), Stanzel (1971), Uspensky (1973), Cohn (1978), Genette (1980), and Lanser (1981), the last providing a history of approaches to point of view in the European literary tradition.
5 One cannot help but be struck by the extent to which the metalanguage used in descriptions of narrative structure is drawn from the domain of grammar, in particular from grammatical categories associated with the verb. Among the more systematic typologies proposed by literary theorists,

Todorov (1966) operates with the parameters *time, aspect* (= point of view), and *mode*, which may have inspired Genette's analysis (1980) in terms of the *order* (= tense), *duration* (= aspect), and *frequency* (= *Aktionsart*, e.g. singulative/iterative) of events and the *mood* and *voice* through which narration is carried out. It is not gratuitous that the grammar of natural languages provides the conceptual and terminological metaphors for "grammars" of narrative. And the centrality of the categories of tense, aspect, voice, etc., in the accomplishment of certain narrative tasks is no doubt what motivates the choice of the verb as the dominant metaphorical template for descriptions of narrative structure.

6 This distinction between the speaking subject and the source of subjectivity was first suggested by Brooks and Warren (1943), whose term "focus of narration" inspired Genette's label "focalization," coined to avoid the specifically visual connotations associated with the roughly equivalent terms "point of view," "vision" (Pouillon 1946), or "field." After Genette made focalization a topic of critical interest, his typology was refined, notably by Bal (1977, 1983) and Vitoux (1982) (see section 2.2). Whereas the thrust of all these discussions has been toward a conceptual *separation* between narrative "voice" and "point of view," Paul Ricoeur, one of the most penetrating intellects to speak on the subject of narrative, sees these two categories of the narrative metalanguage as being in the final analysis inseparable – a single function considered from the perspective of two questions:

> Point of view answers the question "From where do we perceive what is shown to us by the fact of being narrated?" Hence, from where is one speaking? Voice answers the question "Who is speaking here?" If we do not want to be misled by the metaphor of *vision* when we consider a narrative in which everything is *recounted*, then vision must be taken to be a concretization of understanding, hence, paradoxically, an appendix to hearing. (Ricoeur 1985: 99)

As we shall see below, and as Genette recognized also, the categories of "voice" and "point of view" cannot in practice be analysed entirely independently of one another, even if we do not go so far as to conflate them at the theoretical level, following Ricoeur.

7 From *Les Châtiments* (1853). Under orders from Napoleon, the French general Grouchy was to pursue the Prussian army, led by Blücher, then continue the march on to Waterloo. Instead, Grouchy was tricked and it was Blücher who arrived at Waterloo to reinforce the English.

The following typographic conventions will be used throughout this chapter to code tense-aspect categories, abbreviated as follows:

PS	simple past/preterit	*italic*
Imp	(past) imperfect	UPPER CASE
P-Prog	past progressive	UPPER CASE
Pr, HPr	present, historical present	*UPPER CASE ITALIC*
PC	compound past	**bold**
Plp	pluperfect/anterior past	***bold italic***
FUT	future	UPPER CASE UNDERSCORING
FUT-OF-P	future-of-the-past	lower case underscoring

Unless otherwise indicated, translations are my own.

8 The distinction French makes between *énonciation* and *énoncé*, between the act of producing an utterance and the utterance itself, provides a convenient terminological shorthand for distinguishing the two levels at which narration simultaneously operates – the diegetic world of the story (*énoncé*) and the extra-diegetic world of its recounting (*énonciation*) by a speaker known as the narrator. Each of these worlds has its own participants and its own time frame. See also note 9 below.

9 This statement requires qualification: the phrase "at the same time" refers to the coincidence of two instances (both marked "t_1") which are understood to pertain to different time frames – the time frame of *énonciation* and that of *énoncé* – corresponding respectively to the world of the narrator (W_N) and that of the story (W_S). As narratologists, Genette in particular, have pointed out, the length of time required to narrate a sequence of events (in the time of *énonciation*) is never, save for certain experimental texts, the same as the time required for those events to take place in a real or fictional world (the time of *énoncé*), whence the various "anachronies" between narrating time and story time (see in particular Genette 1980: chap. 2). The distinction between "narrative" and "commentative" modes is developed in Weinrich (1973).

10 According to Barthes (1966: 18, 1975: 262), the criterion for internal focalization is the possibility of rewriting a narrative sequence in the first person – if it is not in that person already – with a pragmatically felicitous result. Already we begin to see how the categories of "voice" and "point of view" become entwined. I would point out, however, that while this first-person substitution test is a necessary condition for internal focalization, it is not sufficient. In first-person narration the grammatical "I" typically encodes the voice of both the narrating-self and the experiencing-self, as we shall see (section 5). The distinction of "voice" in fiction, i.e. between first and third person, corresponds *grosso modo* to the distinction drawn by natural narrative analysts between "experiential" and "vicarious" narration. Thus many of the observations made here with respect to the two categories of voice in fictional narration are also applicable to their counterparts in naturally occurring narrations.

11 From the Italian short story "Forze occulte" by Grazia Deledda cited in Herczeg 1958: 378).

12 Whereas most investigators situate the emergence of free indirect discourse at a point in literary history coinciding with the rise of the modern novel, Cerquiglini (1984) reopens the case for a medieval avatar of the phenomenon in French. Though I do not concur with his interpretation of the Old French data he cites (discussed in Fleischman (1990: Chap. 7)), I will offer an example from Old Spanish in section 5, not of free indirect discourse but of its functional analogue, the "immediate speech" of interior monologue (for definitions, see note 30).

13 Hamburger (1973) considers the term "narrator" appropriate *only* to first-person narration, third-person narration being constituted not through a narrator but through a "narrative function."

14 As Banfield (1982: 195) puts it: "in first-person narration the *I* is divided by time into a SELF caught always in the NOW of consciousness and a SPEAKER narrating in a moment for which the NOW of consciousness is always past." This distinction between "speaker" and "self" has been

discussed by a number of theoreticians using variant nomenclatures: *erzählendes Ich* vs. *erlebendes Ich* (Spitzer 1928), *sujet d'énonciation* vs. *sujet d'énoncé* (Todorov 1970), "narrator-I" vs. "character-I" (Bellos 1978). See also Butor (1969), Bronzwaer (1970), Hamburger (1973).

15 Cited by Banfield (1982: 157).

16 In a paper exploring the boundary between direct and indirect speech and the validity of this distinction as a linguistic universal, Haberland (1986) notes that in certain languages (notably Danish) sentences of "quasi-direct speech" (= free indirect discourse) also occur commonly in conversational narration. Polanyi (1982) seeks to make the same claim for English; however, the examples she cites are problematic, containing none of the characteristic linguistic marks of free indirect discourse (backshifted tenses, third-person pronominal reference for the focalizer, deletion of introduction-to-discourse formulas), and look very much like free direct speech (for discussion, see Fleischman 1990: section 7.3).

17 The quality of "detachment" (from the speaker and speaker's here-and-now) that an event acquires by virtue of being encoded in the *passé simple* is explored in Waugh and Monville-Burston (1986).

18 Translation adapted (notably with respect to tense usage).

19 Briefly, what demarcates sentences of free indirect discourse is the presence of features of direct speech (direct questions, exclamations, fragments, repetitions, deictics, emotive and conative words, overstatements, colloquialisms) reported in the fashion of indirect speech, i.e. with third-person pronouns and backshifted tenses, but normally without the characteristic "inquit" formulas for introducing indirect discourse, such as "X said/thought that, wondered why". For an analysis of this sentence type, see Banfield (1982: Chap. 2), Rimmon-Kenan (1983: 111 ff.), Bal (1985: 138f.).

20 In contrast to third-person fiction, which involves what Cohn (1978) calls the "mimesis of other minds," first-person fiction involves a different kind of mimesis, simulating speech acts such as autobiography or confession.

21 I modify Scott-Moncrieff's translation on occasion for greater parallelism of tense usage, and bracket text that does not figure in the original, having been added for a smoother translation.

22 Genette would regard the sentences in lines 15–17 as *non-focalized*; however, I am adhering to the revised typology (see section 2.2 above) which distinguishes only between external (narrator) and internal (character) focalizations.

23 In a suggestive essay, Banfield (1985) relates the tense-aspect categories available within the French system of narrative tenses to Proust's theory of time and memory as developed in *Recherche*. Relevant here, the two commonly recognized readings of the *imparfait* (the "mass" tense), habitual action and ongoing/durative action, are associated respectively with Proust's notions of voluntary and involuntary memory (the latter encoded by the "past co-temporal with 'now'" reading), while the PS serves to re-count the individualized, whence numerically "countable," events of a past reported not as a remembered past but as divorced from its speaker's memory and objectified, a past "become history" (cf. note 17 above). (The homology Banfield invokes between perfective/imperfective aspect and count/mass nouns has often been pointed out.)

24 The term is from Dorrit Cohn (1978). It refers to the epistemic access of the narrator to the mental states of represented persons and to situations which cannot normally be observed. This cognitive privilege of the narrator is possible only in "constructed" narratives (fiction) which are true in constructed worlds; only in fiction can one presume access to and represent in language the thought, the subjectivity of the Other.

25 Time reference in these two sections of commentary (lines 7–11, 15–17) is neutralized. The invalid is an exemplar whose activities stand in no temporal relation either to the events of the story world or to the context of narration. The Pr is thus used here in its generic or timeless sense, with the PC its corresponding perfect, encoding situations completed prior to the reference point provisionally instituted by the "now" of this timeless Pr.

26 I prefer to speak of two *focalizations* associated with the first-person *voice*. However, as noted above (note 6), Ricoeur does not separate these two categories, whence his reference to "two narrative voices."

27 Further on (p. 193) Genette will argue that it is only in interior monologue that internal focalization can be fully realized.

28 Cohn (1978: 12 f.) presents compelling arguments for not drawing a hard and fast distinction between these two types of thought quotation.

29 Readers unfamiliar with the Labovian model of narrative organization (Labov 1972; Labov and Waletzky 1967), developed with respect to naturally occurring narrations, are referred to Centineo's chapter in this volume. "Orientation" sections are those which provide descriptive or explanatory background material for the events that make up the main narrative line. Clauses of orientation typically sketch the kind of thing that was going on before or at the time of a particular "narrative event," whence the tenses commonly found in these clauses are imperfective pasts and pluperfects, also progressives in languages that have a progressive aspect.

30 The sentence of interior monologue corresponds to what Genette (1980: 174) calls "immediate speech," which he contrasts with "free indirect speech." In the latter mode of representing speech (or thought) the narrator's discourse "takes in hand" the character's words or thoughts by "lending this discourse its voice," while it conforms to the tone of what the character said or thought (Ricoeur 1985: 90 f.). By contrast, in "immediate speech" the narrator is seemingly obliterated and the character substitutes.

31 This episode has received perhaps more critical attention – which will not be surveyed here – than any other in the novel. For one insightful reading of the passage, and of the *Recherche* as a whole, with particular regard to Proust's handling of time, the reader is referred to Ricoeur (1985: 130–52) and the references provided there. Proust's own thoughts on the place of tense in narrative discourse are set forth in his essay "A propos du 'style' de Flaubert" (Proust 1920).

32 I discuss pragmatic functions of the present tense *in narration proper* in Fleischman (1985, 1986, 1990).

33 Text from Wolf and Hoffmann's *Primavera y flor de romances*, 1856; repr. by Marcelino Menéndez y Pelayo as vols 8 and 9, with additions, of his *Antología de poetas líricos castellanos*, Santander: Oldus, 1944 (original edn 1899). Text #185a. This version of the ballad first appeared

in the *Cancionero de Romances* of 1550, Antwerp, folio 198.
34 Among the several varieties of general Pr, those in lines 8 and 10 (*NASCE, SE VIENEN*) correspond to the subtype that I elsewhere label "local," i.e. Prs for which the predication holds true for all time moments within a locally construed world. By contrast, *SABE* (1. 28) and *PARE* (1. 20) have "global" scope: the reference in 1. 20 is atemporal or gnomic: anyone, anywhere, at any time, who speaks Arabic so well must *KNOW* it; similarly, in 1. 28 the old man curses *all* women who *BEAR* only one child, though in context this generic reference must be read also as the personal lament of a father who has lost his only son.
35 These two oppositions – first- and third-person narration (voice) and first- and third-person subjectivities (focalization) – need not coincide, whence my insistence, *pace* Ricoeur, of a separation at the metalinguistic level. First-person narration may embed the unmediated discourse of either the self (examples (14), (15)) or the other (example (13)), while third-person narration, being a non-personal narrative stance, is limited to representing other third-person subjectivities (examples (2), (16)).
36 The term "literary" is used loosely here. Verbal artifacts of traditional popular cultures such as the Spanish *romances* are included under this broad – and for the sixteenth century anachronistic – belle-lettristic rubric mainly because we now encounter these texts in the context of academic literature or folklore courses where we read them divorced from the pragmatic contexts in which they were originally performed. A preferable umbrella term might be "artificial narrative" forms, coined by van Dijk (1975) to distinguish such genres as stories, novels, and other types of literary narrative, as well as myths, folktales, epics, etc., from the "natural" narratives occurring in everyday conversation.

REFERENCES

Bal, Mieke (1977) *Narratologie. Essais sur la signification narrative dans quatre romans modernes*, Paris: Klincksieck.
—— (1983) "The narrating and the focalizing: a theory of agents in narrative," *Style* 17 (2): 234–69.
—— (1985) *Narratology. Introduction to the Theory of Narrative*, trans. Christine van Boheemen, Toronto: University of Toronto Press. (Original title: *De theorie van vettellen en verhalen*, 2nd revised edn, Muiderberg: Coutinho, 1980.)
Banfield, Ann (1982) *Unspeakable Sentences. Narration and Representation in the Language of Fiction*, Boston: Routledge & Kegan Paul.
—— (1985) "Grammar and memory," *Proceedings of the Berkeley Linguistics Society* 11: 387–97.
Barthes, Roland (1966) "Introduction à l'analyse structurale des récits," *Communications* 8: 1–27. (English version: "An introduction to the structural analysis of narrative," *New Literary History* 6 (1975): 237–72.)
Bellos, David M. (1978) "The narrative absolute tense," *Language and Style* 11: 231–7.
Benveniste, Émile (1959) "Les relations de temps dans le verbe français," *Bulletin de la Société Linguistique de Paris* 54: 237–50.
Boyer, Henri (1979) "L'opposition passé simple/passé composé dans le

système verbal de la langue française," *Le Français Moderne* 47 (2): 121-9.
Bronzwaer, W.J.M. (1970) *Tense in the Novel*, Groningen: Wolters-Noordhoff.
Brooks, Cleanth and Warren, Robert Penn (1943) *Understanding Fiction*, New York: Crofts.
Butor, Michel (1969) *Essais sur le roman*, Paris: Gallimard.
Cerquiglini, Bernard (1984) "Le style indirect libre et la modernité," *Langages* 73: 7-16.
Chvany, Catherine V. (1979) "Grammatical categories in the narrative of Elin Pelin's *Zemja*," *Folia Slavica* 3 (3): 296-316.
Cohn, Dorrit (1978) *Transparent Minds: Narrative Modes for Presenting Consciousness in Fiction*, Princeton: Princeton University Press.
Deledda, Grazia (1939) *Il Cedro del Libano, Novelle*, Milan: Garzanti.
Doležel, Lubomir (1967) "The typology of the narrator: point of view in fiction," in *To Honor Roman Jakobson*, vol. 1, The Hague: Mouton.
Ducrot, Oswald (1979) "L'imparfait en français," *Linguistische Berichte* 60: 1-23.
Dujardin, Édouard (1931) *Le monologue intérieur*, Paris: Messein.
Flaubert, Gustave (1954) *L'Education sentimentale. Histoire d'un jeune homme*, ed. Edouard Maynial, Paris: Garnier Frères.
—— (1964) *Sentimental Education*, trans. Robert Baldick, Harmondsworth: Penguin.
Fleischman, Suzanne (1985) "Discourse functions of tense-aspect oppositions in narrative: toward a theory of grounding," *Linguistics* 23: 851-82.
—— (1986) "Evaluation in narrative: the present tense in medieval 'performed stories,'" *Yale French Studies* 70: 199-251.
—— (1990) *Tense and Narrativity: From Medieval Performance to Modern Fiction*, Austin: University of Texas Press/London: Routledge.
Friedemann, Käte (1910) *Die Rolle des Erzählers in der Epik*, Leipzig: Haessel.
Genette, Gérard (1980) *Narrative Discourse. An Essay in Method*, trans. Jane E. Lewin, Ithaca, NY: Cornell University Press.
Givón, Talmy (1982) "Evidentiality and epistemic space," *Studies in Language* 6: 23-49.
Haberland, Hartmut (1986) "Reported speech in Danish," in Florian Coulmas (ed.) *Direct and Indirect Speech*, Berlin: Mouton de Gruyter.
Hamburger, Käte (1973) *The Logic of Literature*, trans. Marilyn Rose, 2nd rev. edn, Bloomington: Indiana University Press.
Herczeg, Giulio (1958) "Valore stilistico del presente storico in italiano," in *Omagiu lui Iorgu Iordan*, Bucharest: Academia Republicii Populare Romîne.
Kamp, Hans and Rohrer, Christian (1983) "Tense in text," in Rainer Bäuerle, Christoph Schwarze, and Arnim von Stechow (eds) *Meaning, Use and Interpretation in Language*, Berlin/New York: Springer.
Labov, William (1972) "The transformation of experience in narrative syntax," in *Language in the Inner City*, Philadelphia: University of Pennsylvania Press.
Labov, William and Waletzky, Joshua (1967) "Narrative analysis: oral versions of personal experience," in June Helm (McNeish) (ed.) *Essays on the Verbal and Visual Arts*, Seattle: University of Washington Press.

Lainé, Pascal (1974) *La Dentellière*, Paris: Gallimard.
Lanser, Susan Sniader (1981) *The Narrative Act: Point of View in Prose Fiction*, Princeton, NJ: Princeton University Press.
Longacre, Robert E. (1976) *Anatomy of Speech Notions*, Lisse: De Ridder.
Martin, Wallace (1986) *Recent Theories of Narrative*, Ithaca, NY: Cornell University Press.
Polanyi, Livia (1982) "Literary complexity in everyday storytelling," in Deborah Tannen (ed.) *Spoken and Written Language: Exploring Orality and Literacy*, Norwood, NJ: Ablex.
Pouillon, Jean (1946) *Temps et roman*, Paris: Gallimard.
Proust, Marcel (1920) "A propos du 'style' de Flaubert," *Nouvelle Revue Française* 14 (1): 72–90.
—— (1954) *À la recherche du temps perdu*, ed. Pierre Clarac and André Ferré, 3 vols, Paris: Gallimard.
—— (1934) *Remembrance of Things Past*, trans. C.K. Scott-Moncrieff, 2 vols, New York: Random House.
Raimond, Michel (1966) *La Crise du roman, des lendemains du naturalisme aux années 20*, Paris: Corti.
Ricoeur, Paul (1984, 1985, 1988) *Time and Narrative*, 3 vols, trans. Kathleen McLaughlin (vol. 3 Kathleen Blamey) and David Pellauer, Chicago: University of Chicago Press. (Original title: *Temps et récit*, 3 vols, Paris: Seuil, 1983, 1984, 1985.)
Rimmon-Kenan, Shlomith (1983) *Narrative Fiction*, London: Methuen.
Sartre, Jean-Paul (1947) *Situations*, I, Paris: Gallimard.
Spitzer, Leo (1928) "Zum Stil Marcel Prousts," in *Stilstudien* 2: 365–497.
Stanzel, Franz (1971) *Narrative Situations in the Novel*, trans. James Pusack, Bloomington: Indiana University Press. (Original title: *Die typischen Erzählsituationen im Roman*, Vienna: Braunmüller, 1955.)
Todorov, Tzvetan (1966) "Les catégories du récit littéraire," *Communications* 8: 125–51.
—— (1970) *L'Énonciation*, Paris: Didier-Larousse.
Uspensky, Boris (1973) *A Poetics of Composition: The Structure of the Artistic Text and a Typology of Compositional Form*, trans. Valentina Zavanin and Susan Wittig, Berkeley and Los Angeles: University of California Press.
van Dijk, Teun A. (1975) "Action, action description, and narrative," *New Literary History* 6: 273–94.
Vitoux, Pierre (1982) "Le jeu de la focalisation," *Poétique* 51: 359–68.
Waugh, Linda R. and Monville-Burston, Monique (1986) "Aspect and discourse function: the French simple past in newspaper usage," *Language* 62 (4): 846–77.
Weinrich, Harald (1973) *Le Temps*, trans. Michèle Lacoste, Paris: Seuil. (Original title: *Tempus*, Stuttgart: Kohlhammer, 1964.)

4 Tense switching in Italian: the alternation between *passato prossimo* and *passato remoto* in oral narratives[1]

Giulia Centineo

1. INTRODUCTION

Traditional accounts of the difference between the *passato prossimo* ("near past") (PP) and *passato remoto* ("remote past") (PR) underscore the point that in modern standard Italian the two tenses contrast only in written literary discourse, since PR has almost disappeared from conversational use.

In the "familiar" speech of most northern Italian regions, the PR is said to have been replaced by the PP (Rohlfs 1986; Lepschy and Lepschy 1981; Harris 1982), while in central and southern Italy the PR is still used. There are contrasting opinions on the extent of the use of the PR in central Italy. For instance, Rohlfs says that "in central Italy the *passato remoto* begins to lose ground: in Florence it is not much in use" (1966: 45–6); while Lepschy and Lepschy state that both the PR and the PP are found in Tuscany and central Italy and that they have different meanings which are mirrored in literary/written language.

In a written text both PP and PR are said to be tenses which report past events. The PR encodes events which have no relationship with the present and which take (or may have taken) place in a distant past. PR emphasizes an action/state as such, its happening, becoming, and completion (i.e. inchoative or completive aspect). The PP describes past events which are somehow related to the present, i.e. events that took place in a time period which has not yet ended, events in the near past, or events which still affect the present.

Consider the following examples (from Rohlfs 1966 and Lepschy and Lepschy 1981) where PR and PP are contrasted (PR predicates are italicized, PP predicates in bold.[2]

(1) a. Ieri *visitammo* il museo, oggi **siamo andati** al castello.

"Yesterday we *visited* the museum, today we **went** to the castle."
b. Era domenica ieri e *uscimmo*, non **ho potuto** studiare.
"It was Sunday yesterday and we *went out*, I **couldn't study**."
c. Mi **ha dato un calcio** (e mi fa ancora male).
"S/he **kicked (me)** (and it still hurts)."
d. *Mi diede un calcio* (ma ormai non ci penso più).
"S/he *kicked me* (but I don't think about it any more)."
e. Negli ultimi dieci anni **abbiamo cambiato casa** sette volte.
"In the last ten years we **have moved** seven times."
f. In quei dieci anni *cambiammo casa* sette volte.
"In those ten years we *moved* seven times."

Such meaning differences can be captured better in terms of the tense-aspect categories "present perfect" and "preterit." Thus, according to traditional grammatical descriptions, the PR is a "preterit," the PP a "perfect." The two forms contrast with respect to the feature of "present relevance," the presence or absence of which may also distinguish the two forms at the temporal level; i.e. lack of present relevance may imply temporal distance, while present relevance often implies temporal closeness (see Fleischman 1982; Harris 1982; Dahl 1983; Bertinetto 1986).[3]

In modern Italian, however, the PP has assumed, in addition to its perfect meaning, also a preterit meaning:

(2) L'anno scorso Marco **è andato** in Cina.
"Last year Marco **went** to China."

A consequence of the merging of the two categories preterit and perfect into the PP and of the overlap in meaning of PR and PP, is the gradual disappearance of the PR from conversational Italian and its restriction to particular contexts: formal written discourses. Whenever the two preterit forms co-occur in a narrative, the PR presumably encodes narration *per se*, while the PP appears in direct quotes (see Rohlfs 1966; Lepschy and Lepschy 1981; Bertinetto 1986). The language of direct quotes mimics the conversational usage of the form. The following passage from Pratolini, quoted in Lepschy and Lepschy (1981: 200), exemplifies this contrast:

(3) Il plotone dei fazzoletti rossi si *schierò*, *fece fuoco*, i tre al muro *gridarono*: "viva," e *non si seppe* viva cosa, *non ebbero il tempo di finire*.
"**Sono cascati** come burattini," *disse* Tosca. Una donna, una sposa, accanto a lei *si fece il segno della croce*; Tosca *la guardò, sorrise*.

"Forse **ho detto male?**" *le chiese, e si fece il segno della croce.*
"The red-handkerchiefed squad *lined up, fired*, the three against the wall *shouted*: "long live," and we *did not know* long live what, they *did not have the time* to finish.
"They **fell** like puppets," *said* Tosca.
Next to her, a woman, a wife *crossed herself*; Tosca *looked at her, smiled.*
"Perhaps I **said something wrong?**" she *asked her*, and *crossed herself*."

We note, however, that in this example the PP is the only tense possible in those sentences in which it occurs not because it represents conversational usage, but because it reports events located in a very near past. In standard *spoken* Italian, utterances such as "*Cascarono* come burattini" or "Forse *dissi* male," would be ungrammatical if used in this context.[4] In literature, the PR can also appear in direct quotes when the event occurs prior to the moment of speech and has no bearing on it, or is temporally distant from it as in (4):

(4) Poi guardando me che vergognosa abbassavo il capo, *domandò*: questa, è una figlia tua? Lo *seppi*, lo *seppi*, – *aggiunse* frettolosa, – che t'eri sposato – . (Morante 1982: 463)
"Then looking at me as I was bashfully bowing my head, she *asked*, 'And this one, is she a daughter of yours? I *found out*, I *found out*,' she *added* hastily, 'that you had gotten married.' "

Linguists have explained the appearance of the PR beside the PP in modern spoken Italian either in terms of a diachronic process not yet completed, or as an instance of dialectical usage. That is, this use of the PR may be a remnant of an earlier state of the language when PR was the only preterit form or when the possibility of neutralizing present relevance had not yet occurred (Rohlfs 1966; Lepschy and Lepschy 1981; Harris 1982). Alternatively, especially in southern Italy, this use of the PR has been interpreted as an instance of interference from dialects (e.g. Sicilian) in which PR is the only preterit (Rohlfs 1966; Harris 1982).

What these investigators seem to overlook are cases in which the PR and PP coexist in spoken discourse, both with preterit meaning. My data show that the PR not only occurs in oral narrative contexts, but frequently co-occurs with the PP, a situation that suggests that this usage cannot be explained simply as one of free variation; nor can it be accounted for in terms of the correlations that obtain in literature, i.e. PR for narration, PP for direct quotes; nor can it be explained in terms of temporal distance, since the two forms can occur in the same story with reference to events which are equally distant from the moment of speech.

The goal of this chapter is to investigate tense selection and alternation in Italian oral narration, with special reference to the switching between PR and PP. In the course of my discussion I will attempt to answer the following questions: (1) What is the relationship between these two tense forms and the structure of narrated events? (2) What is the function of the switch between PR and PP in oral narration? (3) What are the functions of the tenses themselves in the context of oral narration?

2. DATA AND METHODOLOGY

The data consist of 41 tape-recorded narratives taken from 23 women and 17 men over a period of three months in 1983-4. One narrator provided two versions of the same story. All interviewees were middle class, college educated, 24 to 34 years of age, and native speakers of the Italian spoken in Sicily and at least one variety of Sicilian as well. At the time of the recording, all had lived in Palermo for at least ten years.[5] The social relationship between the interviewer and the interviewees varies from good friends (22), to social acquaintances (10), to first encounters (8).

The interviewees were asked to narrate an incident from their past which had particularly impressed them. About a third of the resulting stories (14) involve a childhood memory; the rest deal with a more recent incident that for some reason struck the narrator as weird, funny, scary, etc.

The framework for the analysis of these stories follows that used in a number of studies on tense switching in oral and written narrative (Wolfson 1979; Schiffrin 1981; Silva-Corvalán 1983; and Fleischman 1985, 1986), which draw on the work of Labov and Waletzky (1967) and Labov (1972) on the structural organization of oral narrative.

3. STRUCTURAL CHARACTERISTICS OF ORAL NARRATIVE

Labov and Waletzky view narrative as "one verbal technique for recapitulating experience, in particular, a technique of constructing narrative units which match the temporal sequence of that experience" (1967: 13). They also define a well-formed narrative as one which serves at one and the same time a "referential function," i.e. providing (new) information, and an "evaluative function," i.e. "indicating the point of the narrative, its raison d'être: why it was told, and what the narrator is getting at" (Labov 1972: 366).

Labov and Waletzky define the clause as the basic unit of linguistic expression within the context of a narrative. To them, in fact, a narrative is a sequence of (a minimum of two) clauses which "recapitulates experience in the same order as the original events" (1967: 21). They propose the following classification of clause types:

(a) *narrative clauses*, i.e. clauses which refer to temporally ordered events; the order of these clauses cannot be changed without altering the semantic interpretation of the sequence of events. Syntactically, narrative clauses are independent clauses. The temporally ordered series of these clauses represents the blueprint of the story, or "primary sequence";
(b) *free clauses*, i.e. clauses which do not have a fixed relation to a temporal order and can, therefore, range freely through an entire narrative;
(c) *co-ordinate clauses*, i.e. clauses whose "displacement" within a narrative is permissible only with respect to each other;
(d) *restricted clauses*, i.e. clauses "which are neither free nor temporally ordered in the strict sense" (Labov and Waletzky 1967: 23); they can be displaced across limited sections of the narrative.

The narratives analysed by Labov and Waletzky are all well-structured texts which consist of a series of basic functional components: (a) abstract, (b) orientation, (c) complicating action, (d) evaluation, (e) resolution, and (f) coda. Each constituent part can be viewed as the answer to a specific underlying question:

    a. Abstract: what was this about?
    b. Orientation: who, when, what, where?
    c. Complicating action: then what happened?
    d. Evaluation: so what?
    e. Result: what finally happened?
    f. Coda: how does this relate to the present discourse context?
                              (Adapted from Labov 1972: 370)

This structure is exemplified by the following narrative:[6]

(5)   dunque perciò   ABSTRACT
      devo raccontarti questo fatto che

	quando ero piccolo e andavo alle scuole elementari	ORIENTATION
	la la nostra suora	
	cioè la nostra insegnante	
	si si seccava molto del fatto che	
	noi bambini sottraessimo dei fogli	
	dei fogli dal quaderno di bella	
	va bene?	
(a)	una volta *venne a scoprire* che nel mio quaderno	COMPLICATING ACTION
	che si chiamava "zibaldone"	
	perchè raccoglievamo	
	questo zibaldone ... tutte le notizie	
	che so	EMBEDDED ORIENTATION
	formule di aritmetica, regole di grammatica	
	mancava	
	che so	
	due pagine	
(b)	allora *mi travestì* da bandito	
(b²)	cioè *mi mise*	
	praticamente	
	un cappuccio	
	mi pare che	
	era un cappuccio bianco con due buchi	EMBEDDED ORIENTATION
	non si capisce	
	per fare vedere gli occhi	
	e un cartello davanti al petto con scritto	
	"io rubo i soldi ai miei genitori"	
	io io invece avevo soltanto un foglio così	RESOLUTION
(c)	e *mi fece girare* l'istituto a me piccoletto	
	tutto l'istituto	
	travestito da bandito	
	fu grande lo choc	EVALUATION
	insomma	
	che io *dovetti sopportare* in quella occasione	
	capito?	
	e mi ricordo sempre questa cosa	CODA
	quando penso a questo istituto	
	il fatto che io da bandito *girai* tutto	
	sotto il	
	additato da dagli altri compagni come un delinquente ***	
	sottoposto a questo ludibrio.	

"So, I must tell you this fact that when I was little and I was going to elementary school, our nun, that is our teacher, would get really upset at the fact that we children would steal some sheets from the last-draft notebook, ok? Once she *found out* that my notebook (which we called 'zibaldone,' because we collected in this 'zibaldone' all the information, I don't know, like arithmetic formulas, rules of grammar) was missing two pages, or something like that. So she *dressed me up* as a bandit, that is she *put a hood on me* (I think it was a white hood with two holes, I don't know, eye-holes, I guess) and a sign on my chest that said 'I steal money from my parents.' I ... I had only one sheet [left] so ... She *made me*, just a little kid, *go all around* the school, the whole school, dressed up like a bandit. It was really traumatic what I *had to go through* on that occasion. You understand? And I always remember this thing when I think of that school the fact that I, as a bandit, *went around* the whole ... under the ... pointed at by the other school kids as a criminal. I was a laughing-stock."

It must be emphasized that well-formed narratives need not exhibit the above idealized structure. As Labov and Waletzky note, abstracts, codas, and a separate initial orientation section may be absent in spontaneous (non-elicited) narratives.[7]

4. NARRATIVE STRUCTURE AND TENSE SELECTION IN ITALIAN ABSTRACTS AND CODAS

In the elicited Italian stories that constitute my data, abstracts and codas occur frequently. Abstracts appear in 18 (43 per cent), and codas in 23 (56 per cent) of the 41 stories.

The abstracts, which consist of at least one free clause, are of two types: (a) some summarize the main point of the story (as in (6) below); (b) others are "interactive" in nature, i.e. the narrator makes explicit reference to the interviewer's request to narrate a story, as in (7):

(6) a. Quando **sono andata** in Grecia
   ho avuto l'idea straordinaria di andarci in aereo.
   "When I **went** to Greece I **had** the extraordinary **idea** to go by plane."

   b. **Ho conosciuto** una persona credo fantastica.
   "I **met** a fantastic person, I think."

   c. *Fummo* tutto sommato *fortunati*.
   "All considered we *were lucky*."

(7) a. E allora ti racconto della prima volta che **sono uscita** sola con la macchina.

"So, I'll tell you about the first time I **went out** with the car by myself."
    b. Ti vorrei raccontare una della mie prime riunioni di lavoro.
"I want to tell you about one of my first business meetings."

In all of the above examples, except for (7b), the information encapsulated in the abstract is encoded in the preterit. Of the two tense forms which have preterit meaning, PP is much more common in abstracts. PR occurs only once, in (6c), the abstract of a narrative which exhibited also dialect switch (Italian/Sicilian).

The coda is that section of the narrative which, when present, formally indicates the end of the story. Three types of codas occur in the Italian narratives: (a) codas which mark the end of the narrative and/or of narrated events, as in (8); (b) codas which function to bridge the gap between the time of the resolution of the story and the present, as in (9); and (c) codas in which the narrator says (implicitly or explicitly) that s/he has complied with the interviewer's request to narrate some memorable fact, as in (10a–d), and which at the same time may express some other narrative function such as evaluation, as in (10e).

(8) a. Ed è **finita**.
    "And it **ended**."
  b. E l'avventura **si è conclusa**.
    "And the adventure **came to an end**."
  c. Insomma questo.
    "In short this [was it]."
  d. E niente.
    "That's it." [lit. "and nothing"].

(9) a. E questo lo ricordavamo oggi con le mie cugine.
    "And just today, my cousins and I were remembering this incident."
  b. E con quella scusa Grazia **non è più venuta**.
    "And with this excuse, Grazia's **never come again**."
  c. E mi ricordo sempre di questa cosa quando penso a questo istituto.
    "And I always remember this incident when I think about that school."

(10) a. Non è carina?
    "Isn't it cute?"
   b. E chista è **stata** la cosa più graziosa....
    "And this **was** the nicest thing...."
   c. Ecco questa è una cosa che mi **ha fatto impressione**.

"Here, this is something that really **left an impression on me.**"

d. *Mi fece un'impressione* terribile.
   "It really *struck me*."

e. E questo *fù* il mio battesimo del volante.
   "And this *was* my baptism at the wheel."

5. ORIENTATION

All of the narratives contain orientation clauses in which the speaker provides background information about the participants, time, and location of the narrated events. In 24 of the 41 stories (59 per cent), orientation clauses (free and restricted clauses) occur both at the beginning and at various other points in the text; in the remainder orientation material does not appear enclosed in a separate section at the beginning, but is interspersed throughout the text.

Tense forms with imperfective aspect – *imperfetto* (Imp) and *presente* (Pr)[8] – occur frequently in orientation clauses (cf. Hopper 1979). The Imp reports habitual situations in the past (11), states, and durative situations simultaneous with the narrated events (12). The Pr occurs in statements of generalities ("gnomic" or "omnitemporal" present) (13), and in the description of states and actions which extend from the past up to the moment of speech (14). The *trapassato prossimo*, the Italian pluperfect, encodes all situations which took place before the current narrative plane (15).

(11) a. Quando io ero piccolo
    e andavo alle scuole elementari
    la la nostra suora
    cioè la nostra insegnante
    si si seccava molto del fatto.
    "When I was little and was going to elementary school, our nun, that is, our teacher would get really upset at the fact."

   b. Quando io ero piccola
    leggevo moltissimo.
    eeh soprattutto quando ero in vacanza.
    "When I was little I used to read a lot, especially when I was on vacation."

(12) a. Ero in via Libertà
    e camminavo lungo i vialoni di via Libertà.
    "I was in Libertà Street, and I was walking along Libertà Street."

(13) a. Lo sai quando tu navighi per tanto tempo
e ti trema sempre tutto.
"You know when you have been sailing for a long time and everything is shaking around you."
b. In caduta libera non si vede precipitare qualcuno
ma sembra addirittura di essere fermi.
"In free fall, you don't see anyone fall, actually, everything seems to be still."

(14) a. E allora io faccio il medico.
"So I am a doctor."
b. Dunque io faccio paracadutismo.
"So I do sky-diving."

(15) a. Avevamo finito di studiare con Grazia
e c'era pure Aurora.
"We had finished studying with Grazia, and Aurora was also there."
b. C'era una festa in maschera e Teresa mi aveva invitato.
"There was a masquerade party and Teresa had invited me."
c. Stavano ripitturando la casa
e avevano sverniciato le porte
nelle porte avevano messo il mastice.
"They were repainting the house and they had stripped the doors and on the doors they had put some putty."

6. COMPLICATING ACTION

The complicating action is that part of the narrative which includes the series of sequentially ordered events which constitute "the story" itself. Labov (1972), Hopper (1979), and others have noted that while imperfective aspect tends to encode backgrounded information, perfective aspect expresses foregrounded information, i.e. it characterizes the "narrative events" which constitute the main story-line.[9] The tense form used to report main-line events must have a preterit interpretation.

In Italian there are three tenses which can exhibit the specifications [+ past, + perfective]: PR, PP, and Pr. All three can occur – and as we will see below at times co-occur – within the complicating action. Texts using only one of these tenses to encode the primary sequence of events are common: of the 41 narratives, 9 (22 per cent) choose the PR, 8 (20 per cent) the PP, and 3 (7 per cent) the Pr. The use of each of these as a narrative event tense is independently motivated.

PR (from the so-called Latin perfect) is the tense which continues diachronically the function of narrative tense *par excellence*. This function attaches to the PR from its core/basic preterit meaning and, therefore, from its lack of "present relevance." The absence of present relevance implies psychological and temporal distance of the narrating ego from the narrated event. Temporal and psychological distance from a past event suggest, in turn, *objectivity of representation*. We could, thus, extend to the Italian PR Benveniste's characterization of the French *passé simple*, as "the tense of the event outside the person of a narrator" (1971: 208).

It is because of its special status as a narrative tense that PR still occurs in spoken Italian, in spite of its alleged disappearance. It attributes objectivity and therefore a historical imprimatur to the account of a personal experience. The PR is the tense of history, in the etymological sense of the word, as eyewitness report.

At least two factors seem to influence the selection of PR as a narrative tense: formality and temporal distance (of the nine stories told exclusively in PR, seven (78 per cent) narrate childhood memories; see example (5)). During the interviews I noted a sharp change in register from informal to formal in some narrators. The fact that their stories were being tape-recorded obviously influenced the register switch. These narrators wanted to speak correctly, and thus understandably "chose" to recount their stories in the PR, the past form associated with formal written language and, therefore, with a more prestigious form of discourse.[10] In three instances the change in register was particularly noticeable since the speakers were friends of the interviewer. They recounted their stories in a speech style significantly different from their habitual style, one characterized by a more careful selection of syntactic constructions and lexical items.[11]

The present is the other tense which typically occurs in narrative contexts (both oral and written) with a preterit meaning. This particular usage has been labeled the historical or narrative present. In my data the choice of HPr as a narrative tense also seems to be influenced by the distance of the events from the moment of speech. Five of the six stories narrated in the HPr recount an incident which happened relatively close to the time of its telling. Narratives in which the main story-line is encoded in the HPr also exhibit considerable use of direct speech and imitation of people's voices, mannerisms, and gestures. They exhibit the criterial features of "performed stories" (Wolfson 1978).

It has traditionally been argued that the function of the HPr is to report events as if they were occurring simultaneously with the moment of speech. Like the PR, the HPr is also a tense selected to give an impression of objectivity in the narration of the story. The fact that the narrator portrays the events as taking place before his or her own eyes as well as those of the addressee is intended to dispel any doubt about the objectivity of the account. However, as an indicator of the objectivity of representation, the HPr differs from the PR in that it leaves the interpretation of the events up to the addressee. The PR reports events as if they were factual "history," while the HPr enables the addressee to witness the events and construe them as "history," if so desired.

The occurrence of the PP as a narrative tense is an extension of its conversational usage with preterit meaning. Despite its occurrence in eight stories as the sole narrative tense, the PP seems not to have the same status as PR or HPr as a basic narrative tense. In fact, in some narratives only the first narrative event, or the abstract, is in the PP, while the rest of the story is in either the HPr or the PR, or a combination of the two. At the beginning of a story, in fact, since the narrator is addressing the interviewer, he or she might still be using the preterit form typical of a dialogic conversational exchange, and not yet the preterit deemed appropriate to narration.[12]

What originally distinguished PP and PR (in their perfect and preterit meanings respectively) was the feature of "present relevance." It seems to me that despite their apparent referential synonymy as preterits they are still distinguished by this feature, although at a different level. Apropos of the change in meaning in the compound past forms of certain modern Romance languages, Comrie notes that "there is a discrepancy between form (which includes both present and past) and meaning (which is often just past)" (1976: 106–7). In Italian narrative discourse, however, in which both preterit forms can occur, this discrepancy between form and meaning seems to have been reconciled: inclusion of the present, at the formal level, has the effect of including also the "psychological center" of the narrator. The narrated events, even though past, are viewed somewhat in relation to the present. They are closer to the narrator, temporally and/or psychologically. We could therefore say with Benveniste that in narrative the PR is the tense of historical, objective narration, and the PP the tense of personal, subjective report, "the autobiographical form par excellence" (1971: 210).

It is difficult to find a clear correlation between the selection of PP and temporal distance or formality. At a very impressionistic level, the stories whose main narrative sequence is reported in the PP belong to a past more distant than those reported in the HPr and more recent than those encoded in the PR.

7. OBJECTIVITY AND SUBJECTIVITY OF REPRESENTATION

It must be understood that the qualifications "subjective" and "objective" used in the above discussion of the PR, HPr and PP do not reflect the real-world adherence of the narrated events to "the facts." Rather, these terms describe the speaker's attitude toward the propositional content of an utterance and his or her (covert and perhaps also unconscious) desire that the account be interpreted as either "history" (objective representation) or "autobiography" (subjective representation). Despite the obvious reference to Benveniste, the labels "objective" and "subjective" representation are, *mutatis mutandis*, rather close in meaning to Lyons' objective and subjective modalization.

> The main difference between subjectively and objectively modalized utterances is that the latter, but not the former, contain an unqualified, or categorical, I-say-so component. The speaker is committed by the utterance of an objectively modalized utterance to the factuality of the information that he is giving to the addressee: he is peforming an act of telling.... objective modalization differs from subjective modalization, the very essence of which is to express the speaker's reservations about giving an unqualified, or categorical, "I-say-so" to the factuality of the proposition embedded in his utterance.
>
> (Lyons 1977: 798–9)

Thus a narrative reported in the PR or HPr is parallel to an objectively modalized utterance with an unqualified "I-say-so" component, whereas in a narrative reported in the PP the "I-say-so" component has been qualified by something like "but it is just my impression."

8. TENSE ALTERNATION IN THE COMPLICATING ACTION

In a narrative context, tense alternation is a means both to encode and to decode particular information. As pointed out on p. 64, the distinction between perfective and imperfective aspect, as expressed through tenses, typically separates foreground from background. More troublesome to analyze is the alternation between tenses which, in narrative, appear to possess essentially the same general semantic features, notably PR, PP, and HPr within the complicating action.

As we saw on p. 65, the selection of a particular form of preterit is determined by a variety of factors: formality/informality, temporal distance, objectivity/subjectivity. These factors, however, do not illuminate for us the function of the alternation between one preterit category and another within the same narrative. Consider the following example:

(16) a. una mattina **mi sono svegliata** molto presto
   avevo un forse tre o quattro anni
   b. allora **mi sono alzata** dal letto
   ed ero un pochettino smarrita
   come sempre perchè io al buio ****
   mi sento un pochettino
   mi confondo
   c. e **ho visto** che c'era luce
   d. e allora ticche ticche ticche *andai d'appresso*
   diciamo
   e. a questa luce e *trovai* mia madre che
   all'orario **** delle cinque di mattina
   era messa che faceva marmellata in cucina [laugh]
   ora
   diciamo
   la cosa che più **mi ha sconvolto**
   è
   f. che mia madre *mi rimproverò* terribilmente
   perchè avevo i piedi nudi
   perchè mi ero alzata eccetera
   e invece io trovavo molto molto grazioso
   propio il fatto di andare
   come dire
   spiando muovendomi nella casa eccetera
   propio [laugh] questa è l'unica cosa
   che mi **è rimasta impressa** [laugh]
   cioè la prima cosa che mi rimane impressa del passato.

"One morning I **woke up** very early (I must have been three or four years old); I **got up** from the bed, and I **felt** a little lost, as usual (because in the dark I feel a little ... I get confused) and I **saw** that there was a light on, and so 'ticche ticche ticche' [imitates the sound of her light steps] I sort of *followed* this light and I *found* my mother who, at five in the morning, was there in the kitchen, making some jam. Now let's say, the thing that **shocked me** the most is that my mother *scolded me* harshly because I was barefoot, because I had gotten up, etcetera. Whereas I found really really neat that I was going, how should I say, snooping around, moving around the house, etcetera, really [laugh]. This is the only thing that really **stuck in my mind** [laugh]. That's the first thing that strikes me as unusual from my past."

Note that of the narrative clauses, (a–c) are encoded in the PP, (d–f) in the PR.

For narratives which display tense switching (such as (16) above), an understanding of the general meaning of each category of preterit (used as sole narrative tense) is necessary but not sufficient to interpret the function of a given tense in a tense-switch context. Rather as we shall see, an interpretation of the alternation of tenses in narrative and of the function of each tense in an alternation set will depend crucially on the specific context of usage and on the relationship each tense has with other tenses used in the narrative.

Seventeen narratives (42 per cent) exhibit tense switching between PR and PP (i.e. there is at least one form of each tense) in the complicating action or in the last clause(s) of the complicating action (the resolution). PR and HPr co-occur in four (10 per cent) of the stories, PP and HPr in nine (22 per cent). In five of these nine narratives HPr is used solely before direct quotes, normally with the speech-reporting verb "say" or one of its synonyms.[13]

9. RESOLUTION

The resolution contains the concluding event of the story. In many stories in which the narrative events are encoded in the PR, HPr, or both (as we shall see on p. 78), the PP encodes the resolution, thus underscoring the present relevance or continuing effects of the incident or the relevance of the story to the discourse context into which it was inserted.

(17) a. un ragazzino di sedici anni *riuscì* a prendermi
e **siamo andati sopra.**
"a 16-year-old boy *managed* to get hold of me
and we **went up.**"
b. e finalmente lui *agitò, toccò una cosa*
e *riuscì* a sbloccare la porta
siamo usciti.
"and finally he *shook, touched something* and *managed* to open up the door, we **got out.**"

The "present of result" meaning of the PP often marks off the resolution and coda from the rest of the narrative encoded in PR or PR and HPr.

10. EVALUATION

Narrative is not a mere list of sequentially ordered events. The speaker's evaluation of the recounted material is an essential feature of narrative, as it often communicates the point of the story. Evaluation can occur either in a specific section of the narrative (typically just before and/or after the climactic point in the complicating action or before the resolution) or may be interspersed throughout the text. Narrators have at their disposal a number of formal means to encode evaluation, ranging from the most overt to the more subtle expressions of personal judgment – what, following Labov, we may call *external* and *internal evaluation* respectively.

10.1. External evaluation

A typical external evaluation strategy is for the speaker to interrupt the narrative and comment on its content:

(18) a. Pure te lo racconto perchè
perchè *fu* un episodio particolare
perchè nella tragedia dell'incidente che poteva sopravvenire
... con la caduta di mio fratello la morte
tutto questo per noi bambini *fu* una specie di festa
perchè era l'inseguimento di un cavallo
tipo di noi piccolissimi tutti appresso
tipo gridando come i pazzi
cioè rendendoci conto
nnn nel con nello stesso tempo
d di un incidente grave che poteva succedere
però allo stesso tempo proprio vissuta come festa.
"Why am I also telling you this? Because it *was* a special episode, because in the tragedy of the accident that might have occurred ... with my brother's fall, his death, all that, for us children *was* some kind of a party, because we were chasing a horse, all of us little children were after it, screaming like crazy, and realizing, at the same time that a serious accident could have occurred, but at the same time, [the event] was experienced as a party."
b. è bruttissimo trovarti in acquasott'acqua
non sapere nuotare e sentirti rifiutata
cioè ti buttavano via

perchè io li prendevo per il collo.
"It is awful to find yourself in water, under water, without being able to swim and feel yourself being rejected, that is, they were pushing you away, because I would grab them by their necks."

c. *fu grande lo choc*
insomma che io *dovetti sopportare* in quella occasione.
"In short it *was really traumatic* what I *had to go through* on that occasion."

At times the speaker's opinion may be woven into the narrative fabric and presented as the content of the speaker's words or thoughts as occurring at the time of the event:

(19) a. **Ho detto** "Guarda quel biondino!"
"I **said**, 'Look at that cute blond guy!'"
b. E **ho pensato**
"Guarda per invitarmi vuol dire che è libero
è disponibile, se no non me lo direbbe."
"And I **thought**, 'Look, for him to invite me it means he's free, he's available, otherwise he wouldn't ask me.'"
c. Io **ho pensato** "ora tira un coltello, una pistola
e mi ammazza qui sul posto
qua la fine della mia vita davanti a questo portone."
"I **thought**, 'Now he'll pull out a knife, a gun, and he'll kill me on the spot; here the end of my life in front of this door.'"

Labov finds that external evaluation is a characteristic of middle-class narrators. Moreover, speakers who are particularly concerned with the expression of their opinions often become so entangled in their search for reasons and justifications that they lose sight of the point and plot of the story. What is primarily communicated by at least four of the forty-one Italian narratives in my corpus is the speaker's evaluation of some ill-defined narrative event.

External evaluation implies departure from the main story-line into parentheticals, asides, etc. (contained in restricted and free clauses). Often, as in (20) below, hedges – here understood as parenthetical expressions which mitigate or intensify an utterance and enclosed in angle brackets – introduce evaluative statements:

(20) a. <Non so come> *andai a finire*.
"<I don't know how> I *ended* up."

b. E l'aereo *s'impennò* di colpo durante il decollo
che <ti dico veramente> lo stomaco *mi uscì* dalle nasche.
"And the airplane *jerked up* all of a sudden, during the take-off, and <I tell you> my guts almost *came out* of my nose."
c. <Ti dico> cose da pazzi.
"<I'm telling you>, it was crazy."

Departures from the narrative events may also be indicated at times by switching into tenses other than the main narrative tense. Consider the following three examples in which the speaker switches from HPr into PP (21) and from PR into PP (22–3), when shifting from the narration of events to their evaluation (present in upper case italics):

(21) (A scary encounter with a street person)
MI SI AVVICINA uno
con uno sguardo orribile, vestito in modo orribile
capelli lunghissimi, niente, tremendo
e mi e *MI COMINCIA A DIRE* cose strane sconclusionate
io sul momento avevo un po' di paura
ma non **ci ho dato molto peso**
perchè non diceva niente di particolarmente eee eclatante.
"A guy *COMES UP TO ME* with a horrible look in his eye, dressed horribly, with very long hair, that's it, terrible. And he *STARTS TO TELL ME* really weird things, that don't make any sense. At that moment, I was a little afraid, but I *didn't think too much of it* because he wasn't telling me anything particularly startling."

(22) (A life-threatening experience at sea)
Ad un certo punto questo qua *ebbe un crampo*
e *mi lasciò*
e io in quel momento **ho avuto la sensazione** di
una persona che mi abbandonava
perchè io cercavo di trattenerlo
e lui invece mi buttava via quest
poi **ho saputo** che mio padre si voleva buttare
mia madre si voleva buttare,
Santo si voleva buttare
la cosa invece mia ... cioè **mi sono salvata** io stessa
perchè
mi resi conto immediatamente che l'unica cosa
che dovevo fare per potermi salvare
era quella di non agitarmi.
"All of a sudden this guy *had a cramp* and *let go of me*, and I, at

that moment **had the feeling** of a person who was abandoning me, because I was trying to hold on to him and he, instead, was pushing me away, that's it. Later I **found out** that my father wanted to jump in, my mother wanted to jump in, Santo wanted to jump in. The thing instead that I ... that is I **saved myself**. Why? I *realized* immediately that the only thing that I had to do to be able to survive was not to panic."

(23) (A heat-wave causes an unusual proliferation of cockroaches in the emergency-room where the narrator works nights)
Comunque
diventarono centinaia
tu vedevi nel corridoio la sera entrando
che so vedevi
io ne **ho contati** cento sessanta una sera
e il corridoio è lungo cinque metri
e allora io che fa
e a in quest'occasione *cominciai*
a coricarmi fuori in macchina
perchè mi faceva troppo schifo.

"Anyway, suddenly there *were hundreds of them*. You would see in the corridor, at night as you were getting in, you would see, I don't know you would see... I **counted** 160 of them one night, and the corridor is five meters long. So what could I do? And that night I *started sleeping outside*, in the car, because it really disgusted me."

In these three narratives PP encodes external evaluation (the subjective comment on the events), while HPr (21) and PR (22–3) report the narrative events themselves "as they occurred," ostensibly independently of the speaker as an evaluative filter.

In the following excerpts from two narratives, the pattern is reversed, i.e. the PR encodes external evaluation while the PP (24) and HPr (25) encode the main events:

(24) (The first important business meeting)
Abbiamo ottenuto un grande ne*** per quelli de dell'impresa
per i quali svolgevamo il lavoro
tant'è vero che
eeh ci **hanno fatto i complimenti** e per la nostra pe pe
le nostre lavorazioni
una cosa che *mi colpì* molto in quella riunione
fu il fatto della dell'esperienza
che occorre ee acquisire
nel mondo del del lavoro.

"We **were a big [success]** with the people in the firm for whom we were working. So much so, that they **congratulated** us for our work. One thing that *struck me* much at that meeting *was* the fact that ... the experience that you have to acquire in the work world."

(25) (A doctor visits a Palermo soccer-team fan)
GLI CHIEDO di che colore fossero le feci
che lui aveva fatto l'ultima volta
perchè in genere chi sanguina ce le ha nere
e allora lui
che era distrutto pieno di di di lividi
ubriaco morto di freddo e quindi in una situazione disastrosa
SI ALZA con un sorriso sar radioso sulla barella
e MI *DICE* che le sue feci sono sempre rosa-nero
che è il colore della maglia [laugh] del Palermo [laugh]
mi fece un'impressione terribile.

"I *ASK HIM* what color his feces were, his last bowel movement, because, generally, when one has bleeding they are black. And so, he – who was a wreck, bruised all over, drunk, freezing cold, and therefore in a really sad condition – he *GETS UP* on his cot with a radiant smile and *TELLS ME* that his feces are always pink and black, which is the color of the uniform of the Palermo soccer team. It really *made an impression on me*."

In (21)–(25) external evaluation is expressed by switching into a tense different from the main narrative tense. The data also show that both PP and PR (but not HPr) can be used to encode external evaluation. However, as we will see in section 11, although the evaluative function of PP and PR may be the same, their rhetorical effect is different.

10.2. Internal evaluation

As an alternative to disrupting the narrative line, a narrator can leave the narrative flow intact and encode evaluation directly into narrative clauses by means of lexical or syntactic devices. Labov (1972) notes that departures from the essentially simple declarative syntax of narrative clauses has the marked function of expressing evaluation. The narrative clause may thus perform at one and the same time a referential function (reporting information) and an evaluative one (subjectively modalizing this information).

Internal evaluation devices can serve a variety of functions: they can mark as salient one or more narrative events; or they can select particular narrative events and amplify, highlight, or at times provide a more detailed description of them. Expressive lexical items (e.g. dialect or slang expressions), taboo words, affective suffixes (e.g. diminutive, augmentative *-ino*, *-etto*, *-one*) are often used for internal evaluation; the use of lexical items marked for subjectivity constitutes a departure from a semantically "neutral" narrative clause. Internal evaluation devices also include use of gestures, imitation of the mannerisms or voice of a story participant, and repetitions (cf. example (5) where the main event in the story is repeated twice). In the examples below evaluation devices are enclosed in angle brackets:

(26)   (Taboo words)
    a. E ci *fu* qualche <stronzo>
       che *mi suonò*
       e io mi ricordo che <*mi incazzai*> moltissimo
       "And there *was* some <jerk> who *honked at me*, and I remember I <*got* really *pissed off*>."
    b. Io qualche anno dopo
       intorno ai miei dodici tredici anni
       insomma in pubertà *lo venni a sapere*
       e <**sono rimasta** propio **di merda**>,
       perchè non avevo saputo la verità.
       "Some years later, around 12 or 13, or some time in adolescence, I *found out* and <really **felt like shit**>, because I hadn't known the truth."

(27)   (Evaluative terms)
    a. E c'era questo <povero> ragazzo
       che *ripetè* questa cosa per lo meno venti volte.
       "And there was this <poor> guy who *repeated* this thing at least twenty times."
    b. E non so come ma *diventammo* <amiconi>.
       "I don't know how, but we *became* <great pals>."

In most of the above cases a tense switch co-occurs with internal evaluation devices. In addition, tense switching can itself have an internal evaluation function, highlighting those narrative events which the speaker considers of particular importance. Consider the following narrative where the switch from PP to PR occurs at the resolution (narrative clause e), then again in the evaluation component ("fu una cosa terribile"), and finally in the coda, which reiterates the "resolution" event ("e loro si misero a ridere").

(28) avevo cinque anni e siccome avevo la sorella più grande
di (?) **** due anni **** lei andava in prima elementare
****e io quando lei tornava a casa da scuola no?
mi mettevo accanto a lei
ee vedevo quello che faceva
e così **ho imparato** a leggere e a scrivere
a. dopo a un certo punto i miei genitori **si sono accorti**
che io avevo cinque anni e però io sapevo leggere e
scrivere senza andare a scuola
b. e allora **hanno deciso** di mandarmi a scuola
e io tutta contenta che dovevo andare a scuola
c. u un giorno **sono andata** a casa di mia zia
tutta contenta che mia madre aveva de[tto]
"vabbè d'accordo ti mandiamo a scuola"
d. ****"sai zia io adesso vado a scuola"
c'era mia zia, mio nonno e mia nonna
e. e *scoppiarono* tutti *a ridere*
e *fu una cosa terribile*
una di quelle cose che io mi ricordo ancora
trent'anni fà
io mi ricordo che ero così contenta di questa cosa
particolare
che andavo a scuola ero piccola
però andare a scuola era una cosa di grandi
e loro *si misero a ridere.*

"I was 5 and since ... I had a sister two years older than me ... she was going to the first grade and when she got back home from school – right? – I would sit next to her and would see what she was doing and that way I **learned** to read and write. Then, at a certain point, my parents **realized** that I was 5 but I could read and write without having gone to school, and so they **decided** to send me to school. And I was all happy about going to school. One day, I **went** to my aunt's house, all happy that my mother had said 'All right, we agree to send you to school.' 'You know, auntie, now, I'm going to school.' My aunt, my grandfather, and my grandmother were there, and all of them *burst out laughing*, and it *was terrible*, one of those things that I still remember, thirty years later! I remember that I was so happy about this special thing, that I was going to school, I was little, but going to school was a grown-up thing and they *started laughing*."

As another internal evaluation strategy, a speaker may underscore an event by placing it against the background of some unrealized or expected alternative. Negatives, modals, and clauses introduced by *in effetti* "in fact," *invece* "instead," *ma* "but" are among the elements which perform such a function:

(29) a. **Siamo andati** al supermercato che a noi ci pareva buono
ma che buono *non fu*.
"We **went** to the supermarket, which we thought was good but it *wasn't*."
  b. Il panico totale perchè Franco
che asseriva di conoscere il francese benissimo
in effetti si *rivelò* una cosa a tipo "bonjour" e "bonsoir."
"[There was] total panic because Franco, who claimed to know French very well, in fact, he *turned out* to be something like 'bonjour' and 'bonsoir.'"

Note that in the sentences in (29), both from the same story, there occurs a systematic tense switch from PP, which encodes the main narrative sequence, to PR in a negated environment or one that turns out to be contrary to the narrator's reading of the situation. Particularly interesting in this regard are the versions of the narrative which I recorded in two different tellings (30a–b). The narrator of this story chooses different tenses for the single negated verb of the story. In (30a), where the basic narrative tense is the PP, the negated form is the PR, while in (30b) the situation is exactly the reverse:

(30a) ero bambina
mi **ha preso il libro dalle mani** e
me l'ha strappato
era u[n] libro che io
appunto leggevo dalla mattina
e continuavo a leggere
nonostante che mia madre mi chiamasse ripetutamente
nella speranza di arrivare a finirlo
perchè volevo sapere a tutti i costi come finiva
e invece in quel modo
non riuscii mai a sapere come finiva il libro.
"I was a little girl – [my mother] **grabbed the book out of my hands** and she **tore it up**. – It was a book that, in fact, I had been reading since that morning, and I kept on reading it, in spite of the fact that my mother called me repeatedly, I was hoping to finish it, because I really wanted to know how it

ended, and that way I *never managed to find out* how the book ended."

(30b) era un romanzo di Salgari
e volevo assolutamente terminarlo al più presto
per sapere come finiva
e mia madre
ovviamente
mi chiamò migliaia di volte
e io rispondevo sempre "ora"
alla fine *venne* ...
mia madre *venne* e *mi prese il libro dalle mani*
e lo
proprio *lo strappò*
e per cui **non l'ho potuto più leggere.**
"It was a novel by Salgari and I was determined to finish it as soon as possible, to find out how it ended. And my mother, obviously, *called me* a thousand times, and I always answered 'All right'. In the end she *came* ... my mother *came* and *grabbed the book out of my hands* and really *tore it right up*. And that is why I **wasn't able to read it any more.**"

From both the co-occurrence of tense switching with indicators of speaker evaluation, and its occurrence at climactic points of a story, we can conclude that in Italian oral narrative tense switching has an evaluative function. Furthermore, the selection of a particular narrative tense (PR, HPr, PP) seems to reflect in large part pragmatic considerations. As argued on p. 67, the choice of one tense over another may be ultimately determined by the desire to mark a particular chunk of the narrative as objectively or subjectively reported.

11. TENSE SWITCHING IN NARRATIVE

Linguists who have investigated the phenomenon of tense switching in (oral) narrative have already noted its essentially evaluative function. Their studies are based on the alternation of HPr (or NPr) with a form of the preterit (see Wolfson 1979; Schiffrin 1981; Silva-Corvalán 1983; Fleischman 1986). There is some disagreement, however, as to whether the tenses that occur in alternation themselves express particular evaluative functions. Wolfson (1979) denies that in a tense-switching context HPr has any particular expressive meaning. Rather, she argues that what counts is the switch, whose function is to separate episodes and events from one another. She maintains that a change in verbal person from one episode to another, and the clustering of same-tense verbs to refer to a single event, offer evidence of such a "boundary" function. Other linguists (Schiffrin 1981; Silva-Corvalán 1983; Fleischman 1986) claim that in a tense-switching context a given tense occurs at particular points of the narrative and that this form acquires, in context, a particular evaluative meaning. Thus, while it is true that recounting a story in the HPr does not necessarily make the story more lively (Wolfson 1978: 215–16; Silva-Corvalán 1983: 769), it is also true that where HPr alternates with another past tense form, it tends to encode climactic points of the story. This does not, however, mean that all high points must be encoded as HPr. Furthermore, the evaluative function of the HPr in tense-switching contexts is, in a sense, an extension of the prototypical usage of the form. "Used in the context of the narrative clause to report past events, the present brings those events from the past and presents them as if they were occurring simultaneously with speech event" (Silva-Corvalán 1983: 778).

These analyses seem also to suggest that in all narrative contexts in which tense switching occurs, the functions of the members of the alternation set would remain constant. That is, in the case of the alternation between HPr and preterit, for instance, HPr would always be an (internal) evaluation device.

This does not seem to be the case in Italian. In the first place, there are three verb forms, PR, PP, and HPr, which can alternate as narrative (event) tenses; second, all of these narrative tenses can perform evaluation. Consequently, the three tenses appear to combine in various tense-switching patterns, in which they assume different functions.

The Italian data exhibit a number of well-defined patterns of tense selection and alternation. I have found at least eight such patterns:

(1) The PR occurs throughout the narrative, encoding both the narrative events and their evaluation (six stories (15 per cent)).
(2) The PP occurs throughout the narrative, encoding narrative events as well as their evaluation. This pattern is found in eight (19 per cent) stories.
(3) PR and PP alternate. PR encodes all sequential narrative events, while PP encodes events or states which are not part of the narrative sequence *per se*, but rather constitute an expansion or explanation of the narrative events, i.e. orientation or narrator's commentary. PR occurs only in narrative clauses, while PP appears in restricted clauses, expressing external evaluation.[14] Five narratives (12 per cent) display this type of tense switch.

(4) PP and PR alternate within the complicating action. PP is the main narrative tense, and PR occurs both in narrative and restricted clauses as a marker of evaluation. Twelve narratives (29 per cent) contain at least one instance of PR with this function. Of the two types of evaluation, the PR is more widely used in my data as an indicator of the internal variety.

(5) HPr and PP alternate in five narratives (12 per cent). HPr occurs only in narrative clauses, while PP occurs in restricted clauses and expresses external evaluation.

(6) HPr and PR alternate in the complicating action of three narratives (7 per cent). However, HPr is the main narrative tense, while PR is the tense of (external) evaluation and/or evaluated action, occurring in both restricted and narrative clauses. I would point out that previous studies on the alternation between HPr and a form of the past have never discussed this particular tense-switching pattern. But given the contextual basis of contrastive phenomena like evaluation (or foregrounding; see Fleischman 1990), this pattern should not be regarded as anomalous for narratives in which the HPr is the basic event tense of the narration.

(7) PP and HPr alternate only in one narrative (2 per cent), where PP is the main narrative tense, while HPr occurs as an internal evaluation device to highlight climactic events. HPr occurs only in narrative clauses.

(8) PR and HPr alternate only in one narrative (2 per cent). In this case, as in (7), the function of HPr is to highlight one particular scene or event within the narrative.

It appears that the question of which tense expresses a purely referential function (i.e. which is the unmarked narrative tense) and which also has an evaluative function must be determined on a case-by-case basis. My data suggest strongly that a particular tense – the one most frequently pointed to in this connection being the HPr – does not encode evaluation a priori, but only in relation to the other tense(s) with which it co-occurs in the narrative. In each narrative one tense is selected as the main narrative tense, and one (or two)[15] of the remaining narrative tenses are chosen for evaluation. By "main narrative tense" I mean the preterit form which has the highest frequency in encoding the sequentially ordered events; this will normally also be the tense that occurs in "unqualified" narrative clauses.

We should not think, however, that the assignment of an evaluative function to a particular tense is totally random, or that the three tense categories express the same evaluative meanings. First, each differs from the others in terms of the types of evaluative clauses in which it appears (PR occurs in both narrative and restricted clauses, PP in restricted clauses and HPr in narrative clauses), and in terms of the type of evaluation it expresses (PR expresses both internal and external evaluation, PP external evaluation, and HPr internal evaluation). Second, each tense accomplishes a different evaluative strategy, related to its narrative/referential meaning.[16]

In particular, PR has the function of highlighting a specific scene or event and bringing it to the foreground. The speaker intensifies his or her statement of "facts" by adding the qualification, "What I am telling you is the objective truth. The events are as dramatic as they seem." As an internal evaluation device, PR differs from HPr in that PR forces the addressee to accept a certain interpretation of the facts, while HPr seems to offer the addressee the option to interpret the facts independently (for an analysis of the evaluative function of HPr, see Schiffrin 1981; Silva-Corvalán 1983).

PP has the function of reporting that part of the narrative which constitutes a departure from the main story-line and of presenting it as the speaker's subjective view of the events. By using the PP, the speaker seems to be saying, "This is my personal view of what happened." It is of interest to note that in most cases in which PP occurs as an indicator of external evaluation, the verb form is a first-person singular or plural.

My data show clearly that in some varieties of Italian the replacement of PR by PP in oral narrative has not occurred (yet); and that PR and PP can coexist, each in its own right, as "narrative tenses." (Recall, however, that the choice between these tenses may be conditioned by pragmatic factors.)

Moreover, the synchronic patterns of occurrence of PR and PP – patterns (1)–(4) on pp. 79–80) – can be situated on an ideal continuum represented in Fig. 4.1 which mirrors the gradual (diachronic) shift in meaning of the PR and PP in modern Romance, more specifically in northern Italian, standard French, and standard Romanian, where the evolution has gone the furthest (see Harris 1982).

Figure 4.1 Diachronic shift in meaning of PR and PP

PR	PR / PP	PP / PR	PP
[NT]	[NT] / [EV]	[NT] / [EV]	[NT]

——————————————————>
<——————————————————

At opposite ends of the cline are the PR and the PP in their preterit meaning, each functioning as the exclusive narrative tense (NT). At intermediate points are the patterns of alternation PR/PP (pattern (3)) and PP/PR (pattern (4)). On the one hand, the PR gives way to the PP as the basic narrative tense and becomes an indicator of evaluation (EV) before it disappears from (oral) narrative. On the other, the PP – which entered the narrative genre from spoken discourse through the back door of asides, comments, and other digressions from the diegetic text, i.e. as an indicator of evaluation – has now assumed the function of a narrative tense.

12. CONCLUSION

The selection of PR as a narrative tense in oral story-telling depends on its function of narrative/historical tense *par excellence*. The choice of PP as a narrative tense reflects instead its modern conversational usage with preterit value. The switch between the PR and the PP (and between one of these two forms and the HPr) functions to evaluate narrated events. It is, however, impossible to determine a priori which tense will encode evaluation. The evaluative function of a tense form can be determined only within a specific narrative context.

As an evaluation device, each tense expresses a particular strategy. In particular, the PP represents an act of stepping into the self, into subjectivity, while the usage of the PR is a stepping outside the self, into objectivity. The specific meaning which each form expresses as an evaluation device stems from its basic meaning in ordinary (non-narrative) language. Finally, the various synchronically present patterns of tense selection and alternation appear to correlate with stages in the diachronic development of simple and compound pasts within Romance.

NOTES

1 This work was supported by an Italian-American Fellowship, offered through the University of California at Berkeley for the academic year 1984–5. I would like to thank Ruggero Stefanini and Eve Sweetser for their helpful comments on an earlier draft. I am particularly grateful to Suzanne Fleischman for her comments, insight, and patience. Special thanks go to all the interviewees who kindly provided the data. Needless to say, mistakes and omissions are solely my responsibility.
2 Predicates may include pronominal and nominal direct and indirect objects, locatives, and adverbials.
3 In addition to the feature of "present relevance" Bertinetto (1986)

identifies other traits which distinguish PP and PR in particular contexts. These traits, however, will not be taken into account here as they are not immediately relevant to the present discussion.
4 These utterances would be perfectly grammatical in Sicilian where the PR marks both preterit and present perfect (see Harris 1982).
5 In these data the Sicilian usage of the PR (see note 3 above) does not interfere with its usage in Italian. In both Sicilian and Italian narratives the PR is used with preterit meaning. However, the high frequency of occurrence of the PR may be due to dialectical influence.
6 Coding conventions: HISTORICAL PRESENT; **passato prossimo**; *passato remoto*. Small letters in brackets to the left of the text indicate narrative clauses. Three or four asterisks indicate an unclear passage on the tape, or a pause by the speaker. In my transcriptions the line break does not indicate a segmentation of the story into syntactic units of analysis such as sentence, clause, or phrase. Rather, it marks a pause or natural break in the narrative flow. Repetitions, stuttering, false starts, interruptions, self-corrections are all left in the texts.
7 In my corpus several stories do not conform to Labov and Waletzky's macro-structural model. These narratives were either merely lists of narrative events, with little or no evaluation or elaboration of any kind, or, conversely, just a series of evaluative statements about some ill-defined narrative event. Some other narratives were missing abstracts and/or codas.
8 Pr in the orientation does not include the historical present, which, when it occurs, has a perfective value.
9 Such a schematic binary formulation of the distribution of aspect for narrative grounding has been challenged. For discussion, see Fleischman (1985, 1990: Chapter 6).
10 In their work on the use of the *passé simple* in French newspapers, Waugh and Monville-Burston (1986) note that the normal association of the *passé simple* with particular genres of written discourse results from the feature they refer to as "detachment."
11 In the example below, the speaker chooses a speech style more formal than his habitual style:

> la nostra suora
> cioè la nostra insegnante
> si seccava molto del fatto che
> noi bambini sottraessimo dei fogli
> dei fogli dal quaderno di bella.
> "Our nun, that is our teacher, would get really upset that we children would steal some sheets from the last-draft notebook."

In this example the speaker uses subordinating syntax with the subjunctive instead of the more colloquial co-ordinative syntax with the indicative. Furthermore, the speaker chooses the unusual and irregular verb *sottrarre* "to subtract," "steal," "take away," instead of the more familiar and common *rubare*, *togliere*, or *strappare*. In a more informal register, we would expect something like: "la nostra suora cioè la nostra insegnante si seccava molto quando noi rubavamo/toglievamo/strappavamo dei fogli dal quaderno di bella."

12 Dahl (1983) reports that in many languages which have special narrative tenses (most belong to the Bantu family), these forms appear only after the second narrative clause. Dahl's findings provide additional support for the claim that narrative is a special category of discourse, distinct from conversational language, with its own rules, and more specifically its own tense system.

13 I am not certain that these five narratives actually contain tense switching (see Wolfson 1979: 178–9 for a discussion of tense switching with forms of the verb "say"). I exclude from consideration instances in which in a narrative clause the present of a *verbum dicendi* such as *dire* "say" immediately follows the PR, PP, or HPr of another *verbum dicendi* (*fare* "go" or *dire* "say"). In these cases, in fact, the Pr marks a direct quote and is not a case of HPr.

(1) Mi *FA* dice "Dominga."
"He goes says 'Dominga.' "
(2) Gli *disse* dice "Vieni qua."
"He told says 'Come here.' "
(3) E **ha detto** dice "Porta le chiavi a tua madre."
"And she said says 'Bring the keys to your mother.' "

14 In the narratives which exhibit this pattern, PP may also occur in abstracts (when present), initial narrative clauses, and resolutions. In these contexts PP does not have an evaluative function. Its presence, in fact, could be explained by the fact that it is closely linked to the context of the telling (i.e. the speaker's present), providing transitions between the narrator's world and the story-world.

15 I also found one occurrence of the PR at the climactic point of the story in three of the narratives which exhibit an alternation between the PP and the HPr. In two of these stories the HPr is the main narrative tense.

16 A similar approach to tense functions is adopted in studies by Waugh (1990) and Waugh and Monville-Burston (1986) on the use of *passé simple*, *passé composé*, and *imparfait* in literary and journalistic texts.

REFERENCES

Benveniste, Emile (1971) *Problems in General Linguistics*, Coral Gables: University of Miami Press.

Bertinetto, Pier Marco (1986) *Tempo, Aspetto, e Azione nel Verbo Italiano. Il Sistema dell'Indicativo*, Florence: Accademia della Crusca.

Comrie, Bernard (1976) *Aspect*, Cambridge: Cambridge University Press.

Dahl, Östen (1983) "Temporal distance: remoteness distinctions in tense-aspect systems," *Linguistics* 21: 105–22.

Fleischman, Suzanne (1982) *The Future in Thought and Language: Diachronic Evidence from Romance*, Cambridge: Cambridge University Press.

—— (1985) "Discourse functions of tense-aspect oppositions in narrative: toward a theory of grounding," *Linguistics* 23: 851–82.

—— (1986) "Evaluation in narrative: the present tense in medieval 'performed stories'," *Yale French Studies* 70: 199–251.

—— (1990) *Tense and Narrativity. From Medieval Performance to Modern Fiction*, Austin: University of Texas Press/London: Routledge.

Harris, Martin B. (1982) "The 'past simple' and the 'present perfect' in Romance," in N. Vincent and M.B. Harris (eds) *Studies in the Romance Verb*, London: Croom Helm.

Hopper, Paul J. (1979) "Aspect and foregrounding in discourse," in T. Givón (ed.) *Syntax and Semantics*, vol. 12 *Discourse and Syntax*, New York: Academic Press.

Labov, William (1972) "The transformation of experience in narrative syntax," in William Labov, *Language in the Inner City*, Philadelphia: University of Pennsylvania Press.

Labov, William and Waletzky, Joshua (1967) "Narrative analysis. Oral versions of personal experience," in J. Helm (ed.) *Essays on the Verbal and Visual Arts*, Seattle: University of Washington Press.

Lepschy, Anna Laura and Lepschy, Giulio (1981) *La Lingua italiana: storia, varietà dell'uso, grammatica*, Milan: Bompiani.

Lyons, John (1977) *Semantics*, 2 vols, Cambridge: Cambridge University Press.

Morante, Elsa (1948) *Menzogna e Sortilegio*, Turin: Einaudi.

Rohlfs, G. (1966) *Grammatica storica dell'italiano e dei suoi dialetti*, Turin: Einaudi.

Schiffrin, Deborah (1981) "Tense variation in narrative," *Language* 57 (1): 45–62.

Silva-Corvalán, Carmen (1983) "Tense and aspect in oral Spanish narrative: context and meaning," *Language* 59 (4): 760–80.

Waugh, Linda (1990) "Discourse functions of tense-aspect: dynamic synchrony," in Nils Thelin (ed.) *Verbal Aspect in Discourse*, Amsterdam: John Benjamins.

Waugh, Linda and Monville-Burston, Monique (1986) "Aspect and discourse function: the French simple past in newspaper usage," *Language* 62 (4): 846–77.

Wolfson, Nessa (1978) "A feature of performed narrative: the conversational historical present," *Language in Society* 7: 215–37.

—— (1979) "The conversational historical present alternation," *Language* 55 (1): 168–82.

5 Multivalency: the French historical present in journalistic discourse[1]

Monique Monville-Burston and Linda R. Waugh

1. THE PRESENT TENSE AND THE HISTORICAL PRESENT

It is well known that the French present (Pr) tense[2] is chameleon-like: it can have a variety of contextual interpretations such as gnomic truths, omnitemporal states, durative states, description, temporally bounded events, future time, past time, and so forth. However, it has not been as evident that in certain contexts two or more of these meanings may be simultaneously relevant, thus leading to semantic multivalency. We will study the exploitation in journalistic discourse of this pluralism in meaning and the contextual diversity which results from it for one type of use of Pr: namely, the historical present (HPr).[3] Our aim will be to show that, far from being a question of promiscuous, unrestricted polysemy or of problematic ambiguity, the double (or triple) meanings/readings are controlled by two interrelated factors: on the one hand, the semantic opposition between Pr and the other tenses of French, and on the other hand the symbiotic relationship between Pr (and HPr) and its context; moreover, the meanings created are equally viable in that context.

1.1. The unmarked nature of Pr

The fact that Pr is semantically so rich and can lead to a variety of contextual interpretations is due to its unmarked nature: it is associated with the unmarked poles of the various oppositions which characterize the French tense system, and thus it is unmarked *vis-à-vis* the three tenses which will be of importance here, namely the imperfect (Imp), the simple past (*passé simple*, PS) and the compound past (*passé composé*, PC). Now, the exact nature of Imp, PS, and PC has been a matter of some debate: e.g. should the use of Imp for past time, hypothetico-irreal processes, and "politeness" be unified or not? (We think so; see Waugh 1976; Monville-Burston forthcoming.) But since in their basic uses Imp, PS, and PC have an explicit reference to past time (the difference between Imp, PS, and PC being a further aspectuo-discursive subdifferentiation of this temporal base), and since, as we shall see, the question of time is important also to HPr, the oppositions of primary relevance here are temporal ones.

As the unmarked pole in these oppositions, Pr has a variety of contextual interpretations available to it, of which there are three major types. The first is the *basic meaning*[4] of Pr where there is a reference to present time. The marking associated with the marked opposites is specifically denied and thus Pr in this usage means non-past ([- past]) and non-future ([- future]), if we take into account the future tense(s) of French[5]: by elimination, this means a focus on present time, a simultaneity or synchronicity between the verbal process and "now," the deictic zero point. This basic usage, called "le sens strict" by Grevisse (1969: 667), "le présent momentané" by Wilmet (1976: 9), "le présent-présent" by Monville-Burston and Waugh (1985), we will refer to as present present, PrPr, is the least context-dependent and is typically cited out of context. Consider the following examples, from Grevisse (1969: 667):

(1) J'écris en ce moment même.
    "I'm writing at this moment."
(2) Voici mon frère qui vient.
    "Here's my brother coming."

As several analysts have noted (Martin 1971: 84–5; Larochette 1980: 220–1; Comrie 1985: 38–9), although we can conceive of "now" as punctual, in practice, when we speak, we tend to mitigate the elusiveness of the present instant by seeing it as a segment of time just elapsed followed by a segment of time to come (the "now" with which the process is simultaneous is an "extended now"). The length of these segments is relative and depends upon linguistic and pragmatic factors.

(3) En ce moment même elle fait son heure d'exercice.
    "At this very moment she's doing her hour of exercises."

Example (3) implies a rather extended view of the presentness of the process "to exercise"; this is an example of: "states and processes which hold at the present moment, but which began before the present moment and may well continue beyond the present moment" (Comrie 1985: 37). On the other hand, in (4), the "présent retardé" (Larochette 1980) *appelle* covers the minimal delay between the call and the speaker's reaction to it:

(4) On appelle mon nom. J'y vais.
    "They're calling my name. I'm going."

From the specific basic meaning, restricted in terms of reference, we pass on to the *non-specific meaning*, the second type of contextualization of Pr, in which the mark characteristic of the marked opposites is neither specifically affirmed nor denied contextually. This non-restricted Pr is divided into two subtypes: the omnitemporal, generic present (OPr) and the atemporal, neutral present (APr). In OPr, time is at issue but essentially all of time is covered; Pr refers to both past and non-past ([± past]), future and non-future ([± future]); i.e. Pr is used for omni(or pan)temporal situations which have a continuity from the past to the present and into the future, a more global continuity as in (5):

(5) L'homme est toujours un loup pour l'homme.[6]
    "Man is always a wolf for man."

Or a more conditioned one as in (6):

(6) Jean fume.
    "Jean smokes."

Given that in such cases Pr makes reference to the "constitution of things" (Calver 1946; Bolinger 1947: 434),[7] the occurrence of the process could be verified at any point on the time line when a speaker might utter the verb (cf. "contemporaineté virtuelle" in Wilmet 1976: 14).

Now, the use of Pr for omnitemporal processes (OPr) can be linked with the notions of persistence in time, of eternally present situations; but that which is eternally present is close as well to gnomic "truths," to those states which are unchanging and not subject to alteration of any kind, and which thus can be considered to be atemporal. As a consequence, the unmarkedness of Pr can also be interpreted as [0 past], [0 future]: this is APR (atemporal present) where time is irrelevant. Irrelevance here does not imply that the event can occur at any time, but rather that temporality is not at issue, it is timeless: in such cases, the verbal process alone is in focus, not its eventual placement in time. It is in this sense that Bolinger calls Pr a "base tense, to which all other tenses are oriented, but which itself is oriented to nothing, expressing merely the *fact of process*" (1947: 436; cf. Kiparsky 1968):[8]

(7) Deux et deux font quatre.
    "Two and two are four."

There exist several subvarieties of this type of Pr: the "metalinguistic present" (Larochette 1980: 223), also called the "reproducing present" (Hamburger 1973: 109), which is used to summarize or analyze literary/cinematic works; the "stage directions" present (Wilmet 1976: 9–40); the "synoptic" present found in chapter headings or captions (Casparis 1975: 126–8). In all of these, time is abolished; what remain are "statements about ideal objects" (Hamburger 1973: 109; also Fleischman 1990), i.e. abstracted from and unaffected by any spatio-temporal context.

The common denominator that unites the basic and non-specific meanings is that there is some portion of the situation being described which does, literally, overlap with the present moment (see Comrie 1985: 40). However, what will be more at issue here is that while the basic usage (PrPr) is tied to the present moment, in both of the non-specific subtypes (OPr and APr) Pr has the ability to refer to processes which transcend not only that present moment but also any limit in time and even time itself.

In the third type of usage, and the most important for our purposes, there is no overlap with the present moment. This results in an *inverted meaning* of the unmarked term; the mark is not specifically denied, and contextually the conceptual category particular to the marked term is affirmed. This is HPr (or the "past present"): on the one hand, the context denies the possibility of simultaneity with the deictic zero point; and on the other hand, there is an explicit or implicit contextual reference to past time:[9] more specifically, the global and/or local context, by a variety of factors (e.g. past-tense verbs in the surrounding discourse, temporal adverbs, dating, use of names of persons no longer alive, etc.), makes it clear that past time is meant. Given its unmarked nature, Pr is not incompatible with (does not deny) such a temporal reference; thus, in principle, the unmarked Pr may substitute for its marked opposites (Imp, PC, PS) without altering the past time reference. While it is true that this usage of HPr could be characterized as [+ past], there is a major difference between this contextual meaning and the three given earlier: namely, that Pr does not and cannot make an explicit and direct reference to past time in the same way that it can be used to denote present time, all of time, or timelessness.[10] In the case of HPr, it is the context which specifies past time, not the tense itself; in its basic, omnitemporal and atemporal usages, Pr (along with the context) refers itself to the particular conceptual category.

HPr represents a marked usage of the unmarked category, an optional strategy which is open to speakers and writers who want to give richness and variety to their texts while exploiting the resources afforded by the tense system. As we shall see, however, there may be stylistic, semantic, and discourse differences between HPr and the given past tense substitute.[11] Fig. 5.1 shows the various contextual meanings of Pr.

Figure 5.1 Contextual meanings of Pr

Types of contextual meaning	Contextual meaning		Name
1. basic meaning: present time	[– past]	([– future])	PrPr "present present"
2. non-specific meanings			
a) generic meaning: omnitemporal	[+ past]	([+ future])	OPr "omnitemporal present"
b) neutral meaning: atemporal	[0 past]	([0 future])	APr "atemporal present"
3. inverted meaning: MARKED USAGE			
past time	[+ past]		HPr "historical present"
(future time	[+ future]		"future present")

While the French tense system is dominated by considerations of deictic placement in time (tense, strictly speaking), it is more accurately called a tense-aspect system,[12] especially with regard to the past subsystem, since one (but only one) of the ways in which Imp, PS and PC are differentiated is according to aspect, Imp being unmarkedly imperfective (thus it can be [– perf], [± perf], [0 perf]) and PS and PC being markedly perfective.[13] Pr, on the other hand, is neither perfective nor imperfective in the code, since there is no aspectual opposition in Pr. Consider, for example, the two sentences in (8), which could belong to a live sports report:

(8) Une foule chahuteuse occupe [PrPr (– perf)] les gradins.... Le joueur nantais rattrape [PrPr (+ perf)] le ballon et *shoote* [PrPr (+ perf)].
"A rowdy crowd fills the bleachers.... The player from Nantes recovers the ball and shoots."

Hearers rely on their knowledge of soccer games and the lexical meanings of the verbs to understand that *occupe* is descriptive-durative while *rattrape* and *shoote* are eventive-punctual (although the basic use of PrPr is imperfective). This non-specificity obtains also for HPr (its basic use, in narrative at least, is perfective). Now, since HPr can substitute for either Imp, PS, or PC, the following differences are relevant for the interpretation of a given HPr: event vs. description (PS vs. Imp), figure vs. ground (PS vs. Imp), focused vs. non-focused events (PS vs. Imp), past event without current relevance vs. past event with current relevance (PS vs. PC), single, semelfactive event vs. durative, repetitive, iterative events (PS/PC vs. Imp).

1.2. Pr in context

Although there are a variety of possible contextualizations of Pr, in many contexts it is clear which one is meant – or ones, since there can be more than one type of Pr used in a given (portion of a) text. Thus, as in example (9), while there is a "mixture" of Prs, including HPrs, there is never any ambiguity, the particular interpretation being determined by the context (see also Fleischman 1990; Blyth and Waugh 1988):[14]

(9) Le procès des meurtriers du père Popieluszko n'a ressemblé à aucun de ceux qui se déroulent [OPr] dans les pays de l'est.... Derrière les quatres accusés se profilent [PrPr] bien des ombres. Soudain le silence *se fige* [HPr] dans la salle. Une atmosphère crispée *succède* [HPr] brutalement à la léthargie.... Les regards *fixent* [HPr] un petit bout de femme qui *s'approche* [HPr] de la barre pour témoigner....
Où une vieille dame se livre (APr)[15] à l'autopsie d'un meurtre.
(*Libération*, February 8, 1985)
[Lead]
"The trial of Father Popieluszko's murderers has been unlike any that has taken place in eastern bloc countries.... Behind the four defendants, many shadows stand out.
[First paragraph, beginning of episode]
Suddenly silence *sets in* in the room. A tense atmosphere abruptly *replaces* lethargy.... Eyes are *fixed* on a tiny little woman who *comes up* to the witness stand [....]
[Subtitle, introducing second paragraph]
Where an old lady performs the autopsy of a murder."

However, despite the fact that HPr is a marked usage of the unmarked Pr, and is thus highly dependent upon the context for its interpretation, since Pr can have more than one value, some contexts may make it difficult to know which one is meant. In such a case, more than one intepretation of a given Pr may be possible in a context, producing double (or multiple) meanings. That is, even though this inverted HPr [+ past] use of Pr refers to a time period specifically denied by the basic meaning PrPr [– past] and not specifically affirmed either by the omnitemporal OPr [+ past] or the atemporal APr [0 past] meanings, there are many primary and secondary effects of these other meanings which are none the less relevant to any use of HPr: paradoxically, even though the time period meant is past, still something of the present or something of the omnitemporal or the timeless Pr is pertinent. It is just such *double entendres* which we will explore here.

1.3. Pr and journalistic discourse

It is crucial for the point we wish to make that we have chosen to focus on journalistic discourse, and not the more prototypical use of HPr in narrative. Journalistic discourse is the ideal environment for the exploitation of the multisemanticity inherent to Pr (and HPr), since it contains a mixture of various perspectives: reporting of recent past events and commentary on their present relevance (cf. van Dijk's (1985) criteria of recency and relevance), filling in of information about events previous to those in focus, discussion of possible consequences, giving of historical background (van Dijk 1988: 17–71). Moreover, newspaper writing is only rarely narrative in structure: rather than tell a story in more or less chronological order,[16] journalists usually take a more explicitly retrospective point of view in which previous events and their context are recounted because of their relevance for the present; so it becomes difficult also to know where the boundary is between the recent past and the extended present ("extended now"). This is particularly important when it comes to the date of publication: in most cases, it seems as if the "now" which is meant is that of the reader (and specified by the date on the paper), not that of the journalist at the time of writing. Furthermore, because the news being reported is of recent date and is thus assumed to be in the memory of readers, only some details are given (others are taken for granted), which then stand metonymically for the whole of the phenomenon being talked about.

This means that in any article of a newspaper there is perforce a mixture of different types of usage, and, as we shall see, the possibility of interpreting a given Pr in more than one way (or of giving multiple interpretations to HPr) arises, leading to multivalency, whether temporal or aspectual in nature. In other words, in all the examples to be discussed, the Pr at issue can be understood as a substitute for some past tense (the data set has been defined methodologically on this basis). However, sometimes there is hesitation between interpreting a Pr as HPr or as PrPr/OPr/APr, since more than one is possible in the context; and at times it may also be unclear which past tense(s) a given HPr is a substitute for – Imp, PS, and/or PC – since the context allows for more than one substitution. The first type of uncertainty leads to temporal multivalency, to be discussed in section 2. The second type is aspectual multivalency, to be treated in section 3; yet, since the temporal perspective is always uppermost in French, such aspectual multivalency is normally accompanied by considerations of placement in time as well.

2. TEMPORAL MULTIVALENCY

2.1. Historical present (HPr), Present present (PrPr)

A first type of ambiguity originates from the fuzziness of the boundary between HPr ([+ past]) and PrPr ([– past]). Since journalistic discourse is by its very nature written to a large extent in the *venir de* mode astride past and present, the subject matter belonging to the recent past and the aim of the discourse being current relevance, journalists take advantage of the ambivalent tool that the linguistic code provides: an unmarked category (Pr) with a [+ past] variant (HPr) which allows oscillation between past and present without operating any morphological shift and thus proves perfectly fitted for much of the material treated.

Ways in which HPr variants can open the text towards the true present (PrPr) are illustrated in example (10) (and (11) below):[17]

(10) On doit lui [M. Berlusconi] reconnaître, tout d'abord, un indéniable savoir-faire financier qui l'*amène* [amena, a amené] dès 1978 à transférer une grande masse de capitaux du secteur en déclin de la promotion immobilière à celui, plus prometteur, de l'audio-visuel. (*Le Monde*, November 20, 1985)

"One must recognize first that he [Mr Berlusconi] has an undeniable know-how in finance, which *leads* [led, has led] him to transfer, starting in 1978, a large amount of capital from the declining sector of property development to the more promising area of audio-visual materials."[18]

Note that if the "absolute" preposition *dès* "from...on," "since," "as early as" were replaced by its deictic equivalent *depuis* "since," the referential meaning of the sentence would not be altered:

94 *Discourse-pragmatics and the verb*

in both cases, Mr Berlusconi started to make transfers of capital and – it is implied – kept/is still making them. The only difference is that *depuis* presents the action from the vantage point of the writer-reader's "now" and could not be associated with a reference to past time. Thus, the HPr *amène* subtly bridges the gap between the completed past (cut off from the writer-reader's "now") and the present (contemporaneous with the writer-reader's "now"): the Pr morphology of *amène*, as well as the inchoative value of *dès*, link the events to present time, while the contextual mention of the date 1978 pulls them back to "before-now." The interplay of verb form and context offers therefore three possibilities, with the HPr clause mediating between the two extremes, as shown in Fig. 5.2.

Figure 5.2 Interplay of form and context

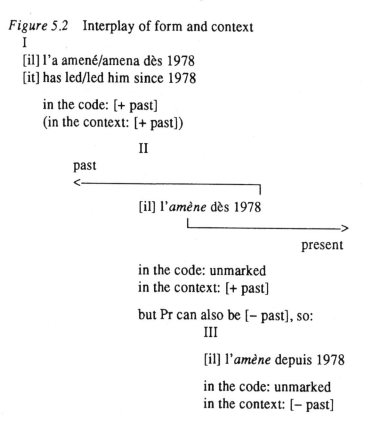

Example (11) unites in a single sentence two co-ordinated Prs, the first clearly HPr, the second one much more uncertain:

(11) En 1984, il [Berlusconi] *met* [a mis] la main sur son dernier concurrent, Rete 4, et règne désormais sur 80% de l'audience de la télévision privée. (*Le Monde*, November 20, 1985)

"In 1984, he [Berlusconi] *takes hold* [took hold] of his last competitor, Rete 4, and ever since has controlled 80 per cent of the private television audience."

It would be natural to understand *règne* as HPr since Berlusconi's ruling over the Italian networks is dated 1984; and indeed, were it not for the adverb *désormais*, it could be glossed by *a régné* (PC). But *désormais* typically means "from the time of the addresser's or addressee's 'now' forward," a meaning which is usually not associated with a reference to past time. If the non-deictic adverbial equivalent *dès lors* "from that time onwards" (or the vaguer *alors* "then") had been used, however, *règne* would quite naturally have received an HPr interpretation (*il règne [a régné] dès lors*: "he *controls* [has controlled] from then on"). Therefore, in (11), *règne* must be understood as a true (extended) present which, associated with *désormais*, strangely draws backwards the speaker's "now" to the point of including 1984. Under formal identity (*met, règne*), we have both a tense switch (past → present) in disguise and a blurring of the past/present distinction.

2.2. Changeable Prs in *Le Monde*

It is sometimes difficult for the analyst of *Le Monde* to determine if a present form is "true" or "historical." This is due to two combined factors, the first one general, the second one particular to the newspaper in question:

(a) as mentioned earlier, all daily newspapers tend to adopt the time of reading as point of reference for deictic constituents (verb tenses and time adverbials);

(b) issues of *Le Monde* are postdated to the next day, and since distribution takes only one day in Paris but two days to the provinces, today's news is presented as tomorrow's to readers living in the Paris region, but not to those in the provinces (see Simonin 1984: 167); (12) is an example of this:

(12) Toutefois, dans un communiqué publié lundi 20 février, le ministère de la justice *corrige* [a corrigé/PrPr] le tir. (*Le Monde*, February 21, 1989)

"However, in a statement published on Monday February 20, the Ministry of Justice *is adjusting* [adjusted] its fire." [dated Tuesday, February 21, but distributed on Monday, February 20, 1989, in Paris]

96 *Discourse-pragmatics and the verb*

In (12) Parisian readers will mentally convert the objective absolute date (Monday, 20 February) to the deictic "today," and consider *corrige* to be a true present, while the readers in the provinces, reading it the next day, will take it to be HPr. This oddity, based on readers' location with respect to publishing place, is of no serious consequence for understanding temporal relations.[19] It shows, however, the precariousness of past/present distinctions in the domain of time that has just elapsed.

2.3. Historical present (HPr), Atemporal present (APr)

Certain Prs, typical of newspaper writing, clearly describe events that occurred in the past (HPr), but are simultaneously permeated by the timeless quality of APr: e.g. the HPr of titles (13), leads (14), news diaries (15), brief biographies in obituaries (16):

(13) M. Mitterrand *demande* [demanda, a demandé] aux Français de faire bloc. (*Le Monde*, September 22, 1986)
"Mr Mitterrand *asks* [asked] the French to unite."

(14) Un virage, une voiture qui *dérape* [dérapa, a dérapé], une cabine téléphonique brisée et la mort *survient* [survint, est survenue]. (*Journal du Dimanche*, March 23, 1986)
"A sharp turn, a car which *skids* [skidded], a shattered telephone booth and death *arrives* [arrived] unexpectedly."

(15) Jeudi 21 Novembre
IRAK. – Les dirigeants de l'Organisation de Libération de la Palestine (OLP) *confirment* [confirmèrent, ont confirmé] leur rejet des résolutions des Nations Unies sur le Proche-Orient qui reconnaissent le droit à l'existence de l'État d'Israel.
  La centrale palestinienne *décide* [décida, a décidé] de s'en tenir fermement au rejet des résolutions 242 et 338 du Conseil de sécurité. ("Sélection hebdomadaire" du *Monde*, November 21–7, 1985)
"Thursday November 21
Iraq. – The leaders of the Palestine Liberation Organization (PLO) *confirm* [confirmed, have confirmed] their rejection of the United Nations resolutions on the Middle East which recognize the right of the State of Israel to exist. The coalition of Palestinian groups *decides* [decided] to hold firm on its rejection of Resolutions 242 and 338 of the Security Council."

(16) Né le 22 juillet 1921, à Nérondes (Cher), Raymond Vilain *est nommé* [fut nommé, a été nommé] après des études à la faculté de

médecine de Paris chirurgien des hôpitaux de Paris en 1963....
En 1973, il *fonde* [fonda, a fondé] SOS-Mains, réseau d'unités de
microchirurgie spécialisées. (*Le Monde*, February 21, 1989)
"Born on July 22, 1921 in Nérondes, Cher, after studying at the
Paris School of Medicine, Raymond Vilain *is named* [was named]
surgeon of the Paris Hospitals in 1963.... In 1973, he *founds*
[founded] SOS-Hands, a network of specialized microsurgery
units."

In the above four examples, the date of the newspaper and/or specific dates found in the immediate environment of the verbs doubtless impose a past reading on the Pr forms.[20] However, this pastness is not pure. The tenselessness of APr [0 past (0 future)] somehow surfaces and solicits the reader as forcefully as contextual pastness. Several reasons can be adduced to explain why it is the neutral, atemporal interpretation of the unmarked Pr which comes to the fore in these cases, rather than the OPr or PrPr, both of which are clearly time-oriented. Because of their special typography (bold/large characters), titles and leads (see examples (13) and (14)) are, so to speak, lifted from the rest of the text and presented as independent statements to be read *in se* and *per se* (see van Dijk 1985: 86). What is emphasized is not time, but pure content, the raw message. The reader is invited to form a framed and simplified picture of the situation (the elementary structure of the sentences, the little circumstantial information), directly apprehended and not mediated through the category of time or any other categories we use to understand the world.

The analogy with immediate visual perception[21] can also be used to explain the atemporal shading of the "présent tabellaire" illustrated in (15) and (16).[22] A sentence like (17):

(17) en 1821, Napoléon *meurt* [mourut, est mort] à Sainte-Hélène
   "in 1821 Napoleon *dies* [died] on Saint Helena"

in a list of the important dates in Napoleon's life is less an inscription of the particular process in time and more an excision of the process from time and its insertion into the timeless realm of those processes which are permanent verities, which everyone knows happened. Casparis, calling the "présent tabellaire" a "pure annalistic present," rightly claims that "it resembles a slide show effect... in that no emphasis is placed on sequential flow, chronological order being simply an order superimposed on a string of isolated events" (1975: 139).[23] As in (13) and (14), the style is bare, emotionless, non-evaluative, it is reduced to essentials, intersentential coherence is not sought after, and causal relationships and relative time are not in focus. It results in a great neutrality, a lack of depth, and the impression that the verbal processes are islands estranged from each other and disconnected from the temporal system.

With respect to time, we have seen that the past interpretation of HPr in *parole* is not absolute or self-sufficient. To be fully grasped, it needs to call on the internalized knowledge that addressers/addressees have of the inherent meaning of Pr in *langue*. As we will see, the same is true with regard to aspect.

3. ASPECTUAL MULTIVALENCY

3.1. Perfectivity and imperfectivity in HPr

As said in section 1, Pr (including PrPr and HPr) is neither perfective nor imperfective. In the case of HPrs, in order to distinguish between perfectivity and its absence, additional help can be supplied by paradigmatic comparison with the other tenses of the past system, since PC and PS are inherently perfective and Imp is imperfective in its basic meaning. Although it should be recognized that in narrative, as well as in many of the examples used here, HPr is more likely to be interpreted as perfective (i.e. is more likely to replace PS or PC – see (18)), there are cases of imperfective HPrs (see (19); also Comrie 1976: 73–4):

(18) Footballeur le dimanche, il travaillait en usine la semaine. Pour 3000 F par mois. Mais en 1978, le Paris Saint-Germain l'*appelle* [appela/a appelé (+ perf)]. (*Le Journal du Dimanche*, March 23, 1986)
"Soccer player on Sundays, he worked in a factory during the week. For 3000 francs per month. But in 1978, the Paris Saint-Germain Club *calls* [called] him up."

(19) Lundi dernier, à Cantin, dans le Nord ... , vers 20 heures 15, une voiture *rate* [rata/a raté (+ perf)] un virage et *percute* [percuta/a percuté (+ perf)] une cabine téléphonique. Dans la voiture, deux jeunes gens et une jeune fille. Ils *reviennent* [revenaient (– perf)] d'un repas de fiançailles. (*Le Journal du Dimanche*, March 23, 1986)
"Last Monday, in Cantin, North ... around 8.15 p.m. a car *misses* [missed] a turn and *hits* [hit] a telephone booth. In that car, two young men and a girl. They *are coming back* [were coming back] from an engagement party."

In the above examples, the recognition of contextual variants is facilitated not only by the grammaticality or non-grammaticality of past-tense equivalents, but also by textual, lexical, and syntactic clues in the passages. Furthermore, situation types (in the sense of Vendler 1967) in particular, confirm perfectivity, or the lack of it: for example, in our passage the achievement phrases (*rate le virage, percute une cabine*) can be replaced far more naturally by a punctual (perfective) past form than can the activity verb *reviennent*.

Therefore, to summarize, if many elements in the context conspire to produce a perfective interpretation, the action in the HPr is viewed as bounded, with possible focus on either endpoint, but particularly on the terminal one. It has the same graphic representation as PS and PC (see Fig. 5.3).

Figure 5.3 Perfective HPr

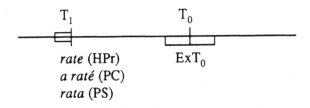

ExT_0 = "extended now," T_0 = writer-reader's "now," and T_1 = the terminal point of the completed/past action

If on the contrary, the context favors an imperfective interpretation, HPr can be represented as Imp (Fig. 5.4).

Figure 5.4 Imperfective HPr

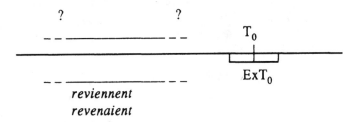

? = absence of focus

Instances can be found, however, where the aspectual quality of an HPr form is not as readily definable. We have then a [+ perf] interpretation of HPr, and as a consequence the analyst may hesitate

100 *Discourse-pragmatics and the verb*

between a substitution by PC/PS or Imp, as in example (20).

(20) Badgés de vert et de bleu, ils [les acheteurs et vendeurs de programmes télévisés] *JOUENT* [jouèrent/ont joué/jouaient (+ perf or – perf)] comme chaque année une grande partie de colin-maillard audio-visuel, dont les points se comptent en dollars et parts d'audience. (*Le Monde*, February 21, 1989)
"With green and blue badges, they [buyers and sellers of TV programmes] *play* [played/were playing], as they do every year, a large audio-visual blind man's bluff game where scores are counted in dollars and percentages of the audience."

Should *jouent* be viewed globally as an unanalyzable whole (perfective) or, on the contrary, should the boundaries of the process be left out of focus (imperfective)? The reader can lean freely toward either interpretation, the context being too weakly constraining.

3.2. HPr, PC, and current relevance

3.2.1.

In cases where an action in HPr is "open" (i.e. imperfective), it can be completed at any time following its inception, and of necessity may run into the PrPr boundary (extended or punctual "now") and impinge upon its domain.[24] Consider passage (21):

(21) Flash back.... C'est en 1976 qu'*apparaît* [apparut, est apparue (+ perf)] cette petite bombe de 105 ch.... La Golf *va* [allait (– perf)] vite, *accélère* [accélérait (– perf)] comme un dragster ... *colle* [collait (– perf)] à la route comme aucune traction avant ne l'avait fait avant elle. Foudroyant succès. (*Le Journal du Dimanche*, March 23, 1986)
"Flash back.... It's in 1976 that this little 105 horsepower bomb *is released* [was released].... The Golf *is* [was] fast, *accelerates* [accelerated] like a dragster, *sticks* [stuck] to the road as no front-wheel drive car has/had ever done before. A smashing success."

The car described by the journalist is still on the market and its qualities (*va vite, accélère, colle*) have to be considered as true at the moment of utterance.

Example (21) illustrates openness to the PrPr period with an imperfective HPr. But even with a perfective HPr, although the action is without doubt completed at some moment in the past, it is not uncommon for its results or consequences to be viewed as encroaching upon the "now" period. In other words, the aspectual non-specificity characteristic of Pr is always ready to reappear and color the perfective usage, if the context is not compelling enough or if some sentential element invites, at the same time, the opposite (imperfective) reading. This second possible interpretation will be indicated as follows: ((−perf)). The potentiality of an imperfective interpretation blending with a perfective one can be observed in examples (22), (23), (24):

(22) Les faux époux Turenge *sont condamnés* [furent condamnés, ont été condamnés (+ perf) ((− perf))]. (*Le Monde*, November 23, 1989)
"The Turenges, who passed themselves off as a married couple, *are convicted* [were convicted, have been convicted]."

(23) Puis elle [la DS] *va* [alla, est allée (+ perf)] percuter la R4. Les deux voitures *sont transformées* [furent transformées, ont été transformées (+ perf) ((− perf))] en un tas de ferraille. *(Le Journal du Dimanche*, March 23, 1986)
"Then it [the Citroën] *goes* [went] and hits [hit] the Renault. The two cars *are turned* [were turned] into a scrap heap."

(24) Dans un fracas épouvantable, la DS *écrase* [écrasa, a écrasé (+ perf)] la cabine dont il ne *reste* [resta, est resté (+ perf) ((−perf))] quelques secondes après que des débris. (*Le Journal du Dimanche*, March 23, 1986)
"In a horrible crash, the Citroen *flattens* [flattened] the phone booth of which only broken fragments *are left* [were left], a few seconds later."

Sont condamnés (22) and *sont transformées* (23) are typically achievement situations since they depict the beginning of a verbal action; *condamner* even has performative force. However, their use in the passive voice weakens this highly perfective quality, and the auxiliary *être* (a stative verb) in Pr[25] allows the basic, imperfective interpretation to intrude. The reader is thus offered a dual perspective on the situation. In (22), for example, the Turenges were declared guilty (punctual action [+ perf]) and since then have been serving their sentence and still are (resulting state [− perf]). In (24), the double reading is due not to the passive syntactic structure, but to the inherent lexical imperfectivity of the verb *rester*, which clashes with the punctual adverbial *quelques secondes après*. Graphically, the situations in (22), (23), (24) can be represented as in Fig. 5.5 (we use the details and vocabulary items pertaining to (22)).

Following Culioli (1980: 187), we can say that the interval to the right of T_1 (endpoint of the completed action) is "open and adjacent." The

Figure 5.5 Double reading of HPr: + perf, – perf

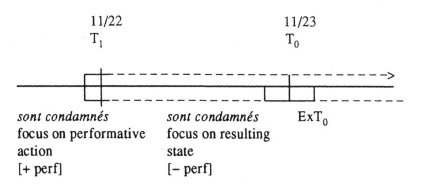

situation therefore has a double property: "fermeture, non rupture" (see also Cintas and Desclés 1984: 83).

3.2.2.

The HPrs just discussed, oriented as they are toward PrPr by the state resulting from the action, recall certain uses of PC. In Waugh 1987, two major contextual variants of PC are distinguished: PC-1, a perfect, and PC-2 (simp), a preterit.[26] Between these two polar interpretations of PC, there exists a continuum of transitional uses, which are types of PC-2 (comp)s. PC-1 focuses "on the present aftermath of an event which was complete by that moment and took place some time anterior to it" (p. 4). It has "current relevance," i.e. the statements, situations, etc., resulting from the past action remain valid at the time of utterance. PC-2 (simp) describes "an event which is complete and past" (p. 6). Thus, when HPr is embedded in a context where it receives an unambiguous and pure perfective interpretation (see Fig. 5.3),[27] it resembles PC-2 (simp) aspectually and temporally. But if contextual elements favor an open perspective toward the *hic et nunc* – which is frequent in newspapers, given the recent nature of many of the reported actions and the attention granted to their consequences – the perfective value is more diluted, less focused upon, and nuances of current relevance may surface. Thus, from an aspectual point of view, these perfective HPrs with current relevance come close to PC-1 (or some version of PC-2 (comp)). Perfective HPrs therefore have affinities with PC, which they do not share with the more semantically restricted PS. This likeness, furthermore, is reinforced by the fact that they are morphologically akin: the auxiliary of PC is in Pr. These two factors may explain certain effects of tense switching that can be observed in newspapers.

Consider the following passages containing respectively a PS → perfective HPr transition (25) and a PC → perfective HPr transition (26):

(25) Il y a un tiers de siècle, lorsqu'il fonda [PS] son entreprise, il choisit [PS] sur un catalogue une couleur qui lui plaisait pour ses camions et ses engins. Nom de guerre de ce minium très orange: minorange. Aussitôt, François Bouygues *s'en empare* [s'en empara, s'en est emparé (+ perf)] comme d'un talisman. (*Le Journal du Dimanche*, March 23, 1986)

"A third of a century ago, when he founded [PS] his business, he chose [PS] from a catalogue a color that he liked for his trucks and machines. Warname for this bright orange red-lead (minium): 'minorange.' Immediately, Francois Bouygues *seizes upon it* [seized upon it] as a sort of talisman."

(26) Des sourires et de la fermeté, les Français en ont ramassé à la pelle.

Fermeté dans le langage et sur le fond du discours. Lorsqu'il *appelle* [appela, a appelé (+ perf)] les Français à "faire bloc" autour des acquis des dernières années ... M. Mitterrand *feint* [feignit, a feint (+ perf)] de s'adresser à tous, mais *parle* [parla, a parlé (+ perf)] essentiellement à la gauche. (*Le Monde*, September 22, 1989)

"The French people have had bucketfuls of smiles and firmness.

Firmness in language, and in the content of the talk. When he *calls on* [called on] the French to 'unite' around the achievements of the last years ... Mr Mitterrand *pretends* [pretended] he's addressing everybody, but *speaks* [spoke] essentially to the left."

In the case of PS → HPr [+ perf] transitions (25), the perfectivity of HPr usually comes out strongly, supported by the perfectivity of the preceding PS; this aspectual continuity, however, is disrupted by the morphological break (PS tense form → Pr tense form) which contributes to creating the often mentioned impression of vividness. In the PC → HPr [+ perf] transitions (26), on the other hand, the HPr perfectivity loses some of its sharpness. This is due to the potential imperfectivity that any Pr verb form contains, associated with the actual (or potential) current relevance that the preceding PC form comprises. We have therefore a continuity of perfectivity watered down by latent imperfectivity. This semantic homogeneity over the tense switch is paralleled by morphological uniformity (a Pr form is maintained on the auxiliary and the lexical verb). Consequently, PC → HPr [+ perf] tense switching does not have the abruptness of PS → HPr [+ perf].[28]

To conclude, then, PC → HPr [+ perf] transitions do not emphasize perfectivity,[29] nor do they exhibit formal discontinuity (and its attendant surprise effect). On the contrary, morphology can be used to articulate effortlessly the passage from PC to HPr. Consider text (27):

(27) La fusillade du 16 juin a mis [PC] le feu aux poudres. En quelques heures Soweto s'est transformée [PC] en un champ de bataille. Les bureaux de l'administration, des véhicules privés, les débits de boisson ... *sont incendiés* [ont été incendiés (+ perf)]. Les établissements scolaires *sont fermés* [ont été fermés (+ perf)] dès le lendemain. Au Parlement le premier ministre, M. John Vorster, *annonce* [a annoncé (+ perf)] que le gouvernement ne se laissera pas intimider. (*Le Monde*, June 16, 1986)
"The shooting on June 16 caused [PC] the situation to explode. In a few hours, Soweto was changed [PC] into a battlefield. Administrative offices, private vehicles, pubs ... *are set on fire* [were set on fire]. Schools *are closed down* [were closed down] from the (very) next day. In Parliament, the Prime Minister, Mr John Vorster, *announces* [announced] that the government will not let itself be intimidated."

Note that *sont incendiés* is the locus of the tense shift. Far from being highlighted (as often happens with tense switching), it seems to be buried in the center of the group of periphrastic verb forms (*s'est transformée, sont incendiés, sont fermés*). It mimics the pronominal PC *s'est transformée* with its passive morphology. On the other hand, *s'est transformée* simulates the neutrality of HPr with respect to perfectivity; it presents the situation described under two different angles: a perfective perspective ([+ perf] marking of PC); telic lexical meaning (achievement) of "to transform," and an open perspective on the results of that transformation. It is only when the one-word (active) HPr *annonce* follows the periphrastic (passive) HPr *sont fermées* that the PC → HPr tense switch appears to have been fully performed. Thus, the PC → HPr transition is developed so smoothly that it passes almost unnoticed.

3.3. Declarative verbs in HPr

In newspaper writing, journalists are often led to quote the speech of the people about whom they are reporting, or who are involved in the story they are telling. To introduce this spoken material, they use a great variety of declarative words: verbs of saying as well as verbs expressing judgments or feelings that can be manifested by speech.[30]

For example: *dire* "say," *affirmer* "state," but also *estimer* "to be of the opinion," *reconnaître* "to acknowledge," *craindre* "to fear," etc. There is a marked tendency for these declarative verbs to be put in Pr. They are found both in non-narrative and narrative passages, in the latter case with or without tense switching on the declarative verb. Speech is reported in direct or indirect (occasionally free indirect) style, but in general at least some element of what was actually said is given in direct quotes. In direct style, the declarative verb is either in proleptic or analeptic position (see Cerquiglini 1981):

(28) (narrative, no tense switching, direct, analeptic)
Il [Me Curry] *commence* [commença, a commencé] sa lecture. D'abord les faits.... "Les accusés agissaient sur ordre et croyaient que leur action était dans l'intérêt de la France", *souligne* [souligna, a souligné] Me Curry. La désapprobation *se lit* [se lut, s'est lue] sur les visages des membres de Greenpeace présents à l'audience. (*Le Monde*, November 23, 1985)
"He [Mr Curry, a lawyer] *begins* his reading. First, the facts.... 'The accused were acting under orders and believed that their action was in the interest of France,' *emphasizes* [emphasized] Mr Curry. Disapproval *is evident* on the faces of the members of Greenpeace present at the hearing."

(29) (non-narrative, direct, proleptic)
Le merveilleux Shergar est-il enterré quelque part en Irelande du Nord...? En tout cas, la compagnie d'assurances, la Lloyd's a du verser 84 millions de francs à ses propriétaires. Roy David *affirme* [a affirmé]: "La police connaît les noms de ceux qui ont fait le coup." (*Le Journal du Dimanche*, March 23, 1986)
"Is marvellous Shergar [a horse] buried somewhere in Northern Ireland...? In any case, Lloyd's insurance company had to pay out 84 million francs to his owners. Roy David *states* [stated]: 'The police know the names of those who did it.' "

(30) (narrative, with tense switching, indirect)
Les rafles ont été opérées dans tous les milieux.... Les exemplaires de deux journaux, le *Weekly Mail* ... et le *Sowetan* ... ont été saisis. D'autre part, le groupe des neuf "éminentes personnalités" du Commonwealth ... *affirme* [a affirmé], dans un rapport rendu public le 12 juin, que Prétoria porte la responsabilité de l'échec de sa tentative de médiation. (*Le Monde*, June 18, 1986)
"Raids were carried out in all areas/social groups.... Copies of two newspapers, the *Weekly Mail* ... and the *Sowetan* ... were

seized. On the other hand, the group of nine 'eminent persons' of the Commonwealth ... *states* [stated], in a report made public on June 12, that Pretoria is responsible for the failure in its attempt at mediation."

Narratologists have observed the same propensity for *verba dicendi*, across languages, to be in HPr in oral story-telling, as well as in some written story-telling genres; various hypotheses for the phenomenon have been put forward:[31] signal of a transition between the narrative and assertive modes (the verb of saying taking by osmosis Pr, characteristic of conversation); highlighting the immediacy and vividness of the spoken words by introducing them with Pr; device to evaluate the story or to "track" its participants; and so forth.

In newspapers, reported speech is not necessarily inserted in narrative texts. It can be included in the summary, in the lead; it can be part of the narrative itself (it may be the very topic of the news story) or of the accompanying declarations or verbal reactions; it is occasionally contained too in the comments section (expectations, evaluations).[32] Given this multifunctionality of speech reporting in news, given too the variety of styles and techniques adopted by journalists to convey verbal interventions,[33] it is difficult to single out one textual criterion to explain the privileged use of HPr with declarative verbs.

We want to suggest that this phenomenon is essentially due to the fact that Pr has no inherent aspectual value. Declarative verbs in HPr normally refer to utterances which are unique and completed in the past. In such cases, they are contextually [+ perf]. Dates, adverbial complements, etc., promote this interpretation (see (30) for an example). But two further points need to be made in relation to quoted speech in newspapers.

First, readers are presented with the utterances (authentic, reconstituted, or summarized) of various people, e.g. people of importance on the socio-political scene, locally or internationally, or the people-on-the-scene who witnessed the event being described. These utterances may be spoken with authority in public/formal settings, they may lend authenticity to the report, and they may even have a performative or quasi-performative force (*décréter*, for example). At least they are judged to be worthy of mention or to carry some weight (see van Dijk 1988: 87). It is often presumed that they may have some durable effect. In (31), for example, the HPr declarative predicates prepare the PrPr and emphasize the stubborn continuity of Mitterrand's philosophy on the matter of Europe's spatial defense; this is corroborated by the title of the article: "Défense: l'obsession de l'espace" ("Defense: the obsession with space").

(31) Février 1984, à La Haye, le chef de l'Etat *explique* [expliqua, a expliqué (+ perf)] à ses partenaires européens: "Que l'Europe soit capable de lancer dans l'espace une station habitée...."

Mai 1985, à Brest, le président de la République ... n'*hésite* [hésita, a hésité (+ perf)] pas à prophétiser: "De mon point de vue la stratégie sera nécessairement spatiale...."

Aujourd'hui, M. Mitterrand réitère sa profession de foi. (*Le Monde*, November 23, 1986)

"February 1984, in The Hague, the Head of State *explains* [explained] to his European partners: 'That Europe is capable of launching into space a manned (space)station....'

May 1985, in Brest, the President of the Republic ... *does* not *hesitate* [did not hesitate] to prophesy: 'From my point of view, the strategy will necessarily be spatial....'

Today, Mr Mitterrand reiterates his profession of faith."

In (32) and (33), the authors of two open letters expect reactions to their petitions and implicitly will keep asking and appealing until they receive the answers for which they are hoping.

(32) Dans une lettre ouverte à M. François Mitterrand, Petr Uhl ... lui *demande* [demanda, a demandé (+ perf)] d'intervenir "publiquement et énergiquement afin d'empêcher la condamnation honteuse de Vaclav Havel." (*Le Monde*, February 21, 1989)

"In an open letter to Mr François Mitterrand, Petr Uhl ... *asks* [asked] him to publicly and resolutely intervene to prevent Vaclav Havel's shameful condemnation."

(33) Dans un texte publié par le quotidien "An Nahar" Mmes J. Kauffmann, E. Fontaine et S. Khoury ... *lancent* [lancèrent, ont lancé (+ perf)] un appel au Jihad islamique: "Au nom de Dieu, nous vous conjurons de mettre un terme à notre attente." (*Le Journal du Dimanche*, March 23, 1986)

"In a text published by the daily newspaper *An Nahar*, Mrs J. Kauffmann, E. Fontaine and S. Khoury ... *appeal* [appealed] to Islamic Jihad: 'In the name of God, we beseech you to put an end to our waiting.' "

Thus, in spite of the fact that the declarative action is telic, it is presented as having a result phase of some relevance: although the agent has ceased to be active, the predicate continues to be valid.

Second, another characteristic of declarative verbs in newspapers is the durability of their aftermath, in particular the fact that they are often predicated on the basis of actual (temporary or permanent) records,[34] which are written or taped. Their existence is frequently mentioned in the body of the article, by references made to *communiqué, décret, dépêche, lettre, message, rapport, texte*, etc., as in examples (30), (32), (33); or it is presupposed by the layout of the text:

(34) Dans une interview qu'il nous a accordée, le lundi 20 février, M. Michel Pezet ... *dément* [démentit, a démenti (+ perf)] que des négociations aient eu lieu. (*Le Monde*, February 21, 1989)
"In an interview that he granted to us on Monday, February 20, Mr Michel Pezet ... *denies* [denied, has denied] that negotiations took place."

This passage is followed by an alternation of questions (by the journalist) and answers (by the socialist candidate). As the final note suggests ("Propos receuillis par Guy Porte"), the journalist simply reproduces a recorded interview.

With declarative verbs, therefore, a perfective HPr, because of the neutrality of Pr with regard to aspect, can support nuances of imperfectivity. These nuances (duration, permanence, orientation toward PrPr in the result phase of the predicate) combine with its basic contextual perfectivity without creating infelicitous utterances.

The degree of imperfectivity in HPr of speech-introducing verbs varies with the context and the situation referred to. It appears limited in (28) where what dominates is the completion of the successive events in an article which is essentially narrative in nature. It is more discernible in (31), (32), (33) (as discussed on p. 107), or in (29), where, in the middle of the evaluative conclusion of the article, *affirme* can refer both to a unique instance of Roy David's expression of his opinion to the reporter, and to potential reiterations of this opinion (see 3.4), which remains the same after having been formulated once. Finally, there are cases where the declarative verb can barely or not at all be replaced by a past tense. At this point, imperfectivity has taken over, and with it stative aspect and non-agentivity. The subject of the declarative verb is no longer a [+ human] entity, but an object, the recorded document itself.

(35) Ce message indique [OPr] notamment: "Le régime raciste a trop longtemps eu les coudées franches." (*Le Monde*, June 18, 1986)
"This message indicates in particular: 'The racist regime has had free play for too long.'"

(36) Le président colombien ... a décrété ... "un état d'urgence social et économique"....Le décret instaurant l'état d'urgence fait référence [OPr] au massacre...."L'ordre économique et social du pays

a été perturbé", indique [OPr] le décret signé par le président Betancur. (*Le Monde*, November 22, 1985)
"The Colombian president ... has decreed ... 'a social and economic state of emergency'....The decree establishing the state of emergency refers [OPr] to the massacre....'The country's economic and social order has been disturbed,' the decree signed by President Betancur indicates [OPr]."

OPrs[35] (*indique, fait, indique*) have replaced HPrs. Their validity started at a moment in the past which could easily be pinpointed, but which is not highlighted. Focus is on the content of the quoted text, not on the act and person at its origin.

There are similarities between certain declarative HPrs [+ perf, with current relevance] (see examples (29), (30)) and the quotative Prs discussed by Casparis (1975: 137). In phrases like "as Plato says [said] in his *Republic*" ("comme Platon le *dit* [a dit] dans la *République*"), used by speakers to substantiate an argument, Pr is not compulsory; however, since Plato's work is still extant, Pr can be selected if the intended meaning is "at any time since the writing of the book and in particular now, for the purpose of my discussion." A past tense is preferred if Plato's utterance needs to be anchored in the past and focus is on its completion, for whatever reason (historical perspective, contrastive effect between then and now, etc.)

Simonin (1984: 181) remarks that declarative HPrs are often not the exact equivalents of pure past tenses, but seem more related to atemporal Prs (APr [0 past, 0 perf]). As a result, one may hesitate about the exact temporal-aspectual value of certain Prs with declarative verbs. This could apply to our examples (32) and (33), where the reader feels no urgent need to adopt a retrospective view of the situation even if past equivalents are acceptable for the Pr forms. Simonin further proposes that the APr interpretation of declarative Prs is due to the frequent reference they make to written utterances. This suggests, therefore, that we conceive of written texts as entities independent of time.[36] This is certainly corroborated by our examples (35) and (36), where Pr is compulsory. The same idea partially underlies Wilmet's discussion of what he calls "présent de persistance," i.e. whose signified has lasting existence (1976: 25).[37] Taking the example of a photograph of Général de Gaulle with the caption:

(37) Accompagné d'un aide de camp, il *arrive* [est arrivé] à la BBC
"Accompanied by an aide-de-camp, he *arrives* [arrived] at the BBC"

Wilmet stresses the importance of the "support matériel," which, he says, "éternise le signifié" (1976: 35–6). In this case the primary perfectivity of HPr (*arrive* represents an achievement situation) is permeated by the imperfectivity that the referent acquires by virtue of being translated on to a durable medium. The contradiction in aspect [+ perf]/[− perf], however, as well as the temporal contradiction between [+ past]/[− past], does not produce any semantic confusion. But it may contribute to a reading of *arrive* which transcends aspect and time, namely an APr reading.[38]

To go back to declarative verbs, before examining the multivalency of other aspectual properties of HPr, the following conclusion can be drawn: newspapers make use of Pr to report speech in two polar ways: on the one hand, with declarative predicates in HPr contextually interpreted as [+ perf, + past]; on the other hand, with declarative predicates in OPr/APr whose interest is independent of an actual, particular, completed occurrence in past time [− perf; ± past/0 past]. In between, there are transitional cases characterized by decreasing focus on perfectivity/past and increasing attention paid to the result phase and permanence of the process.

3.4. HPr and iterativity

Habitual or repeated occurrence is another dimension of aspect associated with perfectivity/imperfectivity. Repetition can be count-quantified[39] (a specific number of instances is involved, e.g. "three times") or mass-quantified (frequency of instances is involved, e.g. "every day"). HPr may refer to both types of situations, the former being associated with perfectivity, the second with imperfectivity as evidenced by the PS/PC or Imp substitutions in (38) and (39):

(38) L'armée de l'air israélienne *abat* [abattit, a abattu (+ perf)] deux appareils syriens. (*Le Monde*, October 22, 1985)
"The Israeli air force *brings* [brought] down two Syrian aircraft."

(39) Il *est* [était (− perf)] agent EDF. Il *se déplace* [déplaçait (− perf)] souvent pour effectuer des dépannages. (*Le Journal du Dimanche*, March 23, 1986)
"He *is* [was] an EDF employee. He often *makes* [made] trips for emergency repairs." [The person in question died the day before in an accident.]

The above examples are straightforward. But HPrs, in relation to iterativity, sometimes demonstrate semantic intricacies, which can be traced once again to the temporal-aspectual unmarkedness of Pr. Consider (40):

(40) Prétoria exécute [PrPr] toujours les criminels de droit commun à un rythme soutenu.... A Addis-Ababa, la prison a compté jusqu'à mille cinq cents prisonniers politiques.... L'armée ougandaise *massacre* [a massacré/PrPr(?)] allègrement des civils – dont une centaine à Namugongo, près de la capitale. (*Le Monde*, November 10, 1985)
"Pretoria still executes common law criminals at a steady rhythm. ... In Addis Ababa, jails have held up to a total of 1,500 political prisoners.... The Ugandan army blithely *massacres* [massacred] civilians – a hundred of them in Namugongo, near the capital."

Although *massacrer* is a "mass verb," it normally denotes an incidental situation (achievement), but in the given context (Amnesty International's reporting on the numerous violations of human rights committed all over the world), the predicate is interpreted as a repeated process. Its iterativity is doubly strengthened by the implicit plurality of the subject mass noun, *l'armée*, and the explicit plurality of the object, *des civils*. As was said above, repetition can be presented as bounded or open. The question is thus: how should *massacre* be read with respect to perfectivity? If it is understood as HPr, given the PC in the preceding sentence and the completion of Amnesty International's investigation, it has to be perfective.[40] But *massacre* can also be a PrPr with extended "now," to be put in parallel with *exécute*. In this case, the process is seen as still repeating itself, and no final endpoint for the repetition is in view. The PrPr interpretation is slightly odd, however, in conjunction with the appended quantification, *une centaine*. This "cardinal count"[41] complement conflicts with the idea of unbounded iterativity, which furthermore may not yet have reached 100 occurrences at the moment of writing/reading. But the grammaticality of the sentence is saved by the possibility offered to the reader to turn back to an HPr interpretation of Pr. What is remarkable, therefore, is that the multivalency of Pr can support such diverse and contradictory perspectives: closed and open iterativity, past and present, simultaneously.

A similar phenomenon can be observed in passage (41):

(41) La grande force de M. Berlusconi est d'avoir investi massivement dès le début pour arracher les droits des meilleures émissions sur le marché international. En spéculant ainsi à la hausse, il *obtient* (obtint, a obtenu (?)/PrPr (?)] l'exclusivité de *Dallas* ou de la

coupe du monde de football. La même surenchère financière lui *permet* [permit, a permis/PrPr] d'enlever aux chaînes publiques leurs animateurs vedettes. (*Le Monde*, November 20, 1985)

"Mr Berlusconi's great strength is to have massively invested from the start in order to snatch away the rights to the best programs on the international market. Speculating on price rises in this way, he *obtains* [obtained] exclusive rights to *Dallas* or the Soccer World Cup. The same financial overbidding *allows* [allowed] him to attract TV stars from government-owned channels."

On the basis of *avoir investi* and other clues in the article, the most natural interpretation of *obtient* (and *permet*) is HPr [+ perf].[42] But in combination with the conjunction *ou* "or," the HPr *obtient*, and its PS and PC equivalents, produce a semantically awkward sentence. The suggestion of an alternative (*Dallas* or the Soccer World Cup) contradicts what is known to be true: Berlusconi did buy both programs.[43] The reader, therefore, mentally replaces *ou* by *et* "and" to create a count-quantified situation (the process occurred twice), which fits the perfectivity of HPr/PS/PC. At the same time, to salvage the disjunctive co-ordination with *ou*, exploiting their internalized knowledge of Pr unmarkedness, readers attempt a non-HPr [– perf] interpretation of *obtient*. From that angle, the two TV programs are viewed as tokens of an unbounded series of acquisitions by Berlusconi: the situation is conceived as mass-quantified, openly iterative, despite the past time context.

In 1.1, the non-specific, contextual, temporal markings of Pr were subdivided into two types: [± past] (OPr) and [0 past] (APr). We suggest that a similar distinction could be made with regard to aspect.[44] In 3.3 many excerpts were provided where Pr (HPr) demonstrates perfectivity in the performance stage of the action and imperfectivity in the result stage. This could be called "double aspect": [± perf]. On the other hand, in 3.4, we have a case of "neutral aspect": [0 perf]. Consider (41) once again. The unbounded iterativity given by *ou* prevents a perfective reading of *obtient*; conversely, the past-completion aspect called for by the context does not agree with an imperfective reading of the verb. Thus, *obtient* in itself is satisfactorily construed as neither [+ perf] nor [– perf]: i.e. it has to be envisaged independently of perfectivity. The context has neutralized the feature and dismissed its semantic relevance.

4. CONCLUSION

In sections 2 and 3, we have discussed various examples of the temporal and aspectual multivalency of HPr. But this contextual richness is not limited to the primary (grammatical) meaning of the categories of tense and aspect. Just as the other French tenses have discourse and expressive functions (see Waugh 1989; Fleischman 1990), Pr – and its HPr version – contribute to the coherence and cohesion, to the evaluative and affective properties, of newspaper articles. In these domains too, the role of HPr is highly diverse, yielding on the one hand to the codal semantic unmarkedness of Pr, on the other to the influence of the surrounding text and wider context. The pragmatic functions of HPr in news reports need further investigation, but possible examples of multivalency would be: distinction or leveling of chronological layers, differentiation or fusion between narrative and commentary, separation or blending of the voice of the journalist and the voice of the news participant in free indirect style.

In the introduction, we underlined the fact that Pr, because of its unmarked nature, is compatible with a context which forces a past interpretation of the verbal process, but cannot itself, by itself, refer to past time. Moreover, again because of its unmarked nature, it can lead a context into a reference either to present time (PrPr) or to omnitemporality or atemporality (OPr or APr): these three contextualizations are inherent to the nature of Pr, and in fact only Pr can be used in this way without other criteria intervening. There is little wonder, then, that in the journalistic context which itself oscillates constantly between (recent) past events/background and present consequences/reactions/events, there should be an intrusion of PrPr/OPr/APr into a potential HPr usage. On the one hand, Pr lends itself more intrinsically to any of these three interpretations; and on the other hand, there is a certain tension between HPr and, in particular, PrPr (this is perhaps partly what Jakobson 1936 was trying to convey by calling the inverted usage "not proper"). This leads to the question: how can the same morphology mean PrPr [– past], its opposite HPr [+ past], their combination [± past], and their neutralization [0 past]? The answer is, as we have seen: with difficulty, only when contextually supported.[45] As soon as the context begins to allow the non-past (whether PrPr, OPr, or APr) to enter in, the various possibilities of semantic multivalency are realized. Likewise with aspect: while one could argue that HPr in narrative and in newspaper writing is more perfective than imperfective (although both are possible), it is clear that PrPr, OPr, and APr tend to be more imperfective. Thus, again, the tendency toward a fluctuation between imperfective and perfective readings of a given HPr (HPr itself – or HPr *cum* PrPr, OPr, or APr).

Such multivalency is, we insist, not to be interpreted as ambiguity to be disambiguated or as polysemy which impedes communication. Just as in visual perception the famous "Necker" cube can be seen as oriented either to the left or to the right, depending on one's perspective, so the unmarked Pr is a rich communicative device which has the potential for two (or more) simultaneous meanings, given the appropriate context. It would be interesting to see whether the semantic multivalency of other unmarked categories is also taken advantage of in those contexts which oscillate between the very categories at issue.[46]

NOTES

1 We would like to thank Jack Burston, Noëlle Collombet-Sankey, and Suzanne Fleischman for their comments on an earlier version of this paper.
2 We use the term tense here (instead of tense-aspect, or even tense-aspect-mood, for example) in accordance with traditional French usage.
3 Historical present is not the term we prefer; we like better the formulation by Wilmet (1976: 11), "présent-passé" (or that of Simonin 1984: 177, "présent à valeur aoristique," for certain uses of HPr). But, given that HPr is the traditional term, sanctioned in the literature, we will use it here.
4 We follow the definition of basic (principal, core, nuclear, central) usage as exemplified in the work of Jakobson (1936), Comrie (1985: 18–23) and others: it is that usage which is most frequent, least contextually determined, and considered to be prototypical.
5 And if we assume that the basic use of at least one of the future tenses is a temporal one. For our purposes, even if the basic meaning of the morphological future is modal (see Fleischman 1982), this does not alter our discussion here, since the basic meaning of the periphrastic future (with *aller*) is future time. In this case, the *aller* future would have displaced the morphological future in the core of the French tense system.
6 The presence of the adverb *toujours* is telling here: it indicates that time is at issue but that an omnitemporal interpretation is meant.
7 Calver and Bolinger use this phrase to characterize English Pr. We cite here and on p. 89 analyses of Pr in Indo-European languages other than French since we feel that all these languages have uses of Pr which fall into the categories given here. The difference may be, for example, that while PrPr is the basic meaning in French, OPr is probably the basic one in English. But such considerations go well beyond the scope of this chapter.
8 Perhaps this is the reason why Wolfson (1982: 52–3) claims that HPr is in itself meaningless, that only the switch into or out of a given HPr in a text is meaningful.
9 The "future present," where Pr is used in a context where there is a reference to future time, is also an example of an inverted meaning.
10 Since this conceptual category is the one categorically denied by the basic meaning ([– past] vs. [+ past]), this type of usage is sometimes called the

"not proper" meaning (Jakobson 1936: 69–70; see also Jakobson 1939). Given the pejorative connotations of the term "not proper," we use instead the term "inverted" because it is an inversion of the basic meaning.

11 Some of these differences are alluded to in previous discussions of the semantic value of HPr and can be related directly to questions of time: HPr has been described as a reactualization of what is known to be a past event, making contemporaneous what is not strictly contemporaneous. This may make it seem like an eye-witness account, a current report, which may then lead to vividness and immediacy. It is not, however, such effects which will be studied here: interestingly, in journalistic discourse there is little of the vividness characteristic of HPr in narrative texts.

12 On combined tense-aspect oppositions, see Comrie (1976: 78–82).

13 Perfective vs. imperfective covers various aspectual oppositions: bounded whole vs. non-bounded process, completed action vs. ongoing process or state, semelfactive action vs. repeated one. For more details and for discussion of other (discourse) functions of PS, see Monville-Burston and Waugh (1985); Waugh and Monville-Burston (1986); and Waugh (1989). For a treatment of the complicated structure of PC, see Waugh (1987), and for an examination of the multiple meanings inherent in Imp, see Monville-Burston (forthcoming).

14 In the examples, French HPrs (and their English equivalents) are in italicized capitals; any Prs printed otherwise are not strictly HPrs.

15 The reason why this Pr is labeled APr will be made clear in section 2.3.

16 See Labov and Waletzky (1967) for an approach to narrative which stresses chronology.

17 For all HPrs we will give in brackets that (or those) past tense substitute(s), whether PS, PC, or Imp, which sound(s) the most natural. In deciding which past tense(s) could be used, we have taken into account the whole of the article: in this section, on tense multivalency, the particular past tense substitute is not crucial (all that is important is that HPr be a substitute for some past tense); thus the context given is enough to show only the temporal interaction itself and may not be long enough (for reasons of space) to show why only the given past tense is substitutable. In the next section, on aspect multivalency, the particular past tense is important to the argument; thus, more context will be given.

18 In the English translations of the example, the French HPr will be rendered by an English HPr (even if it sounds a little artificial at times).

19 Although it is a bit disconcerting, due to the systematic avoidance of *aujourd'hui* "today," to see today always referred to as if it were history.

20 Similarly, the context can impose a future reading, with "not proper" futurity, although examples are rarer. Consider the title: *Jacques Pommatau signe [[+ future] Pr] l'accord salarial* "Jacques Pommatau signs the salary agreement"; this is immediately followed by the introductory sentence of the article, which reads: *La FEN signera [future tense] l'accord salarial proposé la semaine dernière* "FEN [National Education Federation] will sign the salary agreement which was proposed last week."

21 As Bolinger says, HPr "would occur whenever the sensory data are so vivid that they blank out the temporal context" (1947: 436).

22 For other examples, see Wilmet (1976: 35–6). The term "présent tabellaire" is Wilmet's and he distinguishes between it and HPr proper. According to him, the "présent tabellaire" is used in texts starting with an adverbial making past reference and in which the basic tense is the past-present (HPr); the "présent historique" is exclusively a Pr inserted into a narrative for which the basic tenses are PS and Imp.
23 Casparis (1975) mentions the following characteristics of the annalistic Pr: an indifference to the causal linking of events, a downplaying of sequential relations, a dechronologization, an obliteration of the distance usually found in past tenses – in short, an abolition of everything irrelevant to the process including time.
24 See our discussion in section 1.1 on the difficulty of establishing a strict boundary between past and present; we conceptualize it as an unclear zone.
25 *Être* in PS would not produce the same effect as PS is perfective. For PC, see discussion on p. 102. On the relationship between aspect and the auxiliaries *être* and *avoir*, see Martin (1971: 58–70).
26 (Simp) stands for simple, i.e. where PC is not perceived as periphrastic, but as an unanalyzable unit. (Comp) stands for compound, i.e. where PC is semantically analyzable into the meaning of the auxiliary and that of the past participle.
27 Fig. 5.3 is in fact a representation of PC-2 (simp) only. PC-1's representation would be comparable to Fig. 5.5.
28 It is not the purpose of this chapter to establish a typology of tense switching involving HPr. Note, however, that when Imp → HPr transitions occur, they are normally accompanied by an aspectual change: [− perf] → [+ perf]. See example (19).
29 See Simonin's remark: "Si les transitions ps–prs [PS–Pr] sélectionnent la valeur aoristique [here (+ perf)] du prs, les transitions pc–prs [PC–Pr] sont plus ambiguës" (1984: 179).
30 Munro (1982: 316) notes "the general human reaction to speech as a characteristic indicator of personality and intention."
31 See Fleischman (1990) for a useful survey.
32 We follow here van Dijk's thematic tree structure of news discourse (1985: 84–8, 1988: 55).
33 See above examples (28), (29), (30) which are but a sample.
34 See further discussion in 2.3.2. See also van Dijk's list of types of source texts (oral and written) which are immediately available to reporters (1988: 126–9).
35 In the introduction, we defined OPr as [± past]. From the point of view of aspect, it is [− perf]. It is difficult, when treating tense and aspect in French verbs, to separate the two categories completely. Hence, in this section, the use of a term which refers to time (OPr) to discuss questions related to aspect.
36 As Simonin remarks, "On peut se demander si la fréquence des présents se référant à des discours écrits ne reflète pas une conception atemporelle du texte écrit" (1984: 181).
37 See his example: "Bourdaloue ne *RECOMMANDE* [recommanda, a recommandé] pas une charité passive" ("Bourdaloue [a moralist writer] *DOES NOT ADVOCATE* [did not advocate] passive charity"). There is, however, a difficulty with Wilmet's (1976) definition of the "présent de persistance." On p. 35, this Pr is said to be permutable with past tenses; but on p. 25,

the following types of Prs are included in the category: stage directions, titles of paintings, plot summaries, all of these being Prs which do not have past-tense equivalents. This shows how slippery Pr tense classifications are. As Wilmet notes himself, "le glissement est insensible" between his three kinds of past-presents (1976: 35–9): the "présent de persistance," the "présent tabellaire," and the "présent historique" (see note 17). In fact, it is also difficult to make a clear difference between the perfective HPrs with current relevance (a type of "présent de persistance") and the OPr/APr "présents de persistance" [± past/0 past, – perf].

38 For more discussion, see Fleischman (1990) on the *récit de vie* genre, which "freezes" events as in a photograph. In addition, according to Fleischman (personal communication),

> the use of AP to discuss a discourse often implies a *spatial* rather than a *temporal* conceptualization of that discourse – something we would expect to go along with writing. Conversely, a discourse described in temporal terms (i.e., as unfolding through time) correlates more with speech. Thus we have the associations:

Spatial	Temporal
Writing	Speech
Static	Dynamic
AP	Tenses with temporality (Past tenses, PP).

39 See Mourelatos (1981: 202–10), on the relation of aspect and the mass-count distinction.

40 Furthermore, its PC equivalent *a massacré* would be PC-2 (simp). The [–perf] equivalent *massacrait* (Imp) would be much less likely to occur because the whole article is an enumeration of unlawful acts or situations presented as events. An imperfect here would probably be interpreted as background information (rather than as a "narrative imperfect"), which is not the intended message.

41 By opposition to a vaguer "frequency" complement. See Mourelatos (1981: 205).

42 It would be impossible to substitute an Imp here because, as in (40), the processes are not backgrounded; and an imperfect would most likely be interpreted as filling this function.

43 It is implied that the informed reader is aware of other such deals. On presupposition, entailment, and implicitness in news reports, see van Dijk (1986: 62–4, 121).

44 However, again, aspect being a category subordinated to tense in the French verbal system, one would look in vain for examples illustrating "pure" aspectuality.

45 As in narratives about the past for example, which is the main type of HPr which has been discussed recently.

46 In chapter 7 of this volume, Lunn and Cravens investigate a case of "simultaneously available" meanings for *-ra* in Spanish: pluperfect (aspectual) and known proposition (modal), which they call "semantic coexistence," "coexistence which is to be expected due to the natural symbiosis of function in many contexts." What we have tried to show here is the natural symbiosis between the various functions of Pr and the context of journalistic discourse.

REFERENCES

Baldi, Philip (ed.) (1982) *Papers from the XIIth Linguistic Symposium on Romance Languages*, Amsterdam: John Benjamins.

Blyth, Carl S., Jr and Waugh, Linda R. (1988) "Making a scene: the historical present and tense switching in French narrative" (MS).

Bolinger, Dwight L. (1947) "More on the present tense in English," *Language* 23: 434–6.

Calver, Edward (1946) "The uses of the present tense forms in English," *Language* 22: 317–25.

Casparis, Christian Paul (1975) *Tense Without Time: the Present Tense in Narration*, Bern: Francke.

Cerquiglini, Bernard (1981) *La Parole médiévale*, Paris: Éditions de Minuit.

Cintas, Pierre F. and Desclés, Jean-Pierre (1984) "Formal representations of the French present tense," in Philip Baldi (ed.) *Papers from the XIIth Linguistic Symposium on Romance Languages*, Amsterdam: John Benjamins.

Comrie, Bernard (1976) *Aspect*, Cambridge: Cambridge University Press.

—— (1985) *Tense*, Cambridge: Cambridge University Press.

Culioli, Antoine (1980) "Valeurs aspectuelles et opérations énonciatives: l'aoristique," in Jean David and Robert Martin (eds) *La Notion d'aspect*, Metz: Centre d'analyse syntaxique de l'université de Metz.

David, Jean and Martin, Robert (eds) (1980) *La Notion d'aspect*, Metz: Centre d'analyse syntaxique de l'université de Metz.

Fleischman, Suzanne (1982) *The Future in Thought and Language*, Cambridge: Cambridge University Press.

—— (1990) *Tense and Narrativity. From Medieval Performance to Modern Fiction*, Austin: University of Texas Press/London: Routledge.

Grésillon, A. and Lebrave, J.L. (eds) (1984) *La Langue au ras du texte*, Lille: Presses Universitaires de Lille.

Grevisse, Maurice (1969) *Le Bon Usage*, Gembloux: Duculot.

Hamburger, Käte (1973) *The Logic of Literature*, trans. Marilyn Rose, 2nd rev. edn, Bloomington: Indiana University Press.

Helm, J. (ed.) (1967) *Essays on the Verbal and Visual Arts*, Seattle: University of Washington Press.

Herring, Susan C. (1985) "Marking and unmarking via the present tense in narration: the historical present redefined," Special field examination paper, Dept of Linguistics, University of California, Berkeley.

Hopper, Paul J. and Thompson, Sandra A. (eds) (1982) *Syntax and Semantics*, vol. 15 *Studies in Transitivity*, New York: Academic Press.

Jakobson, Roman (1984) "Contribution to the general theory of case: general meanings of the Russian cases," in Linda R. Waugh and Morris Halle (eds) *Russian and Slavic Grammar: Studies 1931–1981*, Berlin: Mouton.

—— (1984) "Zero sign," in Linda R. Waugh and Morris Halle (eds) *Russian and Slavic Grammar: Studies 1931–1981*, Berlin: Mouton.

Kiparsky, Paul (1968) "Tense and mood in Indo-European syntax," *Foundations of Language* 4: 30–57.

Labov, William and Waletzky, Joshua (1967) "Narrative analysis: oral versions of personal experience," in J. Helm (ed.) *Essays on the Verbal*

and Visual Arts, Seattle: University of Washington Press.
Larochette, Joe (1980) *Le Langage et la réalité: l'emploi des formes de l'indicatif en français*, Munich: Wilhelm Fink.
Martin, Robert (1971) *Temps et aspect: essai sur l'emploi des temps narratifs en moyen français*, Paris: Klincksieck.
Monville-Burston, Monique (forthcoming) Imparfait: la narration déstructurée.
Monville-Burston, Monique and Waugh, Linda R. (1985) "Le passé simple dans le discours journalistique," *Lingua* 67: 459–508.
Mourelatos, Alexander P. D. (1981) "Events, processes, and states," in Philip J. Tedeschi and Annie Zaenen (eds) *Syntax and Semantics*, vol. 14 *Tense and Aspect*, New York: Academic Press.
Munro, Pamela (1982) "On the transitivity of 'say' verbs," in Paul J. Hopper and Sandra A. Thompson (eds) *Syntax and Semantics*, vol. 15 *Studies in Transitivity*, New York: Academic Press.
Simonin, Jenny (1984) "Les repérages énonciatifs dans les textes de presse," in A. Grésillon and J.L. Lebrave (eds) *La Langue au ras du texte*, Lille: Presses Universitaires de Lille.
Tedeschi, Philip J. and Zaenen, Annie (eds) (1981) *Syntax and Semantics* vol. 14 *Tense and Aspect*, New York: Academic Press.
van Dijk, Teun A. (ed.) (1985) *Discourse and Communication: New Approaches to the Analysis of Mass Media Discourse and Communication*, Berlin: Walter de Gruyter.
—— (1988) *News as Discourse*, Hillsdale, NJ: Lawrence Erlbaum Associates.
Vendler, Zeno (1967) *Linguistics in Philosophy*, Ithaca, NY: Cornell University Press.
Waugh, Linda R. (1976) "A semantic analysis of the French tense system," *Orbis* 24 (2): 436–85.
—— (1987) "Marking time with the passé composé: toward a theory of the perfect," *Linguisticae Investigationes* XI (1): 1–47.
—— (1989) "Tense-aspect, discourse functions, and pragmatic, textual, modal, expressive and referential meanings," in Linda R. Waugh and Stephen Rudy (eds) *New Vistas in Grammar: Invariance and Variation*, Amsterdam: John Benjamins.
Waugh, Linda R. and Halle, Morris (eds) (1984) *Russian and Slavic Grammar: Studies 1931–1981*, Berlin: Mouton.
Waugh, Linda R. and Monville-Burston, Monique (1986) "Aspect and discourse function: the French simple past in newspaper usage," *Language* 62: 846–77.
Waugh, Linda R. and Rudy, Stephen (eds) (1989) *New Vistas in Grammar: Invariance and Variation*, Amsterdam: John Benjamins.
Wilmet, Marc (1976) *Études de morpho-syntaxe verbale*, Paris: Klincksieck.
Wolfson, Nessa (1982) *CHP: the Conversational Historical Present in American English Narrative*, Dordrecht: Foris.

6 The status of imperatives as discourse signals[1]

Béatrice Lamiroy and Pierre Swiggers

1. INTRODUCTION

1.1. Theoretical introduction

The last decades have witnessed a strong interest in theories of *énonciation*, and, at a deeper level, a move away from a grammar-focused approach toward a communication-centered one.[2] In two recent books, Hagège (1982, 1985) has integrated the latter type of approach into a general theory of language, relating it to an "enunciativehierarchical point of view." This contrasts with a morphosyntactic point of view, which focuses on formal (including positional) and functional aspects of linguistic units above the phoneme-level. By "function" we understand here "internal function," thus a reference to the relation of linguistic units to the language system. In such a view "function" can be opposed to "use." (One could also speak of function 1 and function 2, the latter referring then to the relation between language units and language users.[3])

The grammatical tradition has largely eschewed usage-based definitions of linguistic units on the morphosyntactic level. While this may be due to an awareness (never explicitly acknowledged) that form and function (i.e. function 1) allow one to define linguistic units in a much more operational way, one might well wonder whether this situation is not due to a "subordinative" attitude on the part of grammarians, who often prefer (or preferred) to walk in the footsteps of logicians and language pedagogues who have insisted on formal and content-based classificatory criteria. This is not the proper place to embark upon a broad-gauged investigation of a striking inertia in the history of linguistics. However several observations are relevant in this context:

(a) the remarkable longevity of the parts-of-speech approach (cf. Swiggers and Van Hoecke 1986), which is still adopted, without question, in various modern theories of grammar;

(b) the narrow conception of syntax adhered to throughout the history of linguistics. If one excludes certain rare intrusions of rhetorical theory into the field of grammar,[4] the prevailing conceptions of syntax can be reduced to a functional explanation of inflectional markers or to an account of word combinations in terms of "rules and principles."[5] It is almost an irony of the history of grammar that, although much has been written about linguistic competence (with special reference to "syntactic knowledge"), syntactic theory never raised, let alone answered, the question: "Why do people (mostly) speak in sentences?"

This chapter is not intended as a plea for a new model. Our aim is less ambitious, and as a consequence its focus will be descriptive (i.e. classificatory) and interpretive. Our description aims at clarifying one aspect of communicative competence,[6] which is interesting from a triple point of view:

(a) as a particular instance of speakers' reflexive attitude towards their utterances;
(b) as an example of a functional "displacement" of a particular word-class;
(c) as a case of diachronic "emptying" of word meaning(s) and, indirectly perhaps, as an illustration of the secondary nature of word meaning.

The aspect of communicative competence that will be studied here is the use of discourse signals, a concept that will be defined below (1.2). These signals include a number of forms with a rather heterogeneous morphosyntactic status, which share, however, a "connecting" function (cf. the French term *connecteurs*). Here "function" must be understood as a cover term for both "function 1" (= internal function) and "function 2" (= use), since these connecting elements can serve as linkers between a number of segments within the utterance, and/or between the participants in a communicative exchange. We will limit our analysis to verb forms, and more specifically to imperatives. In their capacity as discourse signals, these forms illustrate the three characteristics mentioned above. By way of illustration, consider the example in (1), from a dialogue in Capus' play *La Bourse ou la vie*:

(1) PLESNOIS. Mme Herbault n'a pas trouvé grâce devant ses petites perfidies.
    JACQUES. Tiens! Tiens! il dit que ma femme a un amant?
    "Mrs Herbault has not found mercy for her little treacheries."

"Well, well [lit. '(be)hold'], is he saying that my wife has a lover?"

This exchange involves a (repeated) use of *tiens* (literally the imperative singular (sg.) of the verb *tenir* "to hold"), which is remarkable in a number of respects:

(a) although formally an imperative, the verb form is not used here to convey an order;
(b) the verb shows no congruity with the addressee, turned into a third-person role (*il dit*), or with the implicit or "indirect" participants (the audience);
(c) the verb form has a specific function: it changes what normally would count as an observation (*il dit que ma femme a un amant*) into an emotive reaction – one of surprise, and perhaps also of indignation.

This example offers a nice illustration of how the speaker is primarily an "actor," playing with his utterance, before an "audience." We are convinced that the study of discourse signals, which is still in its infancy, will contribute to our knowledge of this aspect of a speaker's behavior.

The non-congruity of the imperative with the grammatical person/number of the addressee[7] is a sufficient proof of its functional displacement: the form is no longer used as the expression of a command, but as a polyvalent linking element, which can be attached to predicates of whatever mode, including the imperative as in (3). Or it can be used as an utterance unto itself, as in (4), or as a reaction to a non-linguistic "stimulus," as in (5):

(2) Tiens! c'est vrai.
 "How about that, it's true."
(3) Tiens, dis-moi ce que tu en penses.
 "By the way, tell me what you think of it."
(4) MARGUERITE [to René]. J'ai finalement décidé de me marier.
 "I finally decided to get married."
 RENÉ. Tiens!
 "How about that!"
(5) [Marguerite drops her glass at a party when she sees René]
 RENÉ. Tiens!
 "Ah!"

Finally, the use of *tiens* (or its plural *tenez*) in examples such as (1)–(5) testifies to the loss of the word meaning ("to hold"): it is very hard – particularly in view of the possible absence of grammatical agreement – to establish a constant semantic correlation with *tenir*, although from a strictly formal point of view *tiens* and *tenez* constitute the imperative sub-paradigm of this verb.

1.2. The notion of discourse signals

Linguistic forms can be analyzed from the point of view of their insertion into a sentence (or larger units, such as discourses or texts), from the point of view of their (basic/conceptual) meaning, or from that of their pragmatic function. Much more could be said about this admittedly simplified distinction, which does not do justice either to the integration of these three aspects within a single speech act, or to descriptive methods which take into account several of these aspects, often hierarchized in terms of a means-ends relationship. As for "pragmatic function," we will try to show that a number of linguistic forms which have lost most of their syntactically and semantically coded properties can only be analyzed in a satisfactory way if one takes into account their pragmatic function.

The term "signal" should not be taken in Bühler's sense, as an addressee-oriented sign or sign-value, opposed to "symptom" (speaker- or ego-oriented sign or sign-value) and to "symbol" (referent- or reality-oriented sign or sign-value). Bühler's model, useful as it may be, overlooks the essential discursive relation of signs to their larger context and thereby neglects one of the fundamental features of discursive behavior: the integration or fusion of functions (e.g. integration of symptom and signal, as reflecting the interaction between speaker and hearer). Our use of "signal" is a more neutral one, referring to the relationship between a sign and its discursive context, and with no specific claims as to its connection to the speaker, hearer, or "outside world."

Curiously, one hardly finds lists – let alone detailed descriptions – of discourse signals (for partial lists in French, see Auchlin 1981; Berrendonner 1983; Gülich and Kotschi 1983; for Italian, see the overview in Bazzanella 1985). This state of affairs may be due to the following factors:

(a) discourse signals do not constitute a paradigmatic class (defined in terms of morphosyntactic and/or semantic properties): since forms with a different morphosyntactic status function as discourse signals, there can be no "word class" of discourse signals;
(b) discourse signals do not exhibit a particular syntactic behavior

(unlike auxiliaries, relative pronouns, or conjunctions): conceivably they function outside the syntactic domain of the sentence (cf. Rubattel 1982: 59), whence the difficulty of assigning a particular syntactic function to this composite class;
(c) discourse signals are not amenable to an overall semantic description (i.e. they do not fit within a semantic field or domain): for some of them, no semantic description can be given, and for most others the (surface) semantic description hardly helps to understand their use.

As a consequence of their elusive nature, discourse signals have been the *parent pauvre* of grammatical description;[8] one rarely finds them mentioned in standard synchronic grammars, and they are even more conspicuously absent from historical and comparative grammars. Their problematic status has resulted in their being assigned a variety of labels, ranging from "interjections," "modifiers," and "adverbials" to *connecteurs* (cf. Berrendonner 1983; Roulet *et al.* 1985), *briseurs de chaîne* (cf. Hagège 1982), *marqueurs de structuration* (Gülich 1970), or *mots-phrases*. As a tentative characterization of their status, we propose the following description. Discourse signals are pragmatic units of differing grammatical status (non-lexemes, words, syntagms) that can function either in complete isolation (i.e. as totally free elements, equivalent to a sentence or a set of sentences), or in isolation from the actantial pattern (*schème actanciel*, i.e. the complex of relations built by the verb and its arguments) of the sentence in which they are inserted. They do not introduce a new actantial pattern, and are not subject to a number of phrase-level linguistic operations (such as passivization or topicalization).

Our study of the use of discourse signals, based on a close scrutiny of imperatives, is essentially descriptive. The priority given to description seems justified by a number of considerations: first, the absence of a systematic study of these signals; second, the fact that verb-based discourse signals, which constitute the most neglected type of discourse signals (compared with adverbials and conjunctions), lend themselves to an exhaustive analysis of formal properties, allowing for a number of descriptive generalizations; finally, the implications of the study of "problematic" linguistic elements for grammatical description in general (which is based on more "regular" types of units).

Although the descriptive account given here is self-contained, our contribution also leads to a number of theoretical conclusions (see section 4). While these are suggested by the description and its specific object, we hope that they may stimulate further reflection on the nature of discourse signals, as well as on the linguistic status of sentences and utterances and on the proper object of linguistic description.

2. A TYPOLOGY OF DISCOURSE SIGNALS

2.1.

Given the overall absence of information on discourse signals in the linguistic literature, we will try to outline their typology, with exemplification from three Romance languages: French (Fr.), Italian (It.), and Spanish (Sp.). The occurrence of discourse signals certainly differs according to text types, but the typology proposed here focuses on their formal nature. We do not make a principled distinction between spoken and written language: in fact, many discourse signals traditionally regarded as typical of spoken language frequently occur in written texts. The typology we offer here is a preliminary one in that it does not include certain types of discourse signals, such as:

(a) punctuation marks[9] (which by definition function as connective elements; cf. Harris 1968);
(b) vulgar expressions functioning as discourse signals, mostly in spoken language: e.g. Fr. *je m'en fous* "I don't give a damn," Sp. *¡qué cojones!* "what the hell," It. *cavolo* "damn," etc.;
(c) combinations of elements which function individually as discourse signals (thus we include *eh* "eh" and *bien* "well," but not *eh bien*),
(d) discourse signals resulting from the combination of a relational term and an essentially open series of specifiers. Cases in point are the prepositions Fr. *à* "to, till," Sp. *hasta* "till," It. *a* "to," or the adjectives Fr. *bon*, Sp. *bueno*, It. *buono* "good," combined with time indications. Thus, in French we have *à demain* "till tomorrow," but also *à ce soir* "till this evening," *à cet après-midi* "till this afternoon," *à la semaine prochaine* "till next week," *à l'année prochaine* "till next year," etc. The same holds for Sp. *hasta la vista* "see you," *hasta mañana* "till tomorrow," *hasta la semana/el mes/ el año que viene* "till next week/month/year," and for It. *a più tarde* "see you later," *a questo pomeriggio* "till this afternoon," *a questa sera* "till this evening," *alla settimana prossima* "till next week." It is interesting to note here that some of these productive expressions have

taken on a new pragmatic meaning, different from that of the original discourse signal. In their new meaning these expressions no longer form an extensible group, and as such are again taken into account, e.g. Fr. *bonjour* "hello," Sp. *adiós muy buenas* "farewell, good day," in the following uses:

(6) S'il faut faire tout ce travail manuellement, bonjour!
(7) Acabó el trabajo en cinco minutos. ¡Y adiós muy buenas!

In (6) *bonjour* does not mean "hello," but something like "forget it" ("If one has to do this job manually, forget it"), and in (7) *adiós muy buenas* should be translated as "and that was that" ("he finished the job in five minutes and that was that").

Since the discourse signals considered here constitute an extremely heterogeneous group, it is not an easy task to classify them. Before presenting the results of our classificatory attempt, we will comment on possible taxonomic criteria such as lexical class or, in traditional grammar terms, parts of speech. We will argue for a more operational classification, which is strictly morphological.

2.2.

A common distinction in seventeenth- and eighteenth-century general grammar was that between parts of speech relating to content of thought and parts of speech relating to ways of thinking. Exploring the usefulness of this bipartition for our purpose, we could assume that discourse signals are among the elements that say something about how we think rather than about what we think. However, various word classes can take the role of discourse signals, such as nouns, verbs, and adjectives: e.g. Fr *chapeau* "congratulations" (lit. "hat"), *ma foi* "well" (lit. "my faith"), Sp. *hombre* "hey" (lit. "man"), *venga* "come on," It. *bravo* "bravo," *dai* "come on" (lit. "give"). These forms generally figure in traditional grammars under the heading "interjections" (cf. Grevisse and Goosse 1986: 1588; Dardano and Trifone 1985: 286). Moreover, some of these originally nominal or verbal forms are used exclusively as discourse markers, e.g. Fr. *somme toute* "all in all" (lit. "sum total"), Sp. *venga y dale* "keep insisting" (lit. "come and give"). One could argue that these expressions when used as discourse markers are indeclinable in the same way as other "affective" words (viz. interjections properly speaking). This holds for several cases, in particular nouns (the plural forms *chapeaux, *hombres are not used as discourse signals), but not for all: in Spanish, both *demonio* "devil" and *demonios* "devils," *diablo* "devil" and *diablos* "devils," function as discourse signals. And verb forms functioning as discourse signals usually show paradigmatic variation: Fr. *va* "go," *allons* "let's go," *allez* "go (pl.)"; *tiens, tenez* "hold"; Sp. *digo* "I say," *diga* "tell (me)," *no me digas* "don't tell me"; *anda, ande* "go"; It. *guarda, guardi* "look."

A binary classification into content- vs. modality-centered parts of speech would also be problematic because a large group of discourse signals cannot be assigned to either class: often we use whole phrases as discourse markers, many of which have become fixed idiomatic expressions (Gross 1984). As a result, it is often difficult to identify the head constituent of the phrase, and hence to assign phrasal discourse signals to a lexical class (cf. Fr. *comme quoi* "in sum" (lit. "like what")), *tant qu'à faire* "while [you are] at it" (lit. "so much as to do"); Sp. *visto lo cual* "in view of which" (lit. "seen that what")). Even those connectives that can be identified as formally belonging to a particular lexical class do not show the characteristic use of their class, e.g. Fr. *par contre* "on the other hand" (lit. "by against") or *sur ce* "thereupon" undoubtedly belong to the class of prepositional phrases (PP), but never appear as a PP complement:

(8) a. *Il est tombé sur ce.
    *"He fell on this."
   b. Sur ce, il est parti.
    "Thereupon he left."
(9) a. *Il s'est arrêté par contre un arbre.
    *"He stopped against a tree."
   b. Par contre, il s'est arrêté.
    "On the other hand, he stopped."

The same holds for Fr. *décidément*, an adverb, or for Fr. *somme toute*, morphologically a noun phrase, which show uses different from regular adverbs or noun phrases:

(10) a. * Il a agi décidément.
    *"He acted undoubtedly."
   b. Il a agi avec décision.
    "He acted with decision."
   c. Décidément, il a agi en héros.
    "Undoubtedly, he acted as a hero."
(11) a. *Somme toute a été payée aux travailleurs.
    *"Sum total has been paid to the workers."
   b. Somme toute, on a payé assez.
    "In sum, we have paid enough."

One of the main characteristics of discourse signals that makes their classification intricate is that many of them are "frozen" remnants of former stages of a language, a point to which we will return. It should be clear by now, however, that a typology based on parts of speech will be of little use.

Some grammarians have made a distinction between primary and secondary interjections (cf. Lenz 1916; Alcina Franch and Blecua 1979: 820). Primary interjections have no lexical status: they are sounds (like *ah, hm, ai*) specific to a language community (or to several language communities), which recall certain gestures accompanying speech intended to make sure that the hearer "gets the message." Secondary interjections are lexical items, but their pragmatic meaning is a derived one, thus differing from the "lexical" meaning of the word. For example, Fr. *chapeau*, used as a discourse signal, means "well done!" or "congratulations," but not "hat." Similarly, when Sp. *ojo*, literally "eye," is used as a discourse signal it means "(be) careful."

Although one could argue that a classification into lexematic vs. non-lexematic discourse signals serves only to separate a small class of non-lexemes from a large and heterogeneous group of discourse signals which remain to be classified, the analysis based on the view that discourse signals are pragmatic "doublets" or, seen from the semantic point of view, "metaphors" of lexical items is interesting since it applies to a wide range of discourse signals, e.g. adverbs such as Fr. *franchement* and Sp./It. *francamente* "frankly."

(12) a. Max a parlé franchement.
"Max spoke frankly."
b. Franchement, Max a parlé comme un oracle.
"Frankly, Max spoke like an oracle."

Whereas *franchement* in (12a) is synonymous with *avec franchise* "with frankness," this equivalence does not hold for (12b). The same applies to PPs, e.g. Fr. *au fond*, Sp. *en el fondo* "in fact" (lit. "at the bottom"), and verb phrases (VPs), e.g. Fr. *allons* "come on" (lit. "let's go"), Sp. *vaya* "come on" (lit. "go").

(13) a. Max a trouvé la bague au fond du tiroir.
"Max found the ring at the bottom of the drawer."
b. Au fond, c'est Max qui a trouvé la bague.
"In fact, it was Max who found the ring."
(14) a. Soyons gentils et allons voir notre grand-mère.
"Let's be nice and let's go see our grandmother."

b. Allons, soyez gentils.
"Come on, be nice."

In (13a) *au fond* can be replaced by *au bout (du tiroir)* "at the back (of the drawer)" without a change in meaning; but in the case of (13b) this substitution would result in an unacceptable sentence:

(13) c. ?* Au bout, c'est Max qui a trouvé la bague.
*"At the back, it was Max who found the ring."

Similarly in (14a) *allons (voir)* can be replaced by *courons (voir)* "let's run," without changing the acceptability of the sentence, but this is not possible in (14b). The result is given in (14c):

(14) c. ?* Courons, soyez gentils.
*"Let's run, be nice."

The latter sentence, if grammatical, has a totally different meaning ("please, run with me/us").

This idea leads to the view that discourse signals are lexical elements which have undergone a process of semantic change, analogous to the well-known process of grammaticalization; in the case of discourse signals, however, the meaning of the words does not necessarily fade, but changes, sometimes radically, and the new function of the expressions extends beyond the boundary of the clause or sentence.

The "doublet" hypothesis gains further support from the fact that discourse signals not only differ in meaning from their homonymous counterparts, but also show a different syntactic behavior: in (13b), for example, *au fond* does not allow a nominal complement after it:

(13) d. *Au fond du tiroir, c'est Max qui a trouvé la bague.
*"At the bottom of the drawer, it was Max who found the ring."

Similarly, *allons* allows a locative complement in (14a), but not in (14b):

(14) d. Soyons gentils et allons à la maison voir notre grand-mère.
"Let's be nice and go home to see our grandmother."
e. ?Allons à la maison, soyez gentils.
?"Let's go home, be nice."

The latter sentence is only acceptable in a reading where *allons* is used as a verb of motion.

Although the doublet hypothesis seems valid for some discourse signals in various lexical classes, it is irrelevant to many others.

Several discourse signals listed below (2.3) do not currently have a non-pragmatic equivalent from which they can have been derived: in other words, many discourse signals are used exclusively with a pragmatic function. Cases in point are, among many others: Fr. *certes* "certainly," *assurément* "for sure," *en fait* "in fact," Sp. *en suma* "in sum," *de hecho* "as a matter of fact," It. *infatti* "in fact," *suvvia* "come on," etc. It should also be noted that in certain cases where both a lexical and a pragmatic use occur, the pragmatic use may be the primary one from which the lexical use is derived, and not vice versa, e.g. the case of *bonjour* "good day."

(15) Remettez-lui mon bonjour.
 "Give him my best regards."

Since the traditional criteria that could be invoked to classify discourse signals do not account in a satisfactory way for all cases, we propose instead a formal typology based strictly on morphological criteria.

2.3.

A first distinction to be made is between morphologically non-analyzable and morphologically analyzable discourse signals. The latter class will be broken down into two subclasses, one not manifesting a syntagmatic relation between the morphemes, the other manifesting such a relation. The former subclass is again divided into two groups, depending on whether or not the discourse signal has a paradigmatic relation with other discourse markers. This gives us the following division:

A. Morphologically non-analyzable discourse signals: e.g. Fr. *b(i)en* "well," *donc* "thus," *oh* "oh," *zut* "damn," Sp. *bien* "well," *pues* "thus, so," *uf* "ow," *corcho* "gee," It. *bene* "well," *dunque* "thus," *hm* "hm," *toh* "gee, look."

B. Morphologically analyzable discourse signals:
B.1. Signals not manifesting a syntagmatic relation:
 B.1.1. Absence of paradigmatic alternation: e.g. Fr. *entendu* "OK," *franchement* "frankly," *néanmoins* "yet," *parfait* "great, fine," *seulement* "only"; Sp. *dios* "my God," *francamente* "frankly," *gracias* "thanks," *sólo* "only," *vale* "OK"; It. *inteso* "OK," *francamente* "frankly," *grazie* "thanks," *nonostante* "yet," *perfetto* "great, fine," *soltanto* "only."
 B.1.2. Presence of paradigmatic alternation: e.g. Fr. *va, allez, allons* "come on," *dis, dites* "say," *marche* "go, move on,"

tiens, tenez "hold," *vive, vivent* "long live," *voyons* "let's see"; Sp. *digo, diga* "(I) say," *va, vaya, vamos, anda, ande* "come on," *mira* "look," *oye, oiga* "listen," *viva* "long live"; It. *scusa, scusi* "sorry," *senta, senti* "listen," *guarda* "look," *vediamo* "let's see," *figuriamoci* "let alone," *fila* "move on," *viva* "long live," *capisci, capito* "you see?"

B.2. Signals involving a syntagmatic relation: e.g. Fr. *après tout* "after all," *à propos* "by the way, apropos," *cela dit* "this being said," *en bref* "in short," *en ce qui concerne* "as for," *je vous en prie* "I beg you," *n'est-ce pas* "isn't it," *sans blague* "no kidding"; Sp. *en fin de cuentas* "after all," *a propósito* "by the way, apropos," *es a saber* "viz.," *por supuesto* "of course," *por lo que toca* "as for"; It. *a proposito* "by the way, apropos," *ossia* "viz.," *considerato che* "taking into account," *ciò non toglie* "none the less," *mi raccommando* "please," *per ciò che riguarda* "as for."

A few remarks are in order here. First, nominal and adjectival discourse signals (e.g. Fr. *chapeau* lit. "hat," *ciel* "heaven," *chic* "nice," etc.) should be analyzed as containing a free morpheme and a zero morpheme; they thus belong in subclass B.1.1. This zero morpheme can be regarded as their morphological characteristic, since these nouns and adjectives, unlike verbal forms, do not in general show morphological variation when used as discourse signals.[10] Therefore we have treated them as morphologically analyzable but without any apparent paradigmatic relation.

A second remark concerns the notion of analyzability. All the discourse signals of class B are said to be analyzable into morphemes, and all those of subclass B.2 are characterized by a syntagmatic relation between the morphemes. A major problem here is that many of the expressions that function as discourse signals are historically combinations of morphemes (and thus "syntagmatic" from the diachronic point of view), but are no longer felt as such, e.g. Fr. *cependant* "however," *tant qu'à faire* "while [you are] at it," *peut-être* "maybe," etc. For most speakers of Modern French the relationship between the constituent elements of these discourse signals is no longer transparent: the forms have become fixed idiomatic expressions. Although we are aware of this, we put these cases together with those in which the morphological relationship between the elements is still manifest, e.g. *sinon* "if not," *tu sais* "you know," *si tu veux* "if you will," etc., because the borderline between the "diachronically but not synchronically analyzable" and the "synchronically analyzable" is never clearcut. The degree to which an expression is fixed varies not only for the different forms listed here, but also among different speakers of the language.

Finally, it should be noted that the morphological classification proposed here yields different "natural" classes. The morphologically unanalyzable class contains "inarticulate sounds," conjunctions, and adverbs. The first subclass (B.1.1.) of the morphologically analyzable group contains nouns and adjectives, and a particular type of conjunction and adverb, viz. compound conjunctions (with *que* in Fr. and Sp., *che* in It.) and adverbs in *-ment/mente*. The second subclass (B.1.2.) contains only verb forms, most of which are imperatives. And B.2. consists only of phrases. This group is the most heterogeneous because the phrases belong to various syntactic categories, ranging from noun phrases (NPs) (*somme toute* "all in all"), adverbial phrases (AdvPs) (*jamais de la vie* "never ever") to small clauses (in Williams' (1975) sense; *cela étant* "this being so"), clauses (*s'il te plaît* "if you please") and sentences (*je t'en prie* "I beg you").

In section 3 we will examine in detail a particular subgroup of discourse signals: imperative verb forms. Our analysis will focus on French.

3. IMPERATIVE FORMS AS DISCOURSE SIGNALS

3.1.

The verbal discourse signals considered in this section have a basically pragmatic function, which subsumes a number of morphological, syntactic, and semantic properties. These allow us to define three basic characteristics of verbal discourse signals in general: (a) they are modalizing elements and therefore cannot receive a higher-level modalization (3.1.1.); (b) they are minimally referential (there is no "fit" to the world, in Searle's sense; cf. Searle 1979: 3–5, 14–16), hence the idea of gradual or scalar notions expressed by changes in tense, person, or voice disappears (3.1.2.); and (c) because of their speech-oriented function, they appear as autonomous elements, loosely adjoined to the rest of the sentence, or as separate utterances (3.1.3.).

3.1.1.

Given that one of the main functions of discourse signals is to modalize a stretch of discourse, it is not easy to impose upon them modalizations of a higher level. This is why combinations of an adverbial with a discourse signal are usually ungrammatical. As pointed out by Rubattel (1982), the difference between a predicative adverb (in capitals in the example below) and a corresponding signal is shown by the fact that a modifier (*assez* (16)) is allowed in one case but not in the other:

(16) a. Arthur a assez JUSTEMENT agi.
   "Arthur acted quite properly."
   b. JUSTEMENT, Arthur a eu tort d'agir ainsi.
   "Quite so, it was wrong for Arthur to behave like that."
   c. *Assez JUSTEMENT, Arthur a eu tort d'agir ainsi.
   *"Rather properly, it was wrong for Arthur to behave like that."

The same applies to verbal discourse signals in general (note that the modifiers cannot be excluded on semantic grounds):

(17) a. *Tout compte bien fait, je reste.
   *"Every count well made, I'm staying."
   b. *Réflexion tout à fait faite, j'ai décidé d'acheter une voiture.
   *"Thought completely made, I have decided to buy a car."
   c. *Cela déjà dit, elle fait ce qu'elle veut.
   "This already having been said, she does what she wants."
   d. *Arthur est crétin, n'est-ce pas du tout?
   *"Arthur is a cretin, isn't he at all?"
(18) a. VOYONS vite si Arthur a gagné au lotto.
   "Let's see quickly whether Arthur won the lottery."
   b. Arthur ne gagnera jamais au lotto, VOYONS!
   "Arthur will never win the lottery, you know."
   c. *Arthur ne gagnera jamais au lotto, VOYONS vite!
   *"Arthur will never win the lottery, let's see quickly."

It applies to imperatives in particular:

(19) a. VA, n'exagérons rien.
   "Come on, let's not exaggerate."
   b. VA un peu dire aux voisins qu'ils exagèrent.
   "Go on, tell the neighbours that they're going too far."
   c. *VA un peu, n'exagérons rien.
   *"Go a bit, let's not exaggerate."

3.1.2.

Verbal discourse signals, which are minimally referential, are not subject to morphological variation in tense, person, voice, etc., as the following examples show:

(20) a. Tant qu'à faire, il peut aussi bien vendre le tout.
   "While he is at it, he might as well sell the whole thing."
   b. *Tant qu'à avoir fait, il peut aussi bien vendre le tout.
   *"While he has been at it, he might as well sell the whole thing."
(21) a. Il avait, si tu veux, un don spécial.
   "He had, if you will, a special gift."
   b. *Il avait, si tu voulais, un don spécial.
   *"He had, if you wished, a special gift."

In the case of imperatives, agreement in person with the addressee is not obligatory (cf. Sirdar-Iskandar 1983):

(22) a. Voyons, les enfants, soyez raisonnables.
   "Come on [lit. let's see], children, be reasonable."
   b. Voyons, Arthur, sois raisonnable.
   "Come on [lit. let's see], Arthur, be reasonable."
(23) a. Tiens, vous ici!
   "My gosh, is that you?" [lit. Behold (2 sg.), you (2 pl.) here!]
(24) a. Allons, ne sois pas ridicule!
   "Come on [lit. let's go], don't be ridiculous!"
   b. Allez, arrête ces bêtises!
   "Come on [lit. go (2 pl.)] stop [2 sg.], this nonsense!"

Some second person plural (pl.) imperatives, however, which seem to be the marked form (the unmarked form being the second person sg. imperative) are rarely acceptable without agreement:

(25) a. *Tenez, Arthur, toi ici?
   *"Behold [2 pl.], Arthur, you [2 sg.] here?"
   b. Tenez, Monsieur le Président, vous ici?
   lit. "Behold [2 pl.], Mister President, you [2 pl.] here?"
(26) a. *Dites donc, Arthur, quelle belle voiture tu as!
   *"Say [2 pl.], Arthur, what a nice car you [2 sg.] have!"
   b. Dites donc, Monsieur le Président, quelle belle voiture vous avez!
   "Say [2 pl.], Mister President, what a nice car you [2 pl.] have!"

The low degree of referentiality of verbal discourse signals also accounts for the fact that they cannot be negated:

(27) a. Allons, ne pleure pas.
 "Come on, don't cry."
 b. *N'allons pas, ne pleure pas.
 *"Don't come on, don't cry."
(28) a. Tenez, voilà mon grand-père.
 "Look, there's my grandfather."
 b. *Ne tenez pas, voilà mon grand-père.
 *"Don't look, there's my grandfather."

3.1.3.

In this section we examine four different syntactic parameters relevant to verbal discourse signals. These suggest that verbal discourse signals included within the domain of the sentence itself have rather an adjoined status. The parameters are: valency, embedding, co-ordination, and scope of negation.

As the following examples show, verbal discourse signals in the imperative have no valency, in contrast to full-predicate imperatives:

(29) a. Voyons, ne sois pas ridicule.
 "Come on [lit. let's see], don't be ridiculous."
 b. *Voyons cela, ne sois pas ridicule.
 *"Let's see that, don't be ridiculous."
 c. Voyons cela en détail, nous trouverons peut-être une solution.
 "Let's look at that in detail, maybe we'll find a solution."
(30) a. Dis donc, tu as une chance inouïe!
 "Say, you are incredibly lucky."
 b. *Dis-le donc, tu as une chance inouïe!
 *"Say it, you are incredibly lucky."
 c. Dis-le donc [= avoue]: tu as une chance inouïe!
 "Say it [= admit it]: you are incredibly lucky."

Nor do they allow embedding:

(31) *Il a répondu que dis/dites donc qu'ils devaient y aller.
 *"He answered that say [2 sg./2 pl.] they had to go there."
(32) *Il a répondu que va/allez/allons il ne fallait pas exagérer.
 *"He answered that go [2 sg./2 pl./let's go] one shouldn't exaggerate."
(33) *Il a répondu que tiens/tenez donc son voisin était là aussi.
 *"He answered that behold [2 sg./2 pl.] his neighbour was there too."

This is hardly surprising: several scholars (Blumenthal 1980: 131;

Roulet 1980; Rubattel 1982) in fact consider it a defining property of discourse signals that they cannot appear in embedded sentences.[11] Indeed, we have:

(34) a. Il a répondu: justement.
   "He answered: Precisely."
   b. *Il a répondu que justement.
   *"He answered that precisely."
(35) a. Il a répondu: cela dit, je suis prêt à recommencer.
   "He answered: this having been said, I am ready to start over again."
   b. ?*Il a répondu que cela dit, il était prêt à recommencer.
   ?*"He answered that this having been said, he was ready to start over again."

Another characteristic of verbal discourse signals is that co-ordination with another verb form of the same type is impossible when that form has its pragmatic meaning: co-ordination becomes possible, however, when the verb form has its literal meaning (cf. Sirdar-Iskandar 1983). Compare:

(36) a. Voyons, soyons raisonnables.
   "Come on [lit. let's see], let's be reasonable."
   b. *Voyons et soyons raisonnables.
   *"Let's see and let's be reasonable."
   c. Voyons cela de plus près et prenons ensuite une décision raisonnable.
   "Let's look at this more closely and then make a reasonable decision."
(37) a. Tiens, tu me rends mon livre!
   "Come on [lit. hold], you're gonna give me my book back!"
   b. *Tiens et rends-moi mon livre.
   *"Hold and give me my book back."
   c. Tiens-le et rends-le-moi tout à l'heure.
   "Hold it and give it back to me later on."

This observation seems to apply to the entire class of verbal discourse signals:

(38) a. *Cela étant et ne changeant pas, ...
   *"This being [the case] and not changing. ..."
   b. *Tant qu'à faire et à dire...
   *"So much that to do and to say ..."
   c. *Si tu veux et souhaites ...
   *"If you will and you wish. ..."

d. *Tout compte fait et refait. ...
   *"Every count made and remade. ..."

That these forms function as adjoined elements, loosely attached to the sentence, is finally suggested by the fact that they never fall under the scope of negation of the main verb. This is a well-known property of sentential adverbs, as example (39) shows:

(39) a. Justement, il a agi comme il fallait.
        "Precisely, he acted as he should have."
     b. Justement, il n'a pas agi comme il fallait.
        "Precisely, he didn't act as he should have."

The same holds for our verbal forms:

(40) a. Dis donc, tu as de la chance!
        "Say, are you lucky!"
     b. Dis donc, tu n'as pas de chance!
        "Say, you don't have any luck!"
(41) a. Allez, discutez!
        "Go [on], argue!"
(42) a. Réflexion faite, j'aurais dû partir.
        "Having thought about it [lit. thought completely made], I should have left."
     b. Réflexion faite, je n'aurais pas dû partir.
        "Having thought about it [lit. thought completely made], I shouldn't have left."

Since the four syntactic properties examined thus far are essential characteristics of verbal (predicative) behavior, the fact that verbal discourse signals in the imperative are incompatible with all these properties suggests that they no longer act as verbs, but rather have undergone a process of change from a syntactic to a pragmatic function. In this respect they could be represented, as suggested by Banfield (1973, 1982), within a constituent-structure tree, as a sister node of S', dominated by the supersymbol E, as shown in example (43).

(43)

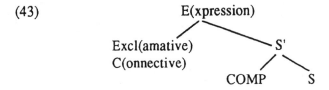

The imperative forms considered here no longer have their inherent (predicative) role, but as is usually the case when words undergo a semantic extension (cf. Lamiroy 1987), one basic aspect (or "pragmatic" function) remains, viz. that of eliciting a reaction from the addressee (or, more generally, from one's audience). In this respect, the imperative discourse markers exactly parallel vocative forms, which have the same pragmatic function. It is noteworthy that the latter are also syntactically outside the domain of the sentence, and that in Indo-European both vocatives and imperatives are originally based on the stem-form.

3.2.

We will conclude our study of the syntactic behavior of verbal discourse signals with a positional analysis of these elements. In general, discourse signals occupy initial position in the sentence; less often, final position:

(44) a. Tant qu'à faire, elle pouvait aussi bien acheter le tout.
 "While she was at it, she might as well have bought the whole thing."
 b. ?Elle pouvait aussi bien acheter le tout, tant qu'à faire.
 ? "She might as well have bought the whole thing, while she was at it."
(45) a. Arthur a eu tort de partir, n'est-ce pas?
 "Arthur shouldn't have left, should he?"
 b. *N'est-ce pas, Arthur a eu tort de partir?
 *"Isn't it, Arthur was wrong to leave?"

Some can also appear within the sentence:

(46) a. Arthur a eu tort de partir, tout compte fait.
 "Arthur shouldn't have left, when you come right down to it."
 b. Tout compte fait, Arthur a eu tort de partir.
 "When you come right down to it, Arthur shouldn't have left."
 c. Arthur, tout compte fait, a eu tort de partir.
 "Arthur, when you come right down to it, shouldn't have left."

It is important to take into account the possible positions each discourse signal can occupy in the sentence because word order can at times disambiguate, as in (47):

(47) a. JUSTEMENT, il a agi [= discourse signal].
"Precisely, he acted."
b. Il a agi JUSTEMENT [= adverb].
"He acted correctly."
c. Il a agi, JUSTEMENT [= discourse signal].
"He acted, indeed."
d. Il a JUSTEMENT agi [= adverb].
"He acted correctly."
e. Il a, JUSTEMENT, agi [= discourse signal].
"He did indeed act."

Concentrating on the imperative forms, we indicate the possible positions for each one in Table 6.1.

Table 6.1 Syntactic position of imperative discourse signals

	Initial	Medial	Final
dis (donc)	+	–	+
dites (donc)	+	–	+
va	+	–	+
allons	+	–	+
allez	+	–	+
voyons	+	–	+
tiens	+	–	+
tenez	+	–	+
marche	+	–	+

As shown, verbal discourse signals in the imperative appear only at the "synapses" of discursive units:
(48) a. N'insulte pas ton père, voyons.
b. Voyons, n'insulte pas ton père.
c. *N'insulte pas, voyons, ton père.
"Come on, don't insult your father."

Interestingly, the pragmatic meaning of a discourse signal can change according to its position in the sentence:

(49) a. TIENS, Arthur n'est pas venu [expression of surprise].
"Well, well, Arthur hasn't shown up."
b. Arthur n'est pas venu, parce qu'il ne voulait pas venir, TIENS [*tiens* as a pragmatic "tail" of an argument].
"Arthur hasn't shown up, because he didn't want to, you see."
(50) a. VOYONS, qu'est-ce que tu me racontes?
"Come on, what are you telling me?"

b. Qu'est-ce que tu me racontes, VOYONS! [mild reproach]
"Now what do you think you're telling me!"

Finally, it should be noted that all discourse signals in the imperative can occur independently, as equivalents of full utterances, a fact that confirms their autonomous status within discourse. Their discursive function is therefore twofold: they establish a link between speaker and hearer (as do vocatives), and they "connect" segments within an utterance (unlike vocatives).

4. CONCLUSIONS

4.1.

Let us first recapitulate our analysis of verb forms used as discourse markers. We have noted that in their use as discourse signals, these verbs do not exhibit most of their "normal" or "prototypical" characteristics. In the first place, they are limited to one or a few forms within the paradigm (*va, allons, allez*); the remaining forms are excluded from this pragmatic function. Also, the forms used as discourse signals are morphologically fossilized; they are not subject to changes of tense, mode, voice, or modality (either internal, e.g. an affirmation turned into a negation, or higher level, e.g. being subsumed under a higher modal predicate). Third, the forms used as discourse signals never appear with their full valency: most often they are used absolutely (without construing government relationships). This special morphosyntactic status is confirmed by a number of syntactic characteristics, most of which are negatively formulated (viz. in contrast with the "normal" behavior of verb forms):

(a) the verbal discourse signals rarely show signs of sentential integration, since they are normally preposed or postposed to predicative units, or inserted parenthetically within them;
(b) the verb forms used as discourse signals can easily function as separate utterances;
(c) they cannot be used in co-ordination with full predicates;
(d) they do not come under scope interpretations affecting the other parts of the sentence.

4.2.

Verbal forms as discourse signals are clearly a result of functional displacement – identified mainly on the basis of negative (or deviant) characteristics – and raise a descriptive problem for traditional grammar. The problem disappears, however, if one adopts a functional approach, focusing on the use of linguistic elements within specific communicative contexts. From a functional point of view, discourse signals may be defined as functors that are related either to extralinguistic stimuli (events or states of affairs, including types of relationships between people), or to predicative structures. In the former case they can be used absolutely, in the latter the functor can affect either the predicative content itself (example (51)) or the speech situation for which a predicate P is used (example (52)):

(51) Allez, suivez-nous!
 "Come on, follow us!"
(52) Dis donc, arrête de l'embêter!
 "Hey, stop annoying him/her!"

The same usages are attested for other discourse markers, such as the class of "adverbials" (cf. Blumenthal 1980).

In the case of imperative forms, we have also observed a number of positive characteristics. First, there is the interesting distribution of person markings in terms of distinctive features. Verb forms used as discourse signals occur in different persons (least commonly in the third-person plural). The use of specific persons is linked to specific functions: first-person singular forms are used to underscore the act of utterance (the *instance d'énonciation*), whereas first-person plural forms are used to signal the solidarity between speaker and hearer as speech partners (whatever their respective social status). Second-person forms are used to elicit the involvement of the addressee, and third-person forms serve variously to mark the utterance content (or its particular linguistic form).

Another positive observation relevant to verbal discourse signals is that they are taken from frequently used verbs relating to the domains of motion and perception, the semantic content of which is emptied.

Finally our analysis allows us to define the general status of discourse signals. As functors, they are: (a) intrinsically modalizing; (b) minimally referential (or non-referential); (c) adjoined or autonomous.

Characteristic (a) refers to their orientation with respect to a predicative structure and, in conjunction with characteristic (c), allows us to account for the fact that no higher-level modalization can be imposed upon these discourse signals. Characteristic (b) refers to the neutrality of discourse signals with respect to fit/non-fit to the world: it accounts for the absence of changes in tense, mood, voice, and, in general, any change involving a scalar or gradual feature. Characteristic

(c) refers to the syntactic properties of discourse signals, which are only minimally integrated into the sentence (when they are not used absolutely).

4.3.

A few theoretical afterthoughts by way of conclusion. Our analysis has tried to convey an idea of the nature and importance of a linguistic-pragmatic approach. We believe that a pragmatic view is extremely useful for the description of linguistic categories (and not only for the study of discursive strategies). Such a view can be coherently articulated at the following levels:

(a) that of the sentence: a sentence is not only a string of words, or the result of a combination of rules and principles. It is also, and perhaps foremost, a way of conveying views, attitudes, and feelings, and of interacting with others. We have tried to show that sentences contain specific signals for this function, and that a systematic account can be given of a particular subclass of these signals;
(b) that of linguistic competence: linguistic competence is not merely a matter of grammatical knowledge, it is an integrated system of strategies (cf. Lundquist's notion of "argumentative program" (1980, 1987)) involving the use of linguistic units in order to perform functionally diversified speech acts;
(c) that of language: language is much more than an inventory of elements and rules; it is essentially an ill-defined system of forms, extensions, and hierarchical sets – all allowing for various groupings – coupled with an array of (socially) stratified functions, which relates to a speech community's experiences of the world.

In sum, the pragmatic view adopted here should be embedded in a pragmatically oriented linguistic theory which starts from the bottom and analyzes linguistic units in terms of their contribution to the discursive event. It seems that no fully articulated theory of that type is yet available, but there are a number of indications that linguists will more and more turn their attention to the study of "the use-in-context of linguistic forms."

NOTES

1 We would like to thank Suzanne Fleischman and Linda Waugh for their comments on an earlier version of this paper. Thanks are also due to our Spanish and Italian informants, Luz Rodriguez and Franco Musarra.
   All examples have been glossed for non-Romance readers (we use quotation marks for translations of acceptable sentences in the source language: non-acceptable sentences are glossed in quotation marks with an asterisk). We have tried to convey as much as possible of the literal meaning of some of the discourse signals, especially since many of them have no straightforward equivalent in English.
2 For a recent example of French *théories de l'énonciation*, see Cosnier *et al.* (1988). Among American linguists communication-centered approaches have been advocated by Hymes (1971, 1974) and Gumperz (1982) in particular, and by their students.
3 For this distinction between two types of function, see Silverstein (1978) and Swiggers (1986).
4 E.g. in Aristotle's *Poetics*, 1456b 9, where syntactic analysis is associated with locutionary types of sentences. An example of a much later intrusion of a rhetorical point of view into syntax is Dumarsais' distinction between *proposition* and *énonciation*, and Beauzée's subsequent discussion of it in the article "Proposition" in the *Encyclopédie méthodique: Grammaire et littérature* (1782–6; cf. Swiggers 1984: 108–15).
5 Chomsky's (1981: 5) definition of grammar lies entirely within this tradition: "U[niversal] G[rammar] consists of interacting subsystems, which can be considered from various points of view. From one point of view, these are the various subsystems of the rule system of grammar. From another point of view ... we can isolate subsystems of *principles*" (italics ours).
6 By communicative competence, we understand (following Hymes 1972) the (native) speaker's control of (1) the grammatical and lexical system of a language L and its "content," (2) a set of uses of this system, in their correlation with (3) a set of utterance situations. This specific control is then actualized by a series of pragmatic operations into (more or less) appropriate texts (= communicative performance).
7 Compare the following utterance: *Vous ici? Tiens! tiens! tiens!* "You here? Well! Well! Well!", also from Capus, *La bourse ou la vie*, IV, 13.
8 On the other hand, some discourse markers (especially adverbs) have been the object of careful, pragmatically oriented studies, e.g. Ducrot (1980, 1984), Ducrot *et al.* (1980), Ducrot and Anscombre (1977). A similar type of "argumentative analysis" has been conducted by Nølke (1983), whose study focuses on adverbs such as *presque, encore, seulement, surtout*; see now also the volume edited by Nølke (1988) on the discursive functions of syntactic operators.
9 Danlos (1988) points out that recording of punctuation marks as connective elements in a dictionary is absolutely necessary in the context of natural language processing: indeed, a grammar developed for computer applications such as language parsing or the generating of language fragments will only be viable if it analyzes and/or generates punctuation marks in a purely mechanical way.

10 There are a few exceptions, such as the above-mentioned Sp. *demonio(s)*.
11 Imperatives, even in their predicative use, do not normally occur in embedded sentences, since they belong by definition to direct speech. The point made here is not trivial, however, since we find examples such as the following in colloquial speech:
   (i) *Il n'aime pas le bruit, de sorte que ne bouge pas* "He doesn't like noise, so [that] don't move" (for a similar example, see Damourette and Pichon 1911–42:, IV, 394). By contrast, when one tries to embed discursive imperatives the result is the unacceptable sentence (ii).
   (ii) **Il n'aime pas le bruit, de sorte que tiens, il est parti* * "He doesn't like noise, so that behold, he has left." The property of excluding embedding (see Rubattel 1982: 39) cannot be generalized to all discourse signals, as example (iii) shows.
   (iii) (a) *Il a répondu: en effet, j'en ai assez* "He answered: indeed, I've had it." (b) *Il a répondu qu'en effet, il en avait assez* "He answered that indeed he had had it."
   This shows, once more, that discourse signals call for a detailed description.

REFERENCES

Alcina Franch, J. and Blecua, J.M. (1979) *Gramática española*, Barcelona: Ariel.

Auchlin, A. (1981) "Marqueurs de structuration de la conversation et complétude," *Cahiers de Linguistique Française* 2: 141–59.

Banfield, A. (1973) "Narrative style and the grammar of direct and indirect speech," *Foundations of Language* 10: 1–39.

—— (1982) *Unspeakable Sentences: Narration and Representation in the Language of Fiction*, Boston: Routledge & Kegan Paul.

Bazzanella, C. (1985) "L'uso dei connettivi nel parlato: alcune proposte," *Sintassi e morfologia della lingua italiana d'uso. Teorie e applicazioni descrittive*, ed. A. Franchi de Bellis and L.M. Savoia, Roma: Bulzoni.

Beauzée, N. (1767) *Grammaire générale, ou exposition raisonnée des éléments nécessaires du langage, Pour servir de fondement à l'étude de toutes les langues*, 2 vols, Paris: J. Barbou (Repr. Stuttgart and Bad Cannstatt: Frommann, Holzboog, 1974.)

Berrendonner, A. (1983) "Connecteurs pragmatiques et anaphore," *Cahiers de Linguistique Française* 5: 215–46.

Blumenthal, P. (1980) *La Syntaxe du message. Application au français moderne*, Tübingen: Niemeyer.

Chomsky, N. (1982) *Lectures on Government and Binding. The Pisa Lectures*: Dordrecht: Foris.

Cosnier, J., Gelas, N., and Kerbrat-Orecchioni, C. (1988) *Échanges sur la conversation*, Lyon: Éditions du CNRS.

Damourette, J. and Pichon, É. (1911–42) *Des mots à la pensée. Essai de grammaire de la langue française*, 7 vols, Paris: d'Artrey.

Danlos, L. (1988) "Connecteurs et relations causales," *Langue Française* 77: 92–127.

Dardano, M. and Trifone, P. (1985) *La lingua italiana*, Bologna: Zanichelli.

Ducrot, O. (1980) *Les Echelles argumentatives*, Paris: Éditions de Minuit.

—— (1984) *Le Dire et le dit*, Paris: Éditions de Minuit.

Ducrot, O. and Anscombre, J.-C. (1977) "Deux *mais* en français?", *Lingua* 43: 23–40.
Ducrot, O. *et al.* (1980) *Les Mots du discours*, Paris: Éditions de Minuit.
Grevisse, M. and Goosse, A. (1986) *Le Bon usage. Grammaire française*, 12th edn, Gembloux: Duculot.
Gross, M. (1984) "Une classification des phrases figées en français," in P. Attal and C. Müller (eds) *De la syntaxe à la pragmatique*, Amsterdam: J. Benjamins.
Gülich, E. (1970) *Makrosyntax der Gliederungssignale im gesprochenen Französisch*, München: Fink.
Gülich, E. and Kotschi, T. (1983) "Les marqueurs de la reformulation paraphrastique," *Cahiers de Linguistique Française* 5: 305–51.
Gumperz, J. (1982) *Discourse Strategies*, Cambridge: Cambridge University Press.
Hagège, C. (1982) *La Structure des langues*, Paris: PUF.
—— (1985) *L'Homme de paroles. Contribution linguistique aux sciences humaines*, Paris: Fayard.
Harris, Z. (1968) *Mathematical Structures of Language*, New York: Wiley.
Hymes, D. (1971) "Sociolinguistics and the ethnography of speaking," in E. Ardener (ed.) *Social Anthropology and Language*, London: Tavistock.
—— (1972) "On communicative competence," in J.B. Pride and J. Holmes (eds) *Sociolinguistics. Selected Readings*, Harmondsworth: Penguin.
—— (1974) *Foundations of Sociolinguistics. An Ethnographic Approach*, Philadelphia: University of Pennsylvania Press.
Lamiroy, B. (1987) "Verbes de mouvement: extensions métaphoriques et emplois figés," *Langue Française* 76: 41–58.
Lenz, R. (1916) *La oración y sus partes*, Santiago de Chile.
Lundquist, L. (1980) *La Cohérence textuelle*, Copenhagen: Nyt Nordisk Forlag.
—— (1987) "Programme argumentatif et stratégies de désambiguïsation référentielle," *Revue Romane* 22: 163–82.
Nølke, H. (1983) *Les Adverbes paradigmatisants. Fonction et analyse*, Copenhagen: Akademisk Forlag.
—— (ed.) (1988) *Opérateurs syntaxiques et cohésion discursive*, Copenhagen: Akademisk Forlag.
Roulet, E. (1980) "Stratégies d'interaction, modes d'implication et marqueurs illocutoires," *Cahiers de Linguistique Française* 1: 80–103.
—— (1987) "Complétude interactive et connecteurs reformulatifs," *Cahiers de Linguistique Française* 8: 111–40.
Roulet, E. *et al.* (1985) *L'Articulation du discours en français contemporain*, Bern: Lang.
Rubattel, C. (1982) "De la syntaxe des connecteurs pragmatiques," *Cahiers de Linguistique Française* 4: 37–61.
Searle, J.R. (1979) *Expression and Meaning. Studies in the Theory of Speech Acts*, Cambridge: Cambridge University Press.
Silverstein, M. (1978) "The three faces of 'function'," in M. Hickmann (ed.) *Proceedings of a Working Conference on the Social Foundations of Language and Thought*, University of Chicago.
Sirdar-Iskandar, C. (1983) "'Voyons!'," *Cahiers de Linguistique Française* 5: 111–30.

Swiggers, P. (1984) *Les Conceptions linguistiques des encyclopédistes. Étude sur la constitution d'une théorie de la grammaire au siècle des Lumières*, Heidelberg: J. Groos.

—— (1986) "La linguistique fonctionnelle du Cercle de Prague," *Philologica Pragensia* 29: 76–82.

Swiggers, P. and Van Hoecke, W. (eds) (1986) *Mot et parties du discours/ Word and Word Classes/Wort und Wortarten*, Leuven and Paris: Leuven University Press, Peeters.

Williams, E. (1975) "Small clauses in English," in J. Kimball (ed.) *Syntax and Semantics*, vol. 4, New York: Academic Press.

7 A contextual reconsideration of the Spanish -*ra* "indicative"[1]

Patricia V. Lunn and Thomas D. Cravens

The Latin indicative pluperfect in -*ra(m)* has had a rough passage into Romance. In some areas the form has died out; where it survives, the morphology carries a variety of meanings. All of these meanings are related semantically, however, in ways that will be discussed in this chapter. The modern outcomes of the Latin indicative pluperfect in -*ra(m)* in a selection of Romance speech types are shown in (1), in traditional classifications.

(1) *amaveram*
    Castilian   past subjunctive (Subj)
    Catalan   – (past Subj in Valencian)
    French   –
    Galician   pluperfect indicative (Ind)/past Subj
    Italian   – (conditional in southern dialects)
    Portuguese   – pluperfect Ind
    Romanian

In Spanish, the -*ra* form has become the dominant member of a pair of synthetic past subjunctives, along with the -*se* form derived from the Latin imperfect subjunctive in -*se(m)*. The -*se* form (early on *amavissem* > *amasse*) remained a past subjunctive in all of the languages listed in (1) except Romanian, where it emerged as a pluperfect indicative.[2]

The functions of the various subjunctive forms in Latin are not neatly distinguishable, as there was some fluidity in usage throughout the language's documented history, as well as a number of tense shifts which are especially evident in Late Latin. Some of these shifts crossed traditional mood boundaries as well. One of the effects which could be produced by the use of competing tense forms has been described as giving "a quasi-subjunctive flavor to indicative forms" (Nutting 1925: 90). Such statements prompt speculation as to just how revealing the traditional terminology is. In this case as in so many others, the convention of labeling in terms of form rather than function inhibits understanding rather than facilitates it.

In the historical developments at issue here, it is clear that the Castilian forms which developed from the Latin -*ra(m)* and -*se(m)* verbs have both come to be used as subjunctives in the modern language. Though there are dialects in which the -*se* form is perceived as archaic, and is therefore used only in highly formal language (cf. RAE para. 3.15.6e), there are also dialects (most, but not all, in Spain) which have both forms in natural registers, in a distribution which has never been described exhaustively (but see Graham 1926 *contra* Dale 1925, also Lemon 1925; Wright 1926a; Staubach 1946; Bolinger 1956; Solaún 1972; Silva-Corvalán 1985).

What is known about this distribution is that the -*ra* form appears in some contexts in which the -*se* form is rarely found. One of these uses is the alleged substitution of the past subjunctive in -*ra* for the indicative pluperfect, which occurs with enough frequency to annoy purists:

> De todos los atentados que con lamentable frecuencia se cometen contra la unidad, la pureza y la corrección de la lengua española, ninguno es a mi juicio, tan grave y peligroso como el que consiste en emplear las formas verbales del pretérito imperfecto de subjuntivo terminadas en "*ra*" (-*ara*, -*iera*) en función de algunos tiempos pasados del indicativo.
>
> (Mallo 1947: 484)

The Real Academia is less vehement, judging what appears as use of -*ra* forms instead of pluperfects to be merely "ajena a la lengua hablada ... más o menos debilitada hasta nuestros días." Instead, the RAE censures employment of -*ra* as "un pretérito cualquiera de indicativo." Apropos of sentences like "'*Se comenta el discurso que anoche pronunciara el Presidente*' (en vez de *pronunció*)," we are told that: "Esta construcción no está justificada en modo alguno por la tradición del idioma," a reference to the Latin pluperfect origin of -*ra* forms (RAE para. 3.15.6b).[3]

In fact, it has been noted that the use of -*ra* forms in place of the indicative pluperfects and preterits predicted by traditional analysis is quite common in journalistic Spanish, precisely in constructions of the type quoted by the RAE.[4] In this chapter, we examine the journalistic use of the verb in -*ra*, and seek to motivate its synchronic classification as a true subjunctive in a unified description of mood choice in Spanish centered on the notion of discourse relevance. This characterization of the subjunctive then provides the descriptive framework for a reappraisal of the traditional understanding of the -*ra* form's function in the earliest Spanish texts. The analysis shows that the usage excoriated by the Real Academia is solidly motivated on pragmatic grounds, and that it has a long history.

Central to our argument is the recognition that the subjunctive in modern Spanish – as in other Romance languages – is not limited to reference to irrealis situations. It is also used to refer to information that is assumed to be factual, i.e. to presupposed information. The sentences in (2) and (3) contain subjunctive verbs which refer to facts.

(2) El hecho de que *haya* [present Subj] centrales nucleares en Europa es preocupante.
"The fact that *there are* nuclear power stations in Europe is worrisome."
(3) Aunque no me *guste* [present Subj], lo tengo que hacer.
"That I don't *like* it doesn't matter; I have to do it."

(*Aunque* + present Subj can also offer the reading "although I may not like it"; this will be discussed on p. 152.)

In journalistic Spanish, the *-ra* form of the past subjunctive conventionally appears in certain sentence types in reference not just to facts, but to well-known facts, i.e. information which can be presupposed as readers' knowledge. Sentences like those in (4) and (5) show the most remarkable of these journalistic uses, as the *-ra* form appears here in non-restrictive relative clauses, an environment in which prescriptive grammars say that the subjunctive should not appear at all.

(4) Don Juan Carlos refrendó con su presencia ... el desagravio de la ciudad al doctor Robert, que *fuera* presidente de la diputación barcelonesa. (*El País*, May 20, 1985)
"Don Juan Carlos lent his presence to the city's recognition of Dr Robert, who *had been* president of the Barcelona Deputation."
(5) La pareja, que se *hiciera* famosa por interpretar el papel de marido y mujer en "El pájaro espino", es en la vida real un matrimonio feliz. (¡*Hola!*, July 6, 1985)
"The couple, who *became* famous for their role as husband and wife in *The Thorn Birds*, is happily married in real life."

Solé and Solé, for example, say that "Subjunctive clauses can only be restrictive since the antecedent has not been previously identified" (1977: 189). Yet non-restrictive relative clauses containing subjunctives are not at all unusual in journalistic style. Something else that Solé and Solé (1977: 189) say in their discussion of relative clauses provides a clue to explaining this usage: "Indicative relative clauses affirm the quality or condition of an antecedent as existing." Affirmation is unnecessary, however, under the pragmatic conditions that obtain in these cases. The information in the subordinate clauses of (4) and (5) needs no affirmation; the editorial assumption is that everybody already knows it. The assumption of prior knowledge motivates the appearance of the subjunctive in such clauses.

The *-ra* form can be used to mark information which readers or hearers of the news are expected to know, i.e. information mentioned in a previous edition or a prior paragraph, or information which is assumed to be common knowledge. In journalistic prose, which is very rich in information, this use of the *-ra* form marks low-priority clauses to which readers can safely pay less attention than they can to high-priority, indicative-marked clauses. An essential characteristic of this style of communication is that readers are treated as if they were familiar with the subjunctive-marked information whether they are or not. This practice, in addition to organizing a text for levels of informativeness, has the effect of including the reader in an idealized, cumulative discourse to which all members of the audience are party.

It might be argued that the journalistic use of the *-ra* form in sentences such as those in (4) and (5) is not a subjunctive at all, but a fossilized relic of the originally indicative pluperfect meaning of the form, particularly in view of the fact that the pluperfect use of *-ra* is claimed to have been revived by consciously archaizing Romantic writers in the nineteenth century. There is synchronic evidence, however, which suggests that the *-ra* form in this journalistic use is indeed subjunctive. The fact that linguistically sophisticated native speakers do not object to this usage (even when it is pointed out that the usual syntactic cues for subjunctive are missing) prompts the search for such evidence, which is found in the use of the unquestionably subjunctive *-se* form to mark well-known information in the same way as the *-ra* form. Both can be used – though with widely varying frequency of selection – not only in indisputably subjunctive slots, but also in reference to factual, previously mentioned information. Examples (6) and (7) show the *-se* form in this usage.

(6) Al día siguiente de que Isabel Preysler ... *iniciase* en un chalet de Marbella su veraneo, según informamos en la página 44 de este número.... (*¡Hola!* August 17, 1985)
"The day after Isabel Preysler *began* her summer vacation in a Marbella chalet, as we reported on page 44 of this issue...."

(7) Las alegrías de Ledesma con su reforma penal, tenían que traer esto. Lo de que, por ejemplo, durante enero y febrero pasados se *cometiese* en Valencia un delito cada veintidós minutos. (Vizcaíno Casas: 1984)

"Ledesma's lovely penal reform had to result in this. That, for example, last January and February in Valencia a crime *was committed* every twenty-two minutes."

Although it is far more common to find the *-ra* form in constructions such as those in (4), the appearance of the *-se* form can be viewed as confirmation that such use is fully subjunctive, and therefore representable by either of the two competing past subjunctive forms (cf. Hernández Alonso 1984: 298, note 27). There is no motivation for the use of the subjunctive morphology in (6) and (7) other than the presumption that the knowledge it encodes is known to the audience.

Consideration of the sources of the sentences in (4)–(7) reveals the context of situation which not only permits, but coherently motivates this usage. The gossip magazine ¡*Hola!* is infamous for its adulation of the rich and titled; the same personalities appear in its pages week after week, with the result that regular readers can be assumed to have a great deal of prior knowledge about any major celebrity. The Madrid daily *El País*, too liberal for the far right and too pragmatic for the extreme left, is the most widely read newspaper in Spain; in its editorial stance, the paper assumes a constant readership familiar with current affairs. Vizcaíno Casas' *100 años de honradez* is a satire on Spanish socialism, written by the well-known conservative champion of "the good old days." Each of these publications has a specific audience, clearly identifiable as regular readers in the case of the periodicals, and as like-minded confederates in the case of the novel. The authors can assume group solidarity with their readers, an appeal which is reinforced frequently, by no means least through use of the "you-already-know-this" subjunctive.[5]

At first glance there may seem to be no relationship between traditional explanations of the selection of subjunctive morphology and the pragmatically controlled conventions suggested for the cases seen above. But the two types can be accounted for in an analysis which examines the overall context in which they are embedded. Pragmatically, the subjunctives in examples (4)–(7), as well as in irrealis propositions, can be interpreted as markers of information which a writer/speaker considers to be of comparatively low relevance in a given discourse context, i.e. information that is relatively less central to the immediate processing needs of a reader/hearer who is developing an understanding of that discourse.[6]

The relationship in Spanish between the semantic nature of subjunctive-marked information and the pragmatic function of this information is schematized in (8). Semantically, irrealis and well-known information make up opposing ends of a continuum of informativeness of which only the middle part is likely to be marked with the indicative. This indicative-worthy information is neither so unreal as to be unknowable (and therefore undeserving of close attention), nor so well known as to be repetitious (and therefore undemanding of close attention).

(8)   Subjunctive   Indicative   Subjunctive
         unreal(ized)........(....................)........well known

There is a language-universal correlation between the left end of the chart and future time, and between the right end of the chart and past time:

> The different temporal locations of an event – past, present, and future – are inherently correlated with differences in mood and aspect. An event that will occur after the speech moment is non-actual and potential. Hence there is a correlation between future tense and non-actual potential mood and, by implication, between non-future tense and actual mood.
>
> (Chung and Timberlake 1985: 206)

Mood in Spanish, however, only partially depends on a semantic actual/non-actual distinction. As already seen in (2) and (3), and, we claim, in (4)–(7) as well, "actual" propositions need not be marked with indicative morphology in Spanish, if it is not productive to pay close attention to them in a given discourse context. The correlation between the right end of the chart and past time in Spanish is that realization of a proposition is a necessary prerequisite to its being well known, though realization is not sufficient in itself to cue selection of the backgrounding subjunctive.

The behaviour of *aunque* "although" with the subjunctive shows that the chart in (8) has identified three real parameters of mood choice. The gloss given for example (3) is only one possible meaning of the sentence, which in an appropriate context can mean: "Although it might turn out that I don't like it [future time], I have to do it." That is, the subjunctive after *aunque* can mark either a proposition which a speaker concedes to be factual but denies is relevant, or a proposition which a speaker concedes may become factual but is as yet unrealized.[7] The indicative is used after *aunque* only when the speaker wishes to concede information which is not flawed by either lack of interest or lack of veracity.

In diachronic studies of Romance, as well as in pedagogically oriented description, it has been traditional to identify the subjunctive mood primarily with the irrealis domain. Though this is, indeed, one of its uses, the traditional focus on irrealis contexts seems to have blinded researchers to other meanings of the contrast between subjunctive and indicative, meanings which are interpretable as manifestations of choices motivated by the principles subsumed in (8).

In Spanish, subjunctive morphology is used to mark both real and irreal information, and what unites the uses of the morphology is not the veracity or lack of veracity of the marked information, but, as suggested above, the limited usefulness of the information to the decoding process. Though it is not our purpose here to go beyond the Spanish data, our approach finds encouragement in Joan Bybee's characterization of mood, based on a language sample which did not include Spanish, as an inflectional category that signals "the role the speaker wants the proposition to play in the discourse" (Bybee 1985: 166).

Basing ourselves, then, on the assumption that modern uses of the -*ra* form like those in (3) are coherently motivated subjunctives, we proceed to look at historical data to see if such usage is a recent innovation in the subjunctive system of Spanish, or if it is of more distant origin. We use data collected by Leavitt Wright in *The -ra Verb Form in Spain* (1932).

Wright analyzed 580,000 lines from early to modern Spanish texts, and concluded that what has been interpreted traditionally as the indicative function of the -*ra* form had ceased to be dominant by the end of the fourteenth century, that indicative usage had virtually disappeared by the end of the sixteenth century, and that it was revived by the Romantics in the early nineteenth century. These conclusions, in essence, are echoed in the Real Academia's *Esbozo de una nueva gramática de la lengua española* (RAE para. 3.15.6b; without reference to Wright's work), and appear to be the standard view on the matter.

Significantly, Wright never defines the terms "indicative" and "subjunctive". The text makes clear, however, that he sees mood choice as being syntactically controlled, so that -*ra* forms which appear in contexts other than the syntactic environments which he accepts as requiring or permitting a subjunctive are excluded from any subjunctive interpretation. The data on which he bases his analysis are thus ripe for reanalysis in an approach which sets syntactic predictions in abeyance in order to examine function from the perspective of discourse context.

In a series of recent synchronic studies, syntactic cues have been shown to be inadequate to account for the appearance of the subjunctive in Spanish (see e.g. Bolinger 1968; Terrell and Hooper 1974; Klein-

Andreu 1975; Lavandera 1983; Lunn 1989).[8] We propose here that a reconsideration of some of Wright's data in the light of a pragmatic definition of the subjunctive produces quite different answers to the question of which -*ra* forms represent principled uses of the subjunctive. This analysis then provides a foundation for understanding the modern journalistic use of the -*ra* form as a pragmatically motivated subjunctive, a coherently describable continuation of options available since the earliest appearances of Spanish.

First, we will look at some of the lines from the twelfth-century epic, the *Poema de mio Cid*, which Wright claims exemplify the continued use, at that early date, of the -*ra* form as an indicative. Of 26 appearances of the -*ra* form in the work, Wright classified 22 as indicatives. The lines discussed here are those which Wright found hard to classify, but ultimately decided contained indicative -*ra* forms. If the discourse context is taken into account, however, it can be shown that the -*ra* forms in Wright's own examples serve a narrative backgrounding function.

In (9), the -*ra* form refers to a battle which is described in detail in the previous stanza, and the verb appears in a short transitional stanza which serves as a bridge to another vivid battle scene. That is, the -*ra* form makes second reference to information which has already been introduced, and it appears during a lull in the narrative action.[9]

(9) Alegre era el Çid e todas sus compañas,
    que Dios le *ayudara* y *fiziera* esta arrancada. (1157–8)
    "Glad was the Cid and all his companions,
    For God *had helped* him and *achieved* the victory."

Wright points out that the lines in (9) would necessarily contain the subjunctive in modern Spanish, but that the conjunction *que* here has a "causal force" (1932: 22), so that the subordinate clause should be analyzed as containing indicative pluperfect verbs. There is no way, however, in the actual contextual embedding of (9), to disentangle the modal and aspectual meanings potentially carried by the -*ra* verbs in the subordinate clause. Pluperfect and known proposition are a symbiotic unit here; the meanings do not cancel one another out, but are simultaneously available. The fact that the past subjunctive and pluperfect meanings of the -*ra* form coexist in modern Galician suggests that such semantic coexistence can be stable.[10]

In (10), the -*ra* form appears in a main clause, which to Wright indicated syntactically that it is an indicative. Still, the two lines quoted appear in a transitional stanza, and right after line 1310 which says "dexare vos las posadas, non las quiero contar" ("I will spare you the stops, I do not wish to tell about them"). Thus the narrator clearly signals that the information he is reciting at that moment is not of central importance to his story.

(10) Demando por Alffonso, do lo podrie fallar;
   Fuera el rey a San Fagunt aun poco ha. (1311-12)
   "He asked for Alfonso, where he could find him.
   The King *had gone* to Sahagún a short time ago."

Not all of the forms in *-ra* which Wright classified as indicative appear in transitional stanzas in the *Poema de mio Cid*; (11) and (12) are two good examples which do not, but which nevertheless illustrate the point at issue. What we see in these lines, again, are *-ra* forms used to refer to information that the narrator does not wish to emphasize. In (11), there are two *-ra* forms which refer to past events that never really happened, though their claim to legitimacy is an important element in the plot.

(11) Delant mio Çid e delante de todos oviste te de alabar
   que *mataras* el moro e que *fizieras* barnax. (3324-5)
   "Before the Cid and before everyone you were heard to
   Brag that you *killed* the Moor and *did* the deed."

In these lines, Pedro Bermúdez taunts the Cid's cowardly son-in-law for not having done the deed that he has taken credit for. The audience is quite aware of what really took place, as the scene in question is recalled immediately before, in lines 3315-23. Here, the *-ra* morphology marks information that is not true, but that is known to the audience, i.e. that is both presupposed and irrealis. Again, assigning only one meaning to the morphology is not realistic, as in a period of fluctuating usage there is no reason to believe that only one meaning was available.

In (12), there is an interesting use of the *-ra* form to background action in the story: the blows struck against the heroic Pedro Bermúdez are described with the *-ra* form, while the hero's blows are described in the preterit indicative. Pedro Bermúdez is the subject of both verbs, of course, but the agent of only the foregrounded indicative. In the analysis proposed here, the choice of forms is quite cogent: the attack on the hero is of little effect, but his response is forceful and effective.

(12) Firme estido Pero Vermuez, por esso nos encamo;
   Un colpe *reçibiera*, mas otro *firio*. (3629-30)
   "Firm stood Pedro Bermúdez, he did not waver;
   He *received* one blow, but *returned* another."

Though Wright found that the -*ra* form was still being used as an indicative in the *Poema de mio Cid*, examples like the ones in (9)–(12) show that consideration of narrative context allows at least some of the -*ra* forms to be reanalyzed as carriers of background information. We suggest that this use is a direct, linear precursor of the pragmatic backgrounding function of the modern subjunctive.

In the pseudo-medieval epic, *El doncel de don Enrique el doliente*, the arch-Romantic Mariano José de Larra tells a story that is old-fashioned not only in content but also in style. According to Wright, indicative use of the -*ra* form had "definitely passed out of the language and was not employed for almost two centuries" (1932: 109), until it was revived by the Romantics. We have found no evidence in the novel, however, to argue for revival of pluperfect use of the -*ra* form rather than survival. The use of -*ra* as a pluperfect is extremely limited; there are only eight occurrences in the book. With one exception, these are governed by the same syntactic and pragmatic conventions which control the use of the -*ra* subjunctive in modern Spanish.[11]

The first two of these perform a function that is stylistically archaizing: they make reference to past events that hearers of a genuine medieval epic might be expected to know, but that nineteenth-century readers certainly did not know. What is archaizing about Larra's use of the -*ra* form in the introductory chapter is certainly not the syntax of his usage, but his preciously artificial assumption that his audience is like a medieval one, knowing about the legendary past of his characters.

(13) Don Juan I había casi abandonado las esperanzas de recobrar aquel reino que indisputablemente le *perteneciera* por su boda con doña Beatriz, hija y única heredera de muerto rey don Fernando. (Larra 1924: 19)
"Don Juan I had almost abandoned hope of recovering the kingdom which indisputably *had belonged* to him because of his marriage to Doña Beatriz, daughter and only heir of the dead King Fernando."

(14) Enrique III, al subir al trono á los catorce años para dar fin á la anarquía, que en el Estado *alimentaran* sus poderosos tutores, había ratificado las ligas hechas por su padre. (Larra 1924: 20)
"Enrique III, upon assuming the throne at the age of 14 in order to put an end to the anarchy which his powerful tutors *had fomented* in the country, had ratified the bonds made by his father."

The -*ra* forms in these two examples do not refer to known information, but Larra uses them to emulate the "you-must-remember-this" introductions of genuine medieval epics. The verbs appear in deeply embedded clauses, and they contain information which is syntactically backgrounded to the modern pluperfects (*había abandonado*, *había ratificado*) in the main clauses.

The only example of a syntactically archaizing main-clause use of a *-ra* form appears in the highly artificial speech of a jester.

(15) Pero, gran señor, tú propio *anduvieras acertado* en restaurar tus fuerzas. (Larra 1924: 29)
"But, my Lord, you yourself *were wise* to get your strength back."

The meaning of the verb is no pluperfect at all, but imperfective. Larra is using the *-ra* form here in the same way that he uses archaic words and spellings throughout the book: as decorative motifs to suggest – but only fortuitously to reproduce – an earlier style whose conventions are alien to him.

Larra's pluperfect use of the *-ra* form is comparable to that of one of the most recent texts examined by Wright, the 1876 novel *Doña Perfecta* by Benito Pérez Galdós.[12] Written only a generation after Larra, yet in a time when literary tastes had changed considerably from those of the Spanish Romantic period, *Doña Perfecta* shows some use of what Wright classifies as *-ra* indicatives. A closer look at these supposedly indicative occurrences, however, reveals that there is nothing indicative about their function in the novel. The indicative in modern Spanish is the mood of assertion, but the information carried by the *-ra* forms in *Doña Perfecta* is not information that is worthy of assertion.

First, all of the fifteen so-called *-ra* indicatives in the novel (of which Wright cites six) appear in subordinate clauses. In *Doña Perfecta* there is no occurrence of a *-ra* form parallel to that in example (10), where it appeared in a main clause. Significantly, these verb forms are found only in syntactic slots in which subjunctives are expected to appear. Moreover, each of them encodes information which contributes very little to the plot, either because it has already been given to the reader (as in (16)), or because it is peripheral to the plot (as in (17)), or because it is piously assumed to be common knowledge (as in (18) and (19)).

(16) Pepe Rey estaba un si es no es turbado a causa del giro que *diera* su tía a una vana disputa festiva en la que tomó parte. (Pérez Galdós 1965: 74)
"Pepe Rey was somewhat disturbed by the turn his aunt *had given* to the silly, playful argument in which he had taken part."

(17) Entretúvose el gran Ramos dando a Librada ciertos recados de poca importancia que una vecina *confiara* a su buena memoria. (Pérez Galdós 1965: 182)
"The great Ramos spent a few moments instructing Librada about some unimportant errands which a neighbor *had entrusted* to his good memory."

(18) Ni qué mejor empleo puede dar un hombre al escaso entendimiento que del cielo *recibiera*, a la fortuna heredada y al tiempo breve con que puede contar en el mundo la más dilatada existencia. (Pérez Galdós 1965: 141)
"Nor can a man make better use of the scant understanding which he *has received* from Heaven, of inherited fortune or of the brief time which even the longest life will spend on Earth."

(19) Y siempre que algún forastero de viso se presentaba en las augustas salas, creíanle venido ... a disputarle por envidia las preeminencias incontrovertibles que Natura le *concediera*. (Pérez Galdós 1965: 106)
"And whenever a distinguished stranger appeared in its hallowed halls, they thought he had come ... to cast envious aspersions on the incontrovertible pre-eminence which Nature *had granted* it."

The last two sentences are very ironic in tone. Sperber and Wilson (1981) define irony in a testable way. They say that irony is a kind of echoic mention, in which such reference is made to a previously used proposition as to make clear that judgment is being passed on its content. This is illuminating of examples (18) and (19) in which Galdós quite typically makes mention of propositions which he expects his readers to have heard, but which he himself cannot be thought to believe. Here, as so often in his novels, Galdós invites the reader to laugh with him at the cherished truisms of conventional society. Significantly, if the *-ra* form is analyzed as a subjunctive which marks well-known information, the source of the irony is accounted for.

The examples discussed in (9)–(19), excluding Larra's artificial (15), suggest that the use of the *-ra* form to mark information that is not of central importance in a given discourse context has a long history, which we have documented only at three points in its diachronic trajectory. We take issue with Wright, whose data we have reanalyzed, because we do not see in his *-ra* indicatives a class of relics holding out against a developing subjunctive use of the morphology. These *-ra* forms, we argue, perform the pragmatic function of backgrounding information which a hearer/reader can safely pay less-than-careful attention to. Far from being an anomaly within the subjunctive system

The Spanish -ra "indicative" 159

of any synchronic state of Spanish examined here, selection of the *-ra* past subjunctive for backgrounding is motivated at all times. It appears to have a long and healthy tradition, in which current usage stands as an exemplification of the continued exploitation of this useful pragmatic device.

The analysis presented here is an illustration of three points of theoretical interest. First, it demonstrates the interdependence of synchronic and diachronic analysis; though a good basic description of the various uses of the past subjunctive could be achieved for any synchronic state, fullest appreciation of the motivation for the synchronic use of the *-ra* subjunctive is found in historical perspective. Second, it brings to the fore the necessity of studying linguistic phenomena with attention to the overall context in which they appear; this is exemplified in the case of the *Poema de mio Cid*, where the backgrounding function of *-ra* forms is unidentifiable without – at the bare minimum – an understanding of the relevant line's force in the ongoing discourse of the poem. Third, and most importantly, the analysis presented here illustrates the fruitfulness of exploring new approaches to old problems; the revised notion of the subjunctive conceptualized in the schema in (8) enables a unified view of the subjunctive in its two major functions, backgrounding both the familiar and the potential.

Consideration of the pragmatic functions encoded in subjunctive morphology prompts a re-evaluation of mood contrasts in earlier stages of the language, resulting from a clearer understanding of language use in that period. The subtleties revealed by this analysis then provide the basis for understanding the principled selection of the *-ra* form in modern Spanish in its role as a signal of typically subjunctive backgrounding. In both cases, whether or not the *-ra* form serves any subjunctive purpose cannot be known unless the narrative context in which the form appears is analyzed. And the analysis cannot be carried out effectively unless the subjunctive is described in adequate pragmatic terms in the first place.

NOTES

1 This chapter is a revised version of a paper presented at the 8th International Conference on Historical Linguistics, held at the University of Lille, August 31–September 4, 1987. We thank discussants there, especially Flora Klein-Andreu, as well as Janet DeCesaris, William Diver, and Suzanne Fleischman for helpful comments. Roger Wright's remarks at an early stage of this study were a welcome stimulus.
2 The imprecision of the label "past subjunctive" instead of the usual

"imperfect subjunctive" is intentional, given the lack of distinction between preterit and imperfect in Romance subjunctive systems.
3 See Mallo (1950: 127–8) and Kany (1975: 170–3) for opinions on the propriety of supposedly non-subjunctive use of *-ra* forms. One voice of reason is Lenz, who finds no motive for condemning "un giro de lenguaje que efectivamente se usa" (1920: 434).
4 Though Wright (1926a) collected examples of the *-ra* forms as presumed indicatives from Latin American newspapers in an attempt to establish the relative frequency of the two, Hernández Alonso seems to have been the first to recognize that the "non-subjunctive" *-ra* form is typically used in journalistic prose. More importantly, Hernández Alonso discovered that the *-ra* verb quite often refers to facts well known to readers, so that *diera* in "la noticia que este diario diera tiene confirmación" carries the meaning "ya ha dado" or "como sabe el lector, ya ha dado" (1935: 52). He also notes that *-ra* forms can be employed when the information is not known to readers, however. The interpretation offered here would predict that the unknown information is of low relevance.

In a second prescriptivist attack, Mallo specifies who in Latin America is most prone to what he sees as abuse of the *-ra* form in writing. It appears only rarely in books of significant literary value "por error o descuido," while third- and fourth-rank writers whose work is less intentionally literary in character use it sporadically at most. It is much more frequent in journalistic prose, not that of "maestros del periodismo," but in the production of "los redactores de categoría inferior ... los que 'hacen' las secciones de deportes, de cines, de vida social, de crímenes y sucesos, de oficinas del gobierno, etc. etc." (Mallo 1950: 135).

Staubach's descriptivist study of Colombian writing revealed that

> The *-ra* form as a past indicative is still a fairly common form in Colombia, among literary artists as well as journalists. The pluperfect value is more common in careful, recognized Colombian writers, while the non-pluperfect values predominate by three to one in journalistic writing (especially the preterit value). The relative clause is by all odds the commonest construction.
>
> (1946: 362)

That the "indicative" use of the past subjunctives can carry the force of a simple past or a pluperfect will not be examined here at length. Though it is often easy to decide which indicative might be substitutable, it is not at all uncommon for an exclusive choice to be very difficult or impossible (cf. Benildo Matías 1943: 531–2; Staubach 1946: 356–7). In the analysis offered in this chapter this fusion is understandable, in that precise relative chronological sequences are non-essential when the verb serves a backgrounding function.
5 Mallo's comments quoted in the previous note are especially telling. The sports, entertainment, and gossip sections of any daily newspaper are no doubt those which can most confidently assume a large constant readership familiar with the subject.
6 The term *relevance* is used in the sense developed by Sperber and Wilson, who say that "the relevance of new information to an individual is to be assessed in terms of the improvements it brings to his representation of

the world" (1986: 103). Unreal and well-known information, as in (8), can bring very little improvement to a hearer's representation of the world. This, we argue, is why such information is marked with the subjunctive in Spanish. For a helpful discussion of the developmental process of understanding, see Fillmore (1984).

7 It is not insignificant that for some speakers, an American English gloss "although I may not like it" can cover both possible readings of the Spanish subjunctive: "that I don't like it is irrelevant," or "though it may turn out that I don't like it." The interpretation can be at either pole of (8) for this construction in either language, and both have the indicative as an option for the unmarked center.

8 For the last two decades linguists have been chipping away at the syntactic description of the Spanish subjunctive, which attributes the presence of subordinate-clause subjunctive verbs to certain (semantic) characteristics of main-clause verbs or subordinating conjunctions. The weight of unexplained, but perfectly grammatical, occurrences of the subjunctive has now become overwhelming. Syntactically embarrassing cases include the use of the past subjunctive of a few verbs in main clauses, such as *Quisiera hacerle una pregunta*, and the discourse-based choice of indicative or subjunctive after *el hecho de que* "the fact that" and *no creo que* "I don't think that." Lavandera (1983) has documented the use of the subjunctive to mark verbs that perform a non-assertive function in discourse. Her pragmatic analysis makes it possible to explain the exceptions to the syntactic analysis in a unified way.

9 Spelling and punctuation follow Colin Smith's edition (1972).

10 Saco Arce gives *fora* for the pluperfect indicative of "be" in Galician, and lists the imperfect subjunctive as *fora, siria,* and *fose,* "si bien es cierto que tal terminación [i.e. -ra] pertenece asimismo al pretérito imperfecto de subjuntivo, es aun más usada en la acepción de pluscuamperfecto de indicativo" (1868: 77). Today, Carballo Calero's *Gramática elemental del gallego común* presents *falara* as the pluperfect indicative of *falar* "speak," with *falase* as the imperfect subjunctive, with the important clarification that "Todos los verbos, como en castellano, admiten otra forma en -ra, -ras, etc., que se confunde con el pluscuamperfecto de indicativo" (1979: 214, n.67).

Though neither of these reports is sufficiently detailed to provide a full understanding of usage, it would appear that in genuine spoken Galician – as opposed to a codified standard which as of 1966 was "más un aspiración que una realidad" (Carballo Calero 1979: 7) – there is no need felt to keep indicative and subjunctive (and to some extent, conditional) neatly separated. Our claim is that this is to be expected on account of the natural symbiosis of function in many contexts.

11 There are many cases in the text of the use of the *-ra* form to replace the conditional in *-ría*. This substitution (one of many archaizing devices in the Sir Walter Scott-like novel) is not analyzed here. See Rojo (1986) on the historical complexities of the Spanish conditional.

12 Benito Pérez Galdós (1843–1920) is a major figure of Spanish realism, and one of Spain's foremost novelists. He defined the novel as *imagen de la vida*, and accordingly made every effort to write in an accessible and representative style. Testimony to his success in this effort is the national

mourning that marked his death, because he "had become known in Spain not through hearsay but through the actual reading of his works" (in Rodolfo Cardona's introduction to Pérez Galdós 1965: 16). Galdós' preoccupation with linguistic realism makes his novels of particular interest as data for linguistic research.

REFERENCES

Benildo Matías, Hermano (1943) *El castellano literario*, Bogotá: Stella.
Bolinger, Dwight (1956) "Subjunctive -*ra* and -*se*: free variation," *Hispania* 39: 345–9.
—— (1968) "Postposed main phrases: an English rule for the Romance subjunctive," *Canadian Journal of Linguistics* 14: 3–30.
Bybee, Joan L. (1985) *Morphology*, Amsterdam and Philadelphia: John Benjamins.
Carballo Calero, Ricardo (1979) *Gramática elemental del gallego común*, Vigo: Galaxia.
Chung, Sandra and Timberlake, Alan (1985) "Tense, aspect, and mood," in Timothy Shopen (ed.) *Language Typology and Syntactic Description*, vol. III *Grammatical Categories and the Lexicon*, Cambridge: Cambridge University Press.
Dale, George Irving (1925) "The imperfect subjunctive," *Hispania* 8: 127–9.
Fillmore, Charles (1984) "Lexical semantics and text semantics," in James E. Copeland (ed.) *New Directions in Linguistics and Semiotics*, Houston: Rice University Studies.
Graham, Malbone Watson (1926) "The imperfect subjunctive in Spanish America," *Hispania* 9: 46–9.
Hernández Alonso, César (1984) *Gramática funcional del español*, Madrid: Gredos.
Klein-Andreu, Flora (1975) "Pragmatic constraints on distribution: the Spanish subjunctive," *Papers from the Regional Meeting of the Chicago Linguistic Society* vol. 11, Chicago.
Larra, Mariano José de (1924) *El doncel de don Enrique el doliente*, Buenos Aires: Editora Internacional.
Lavandera, Beatriz (1983) "Shifting moods in Spanish discourse," in Flora Klein-Andreu (ed.) *Discourse Perspectives on Syntax*, New York: Academic Press.
Lemon, Francis B. (1925) "The relative frequency of the subjunctive forms in -*se* and -*ra*," *Hispania* 8: 300–2.
Lenz, Rodolfo (1920) *La oración y sus partes*, Madrid: Centro de Estudios Históricos.
Lunn, Patricia V. (1989) "The Spanish subjunctive and *relevance*,", in Carl Kirschner and Janet DeCesaris (eds) *Studies in Romance Linguistics: Selected Papers from the Seventeenth Linguistic Symposium on Romance Languages*, Amsterdam: John Benjamins.
Mallo, Jerónimo (1947) "El empleo de las formas del subjuntivo terminadas en 'ra' con significación de tiempos del indicativo," *Hispania* 30: 484–7.
—— (1950) "La discusión sobre el empleo de las formas verbales en 'ra' con función de tiempos pasados de indicativo," *Hispania* 33: 126–34.

Nutting, Herbert C. (1925) "The Latin conditional sentence," *University of California Publications in Classical Philology*, vol. 8, Berkeley and Los Angeles: University of California Press.
Pérez Galdós, Benito (1965) *Doña Perfecta*, ed. Rodolfo Cardona, New York: Dell Publishing Co.
RAE = Real Academia Española (1973) *Esbozo de una nueva gramática de la lengua española*, Madrid: Espasa-Calpe.
Rojo, Guillermo (1986) "On the evolution of conditional sentences in Old Spanish," in Osvaldo Jaeggli and Carmen Silva-Corvalán (eds) *Studies in Romance linguistics*, Dordrecht: Foris.
Saco Arce, Juan A. (1868) *Gramática gallega*, Lugo: Imprenta de Soto Freire.
Silva-Corvalán, Carmen (1985) "Modality and semantic change," in Jacek Fisiak (ed.) *Historical Semantics, Historical Word Formation*, New York: Mouton.
Smith, Colin (ed.) (1972) *Poema de mio Cid*, Oxford: Oxford University Press.
Solaún, Carmen (1972) "Estudio sincrónico de las formas en -ra, -se y -re," *Español actual* 23: 14–17.
Solé, Yolanda R. and Solé, Carlos A. (1977) *Modern Spanish Syntax: A Study in Contrast*, Lexington, MA: D.C. Heath.
Sperber, Dan and Wilson, Deirdre (1981) "Irony and the use-mention distinction," in Peter Cole (ed.) *Radical Pragmatics*, New York: Academic Press.
—— (1986) *Relevance. Communication and Cognition*, Cambridge, MA: Harvard University Press.
Staubach, Charles N. (1946) "Current variations in the past indicative uses of the *-ra* form," *Hispania* 29: 355–62.
Terrell, Tracy and Hooper, Joan (1974) "A semantically based analysis of mood in Spanish," *Hispania* 57: 484–94.
Vizcaíno Casas, Fernando (1984) *100 años de honradez*, Barcelona: Editorial Planeta.
Wright, Leavitt Olds (1926a) "The subjunctive forms in *-ra* and *-se* in Spanish-American speech," *Hispania* 9: 170–3.
—— (1926b) "The indicative forms in *-ra* in Spanish America," *Hispania* 9: 288–93.
—— (1929) "The indicative function of the *-ra* verb form," *Hispania* 12: 259–78.
—— (1932) *The -ra Verb Form in Spain*, University of California Publications in Modern Philology, vol. 15, no. 1, Berkeley: University of California Press.

8 Losing ground: A discourse-pragmatic solution to the history of -*ra* in Spanish[1]

Flora Klein-Andreu

1. INTRODUCTION

The study of linguistic elements as they actually are used, in contexts larger than sentences, has already proved its value in providing an understanding of many synchronic phenomena that were intractable to more traditional approaches (among many recent examples of the newer approach, see e.g. the various articles in Givón 1979b and in Klein-Andreu 1983). I would like to take this opportunity to apply some of the concepts and techniques of discourse-pragmatic analysis toward elucidating a historical problem: namely, the semantic development of the Spanish verb-form ending in -*ra* (as in *(que) yo amara*, now translatable as "(that) I would love").

2. TRADITIONAL VIEW OF THE SEMANTIC DEVELOPMENT OF THE -*RA* FORM

As is well known to students of Romance languages, the Spanish form in -*ra* is descended from the Latin pluperfect indicative in -*eram* (e.g. *amaveram* "I had loved"). At present, however, the -*ra* form is described as imperfect subjunctive – like the verb form ending in -*se*, reflex of the Latin pluperfect subjunctive in -*issem* (e.g. *amavissem* "I would have loved"), whose uses it currently shares.[2] Accordingly, in the development of its present status in Spanish, the original meaning of the -*ra* form has been reanalyzed in two respects: (1) in basic time reference, it has gone from referring to a time before some point in the past to simply referring to the past with no indication of "before-ness"; (2) in modality, it has lost the "assertiveness" (as to the event's occurrence/non-occurrence) that characterizes indicatives in Spanish (see Terrell and Hooper 1974), becoming "non-assertive" – hence its current label as "subjunctive." It is the latter development that is my main concern here.

In general, all accounts of the development of the *-ra* form's modal meaning give primary importance to its early use in the apodosis or consequence clause of conditional sentences, as having set off a chain of events that would eventually lead to its use in the protasis or condition clause, and thence to its current, more general use for non-assertive reference or "as a Subjunctive" (see e.g. Bello and Cuervo 1964: 475, n.94; Wright 1932: 16; Harris 1971: 31). The first step in this process – use of *-ra* in apodoses – seems to be satisfactorily recognized as an instance of the more general (and seemingly universal) use of tenses whose reference is normally to real events in (relatively more) past time, to refer to unreal events in (relatively) less past time – with what Bull called "forward migration" and Rojo calls "dislocation" of their basic time reference (Bull 1960: 61; Rojo 1974, cited in Rojo and Montero 1983: 43. For attempts to explain this phenomenon, see Bello and Cuervo 1964: section 692; Klein-Andreu 1986; Bybee 1987; Fleischman 1987). Thus, tenses whose reference is ordinarily to past time (e.g. the past tense in English, the imperfect and the conditional in Spanish) serve to indicate what might be called "lesser probability" (to the point of actual unreality) in reference to non-past time; similarly, forms whose time reference is basically to time before the past (pluperfects) serve to indicate unreality when they refer simply to the past (giving what Jespersen (1964: 255) called the "preterit and pluperfect of imagination," as in "I wish I had enough money (now)," and the corresponding "I wish I had had enough money (then)").

The problem, however, is that the use of *-ra* in apodoses, while quite plausible in itself, has been taken as explaining the eventual passage of *-ra* to protases, and its consequent disappearance from apodoses – the present situation in most dialects. This view is implicit in most treatments, and is explicitly held at least by Harris, who speaks of a "tendency to formal parallelism between apodosis and protasis of conditional sentences" (Harris 1971: 31). It seems to me, however, that there is little support for any such tendency – at least in Spanish. For we find that other relatively assertive forms – in particular the imperfect indicative and also the so-called conditional – have long been commonly used in apodoses. Yet, they show only a very limited tendency to extend to protases, and even less to disappear from apodoses.[3] As I point out in Klein-Andreu (1986: 106, 116n), what seems to confront us in Spanish (and seemingly in many other languages) is, rather, lack of parallelism between apodosis and protasis. Moreover, this situation is quite plausible pragmatically. Use of more or less "assertive" forms may be expected in apodoses, which must carry some degree of conviction to be interpretable as such: that is, as statements of expectable consequences (Wright 1932: 16, citing Nutting 1925; Hooper 1975). But there is no reason why this should be true of protases, which merely give the condition under which the consequence would be expected (Haiman 1978).[4]

It seems, then, that a different explanation must be sought for the passage of the *-ra* form to protases (and thence to other "non-assertive" or "subjunctive" uses, leading to its eventual loss from apodoses). In my earlier discussion I note that there was an important difference between the *-ra* form and other relatively assertive forms which were likewise used in apodoses but none the less have not been commonly adopted for protases and continue to be used in apodoses. In the case of *-ra*, its original "pluperfect indicative" uses were eventually taken over by a new periphrastic construction, formed with the imperfect of *habere* + the past participle of the particular verb (e.g. *habebam amatum* > *habia amado* "I had loved"). Thus, while the *-ra* form was like other relatively assertive forms in being used to convey relatively greater conviction in apodoses, it was unlike these other forms in that, in time, virtually all of *-ra*'s more assertive ("realis" or "indicative") uses were taken over by a new periphrastic form. I believe it is this circumstance that must be crucial for explaining why the *-ra* form, unlike other assertive forms likewise used in apodoses, was eventually dislodged from its original assertive uses (including its use in apodoses) and came to be used only in relatively unassertive contexts (such as protases of conditional sentences, among others) (Klein-Andreu 1986: 111).

3. AN ALTERNATIVE PROPOSAL

Because I believe the key to the passage of the *-ra* form from its original "indicative" value to its current "subjunctive" use lies in its competition with the new periphrastic pluperfect, I now undertake a brief preliminary examination of the nature of this competition, using techniques and concepts that have proved revealing in synchronic analyses from a discourse-pragmatic point of view. Specifically, I propose to compare the use of the two competing forms in actual usage in which the *-ra* form still occurs preponderantly with its original, pluperfect indicative value (thus, referring to events as actually having occurred before some point in the past), though "alternating" in this sense with the new periphrastic pluperfect. My interest is in determining whether, at a time when both forms were used with the same reference as to both time and modality, one can already discern some other contrast between them that might account for the eventual loss of assertiveness of the -*ra* form.

Of course, to the extent that both forms refer to events as real, and both place them at some time before the past, no meaningful contrast can involve what is traditionally taken as the difference between indicatives and subjunctives – namely realis vs. irrealis reference – nor can it involve time reference; it must be something else. The possibility I have chosen to examine is that, during a time in which the new and the old pluperfect indicatives still appear "in competition" as to both time and realis reference, they are used to distinguish relative degrees of "focus" or attention on the event. Distinctions of this kind have been found by such authors as Reid (1977, 1979) and Pennhalurick (1984); I take them to be more or less equivalent too to what Diver calls distinctions of "relevance" (1969), and to what Hopper and Thompson (1980) call differences in "grounding" (that is fore- vs. backgrounding of the event), also found by other investigators such as Fox (1983) and Fleischman (1986). Specifically, I would expect that the new periphrastic pluperfect should be preferred to refer to events that are placed in relatively higher focus, or foregrounded, so that the old morphological pluperfect – the -*ra* form – would tend to be relegated to describing events that are placed in relatively lower focus, or backgrounded.

There are several a priori reasons why difference in focus seemed a promising possibility. First, it seems to me that the reason why more satisfying explanations for the modal development of the -*ra* form have not been arrived at up to now, despite the apparent interest in the problem, might be because research on this question has concentrated overwhelmingly on its use in conditional sentences. And this special interest in conditionals seems to be based, in turn, on an incorrect view of the difference between indicative and subjunctive in Spanish, as having to do with reference to events as "real" (or "factual") or as "unreal" (or "non-factual"). For in certain respects conditionals can be viewed as occupying an area between the "real" and the "unreal"; thus these concepts are commonly appealed to in their classification and description (e.g. Rojo and Montero 1983; Lavandera 1975).

However, at least in contemporary Spanish (but seemingly also at older stages of the language), forms traditionally called "subjunctive" do not always refer to unreal events, while those traditionally called "indicative" do not always refer to facts. Instead, actual use of indicative vs. subjunctive forms in Spanish seems to reflect what Terrell and Hooper (1974) call "assertion" vs. "non-assertion" of the event's occurrence – an analysis which accounts for a number of facts that were counter-examples to the traditional view based on reality/factuality (see e.g. Klein 1975, 1980; Lunn and Cravens 1987).[5] But, if the semantic difference between "indicative" and "subjunctive" in Spanish is a matter of relative assertiveness, rather than reality or factuality *per se*, then the overriding interest in conditional sentences no longer seems justified. Instead, if we regard change in actual use as reflecting reinterpretation of meaning, then "low focus" on the event appears as a natural candidate for a transitional meaning for the -*ra* form, leading from an original "assertive" meaning (and consequent "indicative" uses) to its current "non-assertive" meaning (and consequent use "as a subjunctive"). Note too that, assuming that exact placement in time should be relatively less important (and so less clear and obvious) in the case of backgrounded events, use of -*ra* as a "low focus" form would also be consonant with its eventual passage from reference to a point before some time in the past (i.e. pluperfect reference), to simple reference to past time – its basic temporal meaning at present.[6]

4. A PRELIMINARY TEST

As a preliminary, "pilot" test of whether this hypothesis is supported by actual usage, I examined all occurrences of -*ra* and of the periphrastic pluperfect in the first forty chapters of a fourteenth-century work: *El Conde Lucanor* by the Castilian author Don Juan Manuel. I chose this text because it appeared, from earlier studies (Wright 1932; Rojo and Montero 1983), to represent a period in which -*ra* was still used largely with both its original temporal and modal meanings – thus as a "pluperfect indicative." This would put it in competition with the new periphrastic pluperfect (henceforward PP) for referring to events as having actually occurred before some time in the past, thus making it possible for the two forms to contrast (only) in some other respect.

According to Menéndez-Pidal (1964: 29), the part of *El Conde Lucanor* under consideration was written between 1328 and 1332. The work is a collection of traditional didactic tales, presented in the form of stories within a story. In each chapter, the "outer" story consists of a dialogue between master (Count Lucanor) and servant/adviser (Patronio), in which the count tells Patronio of some problem that is bothering him at the moment. In order to advise his master, Patronio then recounts a fable or other tale, from which he draws a conclusion that both recognize as applicable to the count's predicament. The stories Patronio tells are known as *enxiemplos* "examples"; they constitute the "inner" story and by far the greater part of the book.

In all, I counted 220 occurrences of the PP and -ra. Of these, twenty examples of -ra are found in an expression that occurs in the same part of each chapter, in virtually identical form, and which I therefore eliminated from further consideration as formulaic. I note, however, that this choice for a predictable expression is consonant in itself with the view that -ra indicates "low focus."[7]

Of the remaining 200 examples, 184 refer to events as real, and only 16 as unreal, as Table 8.1 shows. Of the 16 unreal references, 5 are in protases, 3 in apodoses, 7 in modal expressions, and one in an indefinite expression. All unreal references are in the -ra form – which also is consonant with "low focus."

Table 8.1 Relative frequency of PP and -ra, as a function of realis or irrealis reference

	Total	PP	% PP	-ra	%-ra
Overall	200	49		151	
Realis	184	49	27	135	73
Irrealis	16	0	0	16	100
Distribution of irrealis references					
Protasis		5			
Apodosis		3			
Modal auxiliaries		7			
Indefinite		1			

Where temporal reference is concerned, most examples can be interpreted as pluperfect. This is generally true of the references to real events, which constitute by far the larger part of the data. Thus *El Conde Lucanor* turned out to be a good choice in that, in the great majority of its uses of -ra, it still appears "in competition" with PP as to both temporal and modal reference.

On the other hand, where events are referred to as unreal, it often is very difficult to determine whether their time reference is before-past or simply past.[8]

Consider (1) and (2):

(1) El mercadero, que oyó a su mujer llamar marido a aquel mançebo, pesol mucho ... *Quisiéralos* matar luego, pero acordándose del seso que costara una dobla, non se arrebató. (Manuel 1969: 194)
"The merchant, who heard his wife call that youth 'husband,' was much distressed.... He *wanted* [= would have wanted] to kill

them immediately, but remembering the advice that had cost a doubloon, he restrained himself."

(2) Et después acaesçió otra cosa que *pudiera fazer* por mi, et púsome escusa commo la otra. (Manuel 1969: 94)

"And later there came up another thing that he *could do* [= could have done] for me, and again he gave me an excuse [not to do it]."

Though I have classed these among the "unreal" references, in a sense they bridge the gap between reference to the event as real or as unreal – as well as perhaps between placing it in before-past or simply past time.[9] Strictly speaking, in modal examples such as these only the main verb refers to an "unreal" event, as the reference of the modal (wanting to/being able to) is real enough.

To test whether PP and -ra contrast more generally as to degree of focus, even within references to events as real, I examined whether the relative proportion of the two forms is affected by still other contextual conditions that can be expected, a priori, to tend to make events more or less deserving of attention. I expected that the following should tend to make events relatively more worthy of attention, and so of "high focus." Therefore, if the hypothesis is correct, they should tend to skew the PP/-ra proportion toward a relatively higher use of the PP than would be found otherwise:

(1) reference to transitive events;[10]
(2) reference to events whose subjects are animate (hence, usually people);
(3) reference to events whose accusative objects are animate;
(4) reference to the "outer story" (that is, to events in the dialogue between Count Lucanor and his servant, as compared to those in the traditional tales that the servant tells his master);
(5) mention as first in a sequence of co-ordinated events, in the case of sequences that use both forms.

On the other hand the following were expected to favor backgrounding of the event, and so its mention in "low focus" by -ra:

(1) negation;
(2) reference to a state – specifically by *ser* and *estar* "be" and *haber* "have";
(3) occurrence in a relative clause.

The results are shown in Tables 8.2 to 8.11. Tables 8.2–8 need little comment: only the distribution in Table 8.4, as a function of the object's animateness, does not skew in the direction expected;[11] otherwise, each of the other distributions examined is skewed in the direction the hypothesis predicts.

Table 8.2 Relative frequency of PP and -ra as a function of transitivity

	Total	PP	% PP	-ra	%-ra
Transitive	137	41	30	96	70
Intransitive	47	8	17	39	83

Table 8.3 Relative frequency of PP and -ra as a function of subject's animateness

Subject	Total	PP	% PP	-ra	%-ra
Animate	165	46	28	119	72
Inanimate	19	3	16	16	84

Table 8.4 Relative frequency of PP and -ra as a function of the accusative object's animateness

Object	Total	PP	% PP	-ra	%-ra
Animate	29	7	24	22	76
Inanimate	108	34	31	74	69

Table 8.5 Relative frequency of PP and -ra as a function of reference to "outer" vs. "inner" story

	Total	PP	% PP	-ra	%-ra
Outer story	7	4	57	3	43
Inner story	177	45	25	132	75

Table 8.6 Relative frequency of PP and -ra in sequences as a function of position in sequence

	Total	PP	% PP	-ra	%-ra
First event	5	4	80	1	20
Last event	5	1	20	4	80

Table 8.7 Relative frequency of PP and -ra as a function of whether verb is ser/estar "be" or haber "have"

	Total	PP	% PP	-ra	%-ra
Ser/estar/haber	10	1	10	9	90
Other verbs	174	48	28	126	72

Table 8.8 Relative frequency of PP and -ra as a function of whether event is negated or not negated

	Total	PP	% PP	-ra	%-ra
Not negated	167	46	28	121	72
Negated	17	3	18	14	82

Table 8.9 shows the distribution of the two forms by type of clause: main, complement, relative, and other subordinate clauses (which are mostly expressions of cause). Here we see that difference in the relative proportion of PP to -ra is not so much between relative clauses and clauses of other kinds, but rather between complements and other subordinate clauses, including relatives.[12] As shown more clearly in Table 8.10, it turns out that complements are significantly more hospitable to the new periphrastic form than are other subordinate clauses ($p<.05$, by two-tailed X^2).

Table 8.9 Relative frequency of PP and -ra as a function of type of clause

	Total	PP	% PP	-ra	%-ra
Main	3	1	33	2	67
Complement	58	21	36	37	64
Relative	93	23	25	70	75
Cause, etc.	30	4	13	26	87

Table 8.10 Relative frequency of PP and -ra in complement clauses, compared to other subordinate clauses

	Total	PP	% PP	-ra	%-ra
Complements	58	21	36	37	64
Relatives & cause, etc.	123	27	22	96	78

To test whether the reason for this difference might be that complements are more likely to provide new information than other subordinate clauses, I did another count based directly on the information-status of the verb. As shown in Table 8.11, the results do skew as expected, with unknown events favoring the periphrasis more than events that are already known. Yet the difference is not strong enough to account fully for the difference between complements and other subordinate clauses. But in any event it is consonant with the fact that presentation as a complement seems to be, in itself, more foregrounded than other subordinate presentations. Thus, for example, most complements in this sample are complements of verbs of saying, and so appear as complements as a result of being presented as indirect speech within the narrative; if the speech were quoted directly, it would appear as an independent clause. But the material in the other subordinate clauses – relatives and expressions of cause – would still appear in dependent clauses.

Table 8.11 Relative frequency of PP and -*ra* as a function of whether occurrence of event is already known or not

	Total	PP	% PP	-ra	%-ra
Known event	135	33	24	102	76
Not known	49	16	33	33	67

5. DISCUSSION OF RESULTS

The data from *El Conde Lucanor* support a view of the original pluperfect indicative, the -*ra* form, becoming increasingly relegated to "low focus" reference (that is, to background events), as the new periphrastic pluperfect is preferred for foregrounding. It is not surprising then that -*ra* should be preferred for referring to hypothetical events. This being so, it is also not surprising that -*ra* should go on to be reanalyzed further as indicating "non-assertiveness," and so become specialized for (virtually) exclusive use "as a subjunctive." Thus, the observation that, in conditional sentences, -*ra* appeared first in apodoses, before appearing in protases, would simply reflect its gradual progress from greater to lesser assertiveness. But it is its initial reinterpretation as indicating "low focus" on the event that constitutes the semantic "missing link" between the original more assertive meaning and the later less assertive one. It is this reinterpretation that explains why, of the various more or less assertive forms commonly used in apodoses, only the -*ra* form eventually passed on to virtually exclusive use in environments calling for least assertiveness – such as conditions presented as less likely and other "subjunctive" contexts – becoming unsuited for further use in apodoses.

But there is yet another important reason why use of -*ra* as an indicator of "low focus" appears as a plausible intervening stage between greater and lesser assertiveness, apparently more promising for further investigation than use in different parts of conditional sentences. This is the apparently much greater frequency of occasions for -*ra*'s productive use in contrasts as to (degree of) "focus." In principle, it would seem that a more frequently employed distinction should be relatively more influential in determining subsequent reanalysis of meaning, as compared to a less frequent one.

6. CONCLUSION

In view of the apparent infrequency at this stage of -*ra* with hypothetical reference (and the still greater infrequency of its use in conditional sentences), compared to its relatively frequent use to background events more generally, and considering the a priori plausibility of "low focus" or backgrounding as an intermediate stage in its semantic development, it seems appropriate to ask why this possibility has been overlooked until now. This seems especially remarkable when we consider that there have been many studies of -*ra*'s development, including several (Wright 1932; Mendeloff 1960; Rojo and Montero 1983) based on a considerable amount of data.

I believe the reason for this can only be the traditional tendency to concentrate on semantic differences that affect "truth value": surely this is responsible for the pre-eminence of considerations of "reality," and so for the special interest in expressions of conditions and their consequences. And this position, in turn, seems to have as its methodological counterpart the practise of limiting data to sentences considered in isolation, and so almost necessarily "as propositions" (for typical analytic consequences, see Klein-Andreu 1983).

That the pre-eminence of considerations involving "truth-value" is simply an artifact of the traditional approach itself is abundantly demonstrated in recent work from the discourse-pragmatic perspective. This work reveals, instead, the linguistic importance of distinctions reflecting the language user's choice of how to present the subject matter, based on such considerations as the relative saliency of the various referents to the speaker/writer, and also their expected saliency to the hearer/reader (see e.g. Givón 1979; Marslen-Wilson *et al.* 1982; and many others). As it turns out, these are just the kinds of considerations that account for intuitive differences between apodosis and protasis, and in particular for the traditional impression that it is the apodosis that is "independent," whereas the protasis is "dependent": if "reality" were taken as criterial in itself, then either both clauses would have to be considered hypothetical or (un)real, or if anything the event expressed in the apodosis would have to be viewed as "dependent" on the event in the protasis, since it depends on it for its realization (as noted in James 1982; also Fleischman 1987). Clearly, however, the validity of analyses in terms of such concepts as relative saliency can only be determined, in principle, by considering the context overall.

On the other hand, what leads to envisaging the kind of development indicated here is the view that a form's actual use(s) must be determined by its meaning, so that changes in the form's use(s) over time are expected to reflect reanalyses of meaning. This view of semantic change seems plausible as well as principled, and lends itself well to empirical testing.

In this particular case, the premise that use is determined by meaning leads to the expectation that competition with the new periphrastic pluperfect must have provided the critical impetus for semantic reanalysis of the -ra form. And this leads us to seek evidence of contrast between the two in their actual use at a stage in which they are still predominantly "in competition," both as to time reference and as to reference to events as actually having happened.

NOTES

1 A shorter version of this text was presented orally at the 8th International Conference on Historical Linguistics (Lille, August 1987). I am grateful to Joan Bybee, Erica García, and Suzanne Fleischman for their comments on the earlier version.
2 The converse, however, is still not true; -ra still has uses not available to -se (Klein-Andreu 1986: 112).
3 There are certain localities where the conditional occurs in protases in "non-standard" vernacular: in Buenos Aires (Lavandera 1975) and in the provinces of Logroño and Burgos (Martinez Martín 1983; Silva-Corvalán 1983) and in northern Spain. According to Lavandera, in Buenos Aires this usage leads to the same form occurring in both parts of the conditional sentence. But the peninsular use of the conditional in protases does not lead to formal parallelism, since in Castilla (including the areas in question here and seemingly at all social levels), the imperfect indicative is by far the preferred form for apodoses in speech (Klein-Andreu 1986: 103). In both, however, "if -ra, then -ría" still survives as the normal "formal" pattern for "less likely" non-past conditionals. It seems to me, then, that these local phenomena are of an entirely different order of

magnitude, both geographic and social, from the situation of *-ra*, since *-ra* has lost virtually all its "indicative" uses, in most geographic dialects and stylistic registers (for the apparent exceptions, see Klein-Andreu 1986: 112; Lunn and Cravens 1987).

4 This pragmatic difference between apodosis and protasis is recognized by Harris (1971: 27).

5 For example, the complements of comments or opinions are normally in the subjunctive, even when the events commented on are regarded as actual occurrences. This analysis has the further advantage that assertiveness lends itself easily to being viewed as relative, rather than dichotomous. Thus, it also accommodates quite naturally the present-day verb forms known as future and conditional as intermediate in degree of assertiveness between the traditional indicative and the traditional subjunctive forms, but opposed to each other in their basic time reference as non-past vs. past. This accounts well for the actual uses of the future and conditional – including their common use in apodoses (Klein 1980, Klein-Andreu 1986).

6 That the basic time reference of the *-ra* form is "past" is seen in the fact that it is used to "back-shift" the present subjunctive: that is, to place in past time what the present subjunctive would place in non-past time. For instance, *dudaba que vinieran* "I doubted that they would come" is the exact parallel, in past time, of *dudo que vengan* "I doubt that they (will) come" in non-past time (see Klein-Andreu 1986, Fig. 7).

7 This formula is always used to connect the "outer" and the "inner" stories: when Patronio announces the particular tale he is going to tell the count, this is always followed by *El conde le rogó quel dixiesse commo fuera aquello* "The count begged him to tell him how that had been" (with minimal variations, such as *El conde le preguntó commo fuera aquello* "The count asked him how that had been"). After this Patronio starts his story. Note that the verb in this formula is *ser* "be," which also should favor *-ra*.

8 Part of the difficulty is that translation is useless as a test, since so many languages (including English) use pluperfects to refer to unreal events in past time.

9 The semantic link between "(more) pastness" and "unreality in less-past time" is still the subject of discussion (see e.g. James 1982; Bybee 1987; Fleischman 1987; also the explanation proposed by Diver, summarized in Klein-Andreu 1986).

10 PP is descended from a construction used only for transitive events: it was "passive" in the sense that it referred to the state of an (accusative) object, as a result of the event described by the verb; accordingly, the participle referred to the object's gender and number, by "agreement." In this text, however, of four participles referring to plural objects, only two are plural. This suggests that the periphrasis is losing its passive sense – as is also indicated by the fact that eight (17 per cent) of the occurrences of PP refer to intransitive events. To the extent that this is so, it cannot account for the relatively greater preference for *-ra* with intransitives; this must be due to some other reason, such as the meanings posited here.

11 Erica García observes that this may be because when the accusative object is animate, the subject is usually inanimate – a situation which disfavors PP.

12 It is interesting that PP and -*ra* hardly ever occur in main clauses referring to real events (that is in main clauses other than apodoses). This is perhaps because their temporal meaning, before-past, refers to events prior to the time reference of the body of the narrative: the past.

REFERENCES

Bello, A. and Cuervo, R.J. (1964) *Gramática de la lengua castellana*, 7th edn, Buenos Aires: Sopena.

Bull, W. (1960) *Time, Tense, and the Verb*, Berkeley: University of California Press.

Bybee, J. (1987) "The semantic development of past tense modals in English and other languages," paper presented at 8th International Congress on Historical Linguistics, September 1987, Lille, France.

Diver, W. (1969) "The system of relevance of the Homeric verb," *Acta Linguistica Hafniensia* II: 45–68.

Fleischman, S. (1986) "Discourse functions of tense-aspect oppositions in narrative: toward a theory of grounding," *Linguistics* 23: 851–82.

—— (1987) "Temporal distance: synchronic and diachronic extensions in grammar, discourse, and expressivity," paper presented at 8th International Congress of Historical Linguistics, September 1987, Lille, France. (Printed as "Temporal distance: a basic linguistic metaphor," *Studies in Language* 13 (1989): 1–51).

Fox, B. (1983) "The discourse function of the participle in Ancient Greek," in F. Klein-Andreu (ed.) *Discourse Perspectives on Syntax*, New York: Academic Press.

Givón, T. (1979a) *On Understanding Grammar*, New York: Academic Press.

Givón, T. (ed.) (1979b) *Discourse and Syntax*, vol. 12 *Syntax and Semantics*, New York: Academic Press.

Haiman, J. (1978) "Conditionals are topics," *Language* 54 (3): 564–89.

Harris, M. (1971) "The history of the conditional complex from Latin to Spanish: some structural considerations," *Archivum Linguisticum* II: 25–33.

Hooper, J.B. (1975) "On assertive predicates," in John P. Kimball (ed.) *Syntax and Semantics* vol. 4, New York: Academic Press.

Hopper, P. and Thompson, S.A. (1980) "Transitivity in grammar and discourse," *Language* 56: 251–99.

James, D. (1982) "Past tense and hypothetical: a cross-linguistic study," *Studies in Language* VI (3): 375–403.

Jespersen, O. (1964) *Essentials of English Grammar*, Alabama: University of Alabama Press.

Klein, F. (1975) "Pragmatic constraints on distribution: the Spanish subjunctive," in *Papers from the Eleventh Regional Meeting of the Chicago Linguistics Society*, Chicago: Chicago Linguistics Society.

—— (1980) "Experimental verification of semantic hypotheses applied to mood in Spanish," *Georgetown University Papers on Language and Linguistics*, vol. 17, Washington, DC: Georgetown University Press.

Klein-Andreu, F. (1983) "Grammar in style: Spanish adjective placement," in F. Klein-Andreu (ed.) *Discourse Perspectives on Syntax*, New York: Academic Press.

—— (ed.) (1983) *Discourse Perspective on Syntax*, New York: Academic Press.

—— (1986) "Speaker-based and reference-based factors in language: nonpast conditional sentences in Spanish," in O. Jaeggli and C. Silva-Corvalán (eds) *Proceedings of the Linguistic Symposium on Romance Languages*, vol. XIV, Dordrecht and Riverton: Foris.

Lapesa, R. (1980) *Historia de la lengua española*, 8th edn, Madrid: Gredos.

Lavandera, B.R. (1975) "Linguistic structure and sociolinguistic conditioning in the use of the verbal endings in *si*-clauses (Buenos Aires Spanish)," dissertation, University of Pennsylvania.

Lunn, P.V. and Cravens, T. (1987) "Diachronic consideration of synchronic anomalies: the Spanish unmotivated subjunctive," paper presented at the 8th International Conference on Historical Linguistics, September 1987, Lille, France. (Printed as chapter 7 of this volume.)

Manuel, Don Juan (1969) *El Conde Lucanor, o Libro de los enxiemplos del conde Lucanor et de Patronio*, ed. José Manuel Blecua, Madrid: Castalia.

Marslen-Wilson, W., Levy, E., and Komisarjevky-Tyler, L. (1982) "Producing interpretable discourse: the establishment and maintenance of reference," in R.J. Jarvella and W. Klein (eds) *Speech, Place, and Action*, New York: Wiley.

Martinez Martín, F.M. (1983) *Fonética y sociolingüística de la ciudad de Burgos*, Madrid: CSIC.

Mendeloff, H. (1960) *The Evolution of the Conditional Sentence Contrary to Fact in Old Spanish*, Washington, DC: The Catholic University Press.

Menéndez Pidal, R. (1964) *Antología de prosistas españoles*, 8th edn, Madrid: Espasa-Calpe.

Nutting, Herbert C. (1925) "The Latin conditional sentence," *University of California Publications in Classical Philology*, vol. 8, Berkeley and Los Angeles: University of California Press.

Pennhalurick, J. (1984) "Full-verb inversion in English," *Australian Journal of Linguistics* 4 (1): 33–57.

Reid, Wallis (1977) "Tha quantitative validation of a grammatical hypothesis: the *passé simple* and the *imparfait*," *North Eastern Linguistic Society* 7: 315–33.

—— (1979) "The human factor in linguistic analysis: the *passé simple* and the *imparfait*," dissertation, Columbia University.

Rojo, G. (1974) *Perífrasis verbales en el gallego actual*, Santiago: Universidade de Santiago Compostelo.

—— (1986) "On the evolution of conditional sentences in Old Spanish," in O. Jaeggli and C. Silva-Corvalán (eds) *Studies in Romance Linguistics*, Dordrecht: Foris.

Rojo, G. and Montero, E. (1983) *La evolución de los esquemas condicionales (potenciales e irreales desde el poema del Cid hasta 1400)*, Santiago de Compostela: Verba.

Silva-Corvalán, C. (1983) "Modality and semantic change," MS, University of Southern California.

Terrell, T. and Hooper, J.B. (1974) "A semantically-based analysis of mood in Spanish," *Hispania* 57: 484–94.

Wright, L.O. (1932) *The -ra Verb Form in Spain*, Berkeley: University of California Press.

9 The pragmatics of Spanish mood in complements of knowledge and acquisition-of-knowledge predicates[1]

Jorge M. Guitart

1. INTRODUCTION

I would like to present a pragmatic analysis of Spanish mood in knowledge and acquisition-of-knowledge predicate sentences which I believe is far more descriptive than other proposals known to me. My treatment differs significantly both from traditional accounts and more current treatments, particularly from that given to the same phenomenon by J.B. Hooper and T. Terrell within their broader theory of mood selection in Spanish sentential complements. Their proposal will serve on the other hand as a point of departure for the discussion.

The Hooper-Terrell theory of mood selection hinges upon the notions of assertion and presupposition (Hooper 1974; Terrell and Hooper 1974; Terrell 1976). For Hooper and Terrell a sentential complement is asserted as a proposition when the speaker is establishing it as true, and it is presupposed when the speaker already regards it as true and is making another proposition about it. For instance, in (1) the complement is asserted but in (2) it is presupposed:

(1) Me parece que el bar está cerrado.
 "It seems to me that the bar is closed [complement verb in the indicative, henceforth Ind]."
(2) Lamento que el bar esté cerrado.
 "I regret that the bar is closed [complement verb in the subjunctive, henceforth Subj]."

Within the Hooper-Terrell framework the crucial semantic distinction between these two types of complements is that when the whole sentence is negated a presupposed complement remains presupposed but an asserted complement is no longer being asserted. For example, in (3) the presupposition that the bar is closed remains:

(3) No lamento que el bar esté cerrado.

"I don't regret that the bar is closed [Subj]."

but in (4) the speaker is no longer asserting that the bar is closed:

(4) No me parece que el bar esté cerrado.
    "It doesn't seem to me that the bar is closed [Subj]."

Notice that in (4) the complement is not presupposed either. The same can be said of complements in volitional and dubitative sentences like (5) and (6):

(5) Prefiero que el bar esté cerrado.
    "I prefer for the bar to be closed [Subj]."
(6) Dudo que el bar esté cerrado.
    "I doubt that the bar is closed [Subj]."

One fundamental claim of Hooper and Terrell's is that mood selection in Spanish depends on the attitude of the speaker toward the truth-value of the complement, for as examples (1)–(6) seem to show, asserted complements take the indicative but non-asserted complements (including presupposed ones) take the subjunctive.

2. FACTIVES AND SEMIFACTIVES

In establishing their theory Hooper and Terrell take their lead from Kiparsky and Kiparsky (1970) who endeavor to demonstrate that presupposition has syntactic repercussions in English. The Kiparskys propose a class of factive predicates, which as matrices of complex sentences always take complements that are presupposed as true. In contrast, non-factive predicates take complements not presupposed as true. This is illustrated in (7) (the examples are the Kiparskys').

(7) a. Factive
    { I regret
      I am aware
      I take into account   } that Nixon lied.
      I resent
      I deplore }

   b. Non-factive
    { I assert
      I declare
      It's likely   } that Nixon lied.
      I figure }

Within the Kiparskys' framework, in every sentence in (7a) the speaker presupposes that Nixon lied but this is not presupposed in any of the sentences in (7b).

The Kiparskys show that factive and non-factive predicates differ in their syntactic behavior. For example, only factives can take the noun "fact" as their object; non-factives cannot, as shown in (8):

(8) a. I resent the fact that he wasn't here.
    b. *I assert the fact that he wasn't here.
    c. *I figure the fact that he wasn't here.

There are several other syntactic differences including transformations that are applicable to factives but not to non-factives and vice versa (see their article for details). The Kiparskys conclude that these differences are imputable to the presence or absence of presupposition in the semantic representation of sentences.

Kartunnen (1971) has shown, however, that certain predicates which the Kiparskys list as factive may take complements that cannot be regarded absolutely as presupposed. Consider sentences like those in (9):

(9) Mr Nixon, did you discover/notice/realize that you hadn't told the truth?

These sentences have a factive reading, in which the speaker presupposes that Mr Nixon didn't tell the truth. But they also have a non-factive reading in which the speaker does not know whether Nixon told the truth and is in fact inquiring about it.

Kartunnen coined the term "semifactive" to refer to those factive predicates whose complements can have a non-presupposed reading.

In turn, Hooper and Thompson (1973) noticed that certain semi-factives behave syntactically more like asserted complements than like true factives. The latter for instance cannot undergo preposing whereas the first two types can, as shown in (10):

(1.) It's late, it seems to me [asserted].
    It's late, I noticed [semifactive].
    *It's late, I regret [factive].

This view is incorporated into the Hooper-Terrell framework. According to Hooper and Terrell, that semifactives are more like asserted complements is supported by the fact that in Spanish both take the indicative.

A paradox then arises: though semifactive complements behave syntactically like asserted complements, they behave semantically like presupposed ones, since their truth-value is not affected under negation, as shown in (11) and (12):

(11) Noté que era tarde.
 "I noticed it was late."
(12) No noté que era tarde.
 "I didn't notice it was late."

But by Hooper and Terrell's definition of presupposition, a complement cannot be both asserted and presupposed at the same time. In the face of this, Hooper (1974: 24) suggests two alternatives: one is to redefine presupposition so that it excludes semifactives, the other is to admit that semifactive complements are both asserted and presupposed. Hooper and Terrell opt for the latter: while maintaining that semifactive complements are more like asserted complements, they insist on referring to them as "weakly presupposed" (as opposed to factives which are said to be "strongly presupposed"). This of course is in violation of their own definition of presupposition.

Klein (1977) has pointed out that no paradox exists: semifactive complements can be either asserted or presupposed but not at the same time; when they are being asserted they are asserted complements, and when they are being presupposed they are factive complements. Klein, who apparently sees no need to demonstrate this position, is holding Hooper and Terrell to their definition of assertion and presupposition; for a given reading a speaker is either establishing the complement as true (asserting it) or assuming that it is true (presupposing it) and making another proposition about it, but cannot be doing both at the same time.

(13) Noté que estaba cansada.
 "I noticed that she was tired [Ind]."

Here I am either establishing as true that she was tired or I am assuming that she was tired and am establishing as true only that I noticed this.

3. SEMANTIC PRESUPPOSITION VS. PRAGMATIC PRESUPPOSITION

The problem with Hooper and Terrell's analysis lies in their use of negation as a test for presupposition. This test is used for determining what has been called semantic presupposition, e.g. by Keenan (1971), whom Hooper and Terrell explicitly follow (see Terrell and Hooper 1974: 494, note 4). Semantic presupposition has to do with relations among sentences, relations that are independent of the participants in speech. But, as Kempson (1975) has pointed out, the type of presupposition that is mutually exclusive with assertion is pragmatic presupposition. This term has been variously defined and used in the literature (cf. Keenan 1971; Fillmore 1971; Kartunnen 1973). Here, following the lead of Kempson, I will interpret the distinction "assertion/presupposition" as having to do with the speaker's intention in formulating a proposition *vis-à-vis* what the hearer knows. Roughly, if speakers give a complement as information, they are asserting it; if they comment on it, they are presupposing it. Hooper and Terrell would not disagree with this. What they have failed to notice is that semantic presupposition is independent of assertion. Suppose I say:

(14) Noté que el bar estaba cerrado: no te molestes en ir.
"I noticed that the bar was closed, don't bother to go [Ind]."

Pragmatically I am asserting (informing the hearer of) the proposition that the bar is closed, but semantically I am presupposing it (the complement meets the test of negation: if indeed the bar is closed and I say instead that I did not notice this, I still presuppose the complement of the first sentence as true, and the whole utterance is still felicitous). Klein (1977) has commented that a semifactive complement may be "strongly" presupposed in Hooper and Terrell's sense, and he is right. Suppose that as a rejoinder to (15a) someone says (15b):

(15) a. Creí que había entrado únicamente yo.
"I thought that only I had gone in [Ind]."
b. Pero yo noté que entrabas y te seguí hasta aquí.
"But I noticed that you were going in and I followed you all the way here [Ind]."

In (15b) the speaker presupposes semantically that the addressee went in (the complement meets the test of negation) but also presupposes this pragmatically, since he obviously assumes it to be true; he certainly is not establishing it as true for the sake of the hearer, who already knows it.

In short, semifactive complements are not always pragmatically asserted, but when they are, they are semantically presupposed. The term "weak presupposition" is meaningless unless it is taken to mean "semantically but not pragmatically presupposed," but in that case not all complements of semifactives are weakly presupposed.

4. ACQUISITION-OF-KNOWLEDGE PREDICATES

The term "semifactive" is a negative label: it refers to a set of predicates that do not always behave the way factives do. Semifactives, however, have a positive characteristic of their own: regardless of the truth-conditional status of their complements, they serve to qualify how the information in the complement was acquired, or – in case of negation – how it was not acquired. Consider the sentences in (16), for instance.

(16) $\begin{Bmatrix} \text{Sí} \\ \text{No} \end{Bmatrix} \begin{Bmatrix} \text{me di cuenta} \\ \text{noté} \\ \text{descubrí} \\ \text{vi} \\ \text{sentí} \end{Bmatrix}$ que la plataforma se estaba derrumbando.

"I $\begin{Bmatrix} \text{did} \\ \text{didn't} \end{Bmatrix} \begin{Bmatrix} \text{realize} \\ \text{notice} \\ \text{discover} \\ \text{see} \\ \text{sense/feel} \end{Bmatrix}$ that the platform was collapsing [Ind]."

These tell of different ways in which I came to know that the platform was collapsing or of different ways in which I did not acquire such information; in every case the complement is semantically presupposed though it is pragmatically ambiguous between an asserted and a presupposed reading.

A better label for semifactives is acquisition-of-knowledge predicates (henceforth AK predicates). These include verbs of perception in addition to so-called mental act predicates. Both classes will be seen to behave pragmatically alike in Spanish.

5. MOOD SELECTION IN THE COMPLEMENTS OF SPANISH AK PREDICATES

If a Spanish AK predicate is in the affirmative, there is no contrast of mood in the complement since only the indicative can occur, as illustrated in (17).

(17) $\begin{Bmatrix} \text{Noté} \\ \text{vi} \\ \text{etc.} \end{Bmatrix}$ que la plataforma $\begin{Bmatrix} \text{se derrumbaba} \\ \text{*se derrumbara} \end{Bmatrix}$ [Ind]. [Subj].

Many have noticed, however, that both the indicative and the subjunctive can occur in the corresponding negative and interrogative versions of these sentences, as shown in (18).

(18) a. No {noté / vi / etc.} que la plataforma {se derrumbaba [Ind]. / se derrumbara [Subj].}

b. ¿{Notaste / viste / etc.} que la plataforma {se derrumbaba [Ind]. / se derrumbara [Subj].} ?

But to my knowledge no one has described systematically the differences in meaning conveyed by these differences in mood or the pragmatic conditions that must obtain for the sentences in the subjunctive to be appropriate.

6. NEGATION AND MOOD IN SPANISH AK PREDICATE SENTENCES

When the complement of a negated AK predicate is in the subjunctive, it is not presupposed, not even semantically. For instance, even though (19) is anomalous, (20) is not:

(19) ?No me di cuenta que el bar estaba cerrado definitivamente; es más, creo que está abierto.
?"I didn't realize that the bar was closed for good [Ind presupposed]; what's more, I think it's open."

(20) No me di cuenta que el bar estuviera cerrado definitivamente; es más, creo que está abierto. [Same as 19, with Subj]

Of course, (19) is contradictory because the complement is semantically presupposed to be true: one cannot say, "The bar is closed for good; what's more, I think it's open." But (20) is well formed, for in its first sentence the speaker is saying in effect that he has not perceived the bar as being closed. Thus he is able to think that it is open. The speaker, however, is not ruling out the possibility that the complement may be true. This is shown by the fact that (21) is well formed:

(21) Yo no vi que Oswald disparara, pero puede haber disparado.
"I didn't see Oswald firing [Subj], but he might have fired."

But the effect is one of casting doubt on the likelihood of the situation referred to in the complement. This is true of every sentence in which the complement of an AK predicate is in the subjunctive, whether the verb is one of mental act or of perception.

A pragmatic precondition must be met for a sentence like (21) to be appropriate, and it is that another speaker must have asserted pragmatically the proposition embodied in the complement or some semantic equivalent of it. For example, another speaker must have asserted, prior to the uttering of (21) by the speaker in question, that Oswald fired or that he pulled the trigger or that he used his rifle, etc. This precondition explains the behavior of certain negative particles in AK predicate sentences, which Rivero (1971) had noticed in another connection.

To begin with, even though the sentences in (22) are ungrammatical, those in (23) are not.

(22) { No me di cuenta / No vi } que { a. *pasaba nada / b. *entraba nadie } [Ind]. [Ind].

(23) { No me di cuenta / No vi } que { a. pasara nada / b. entrara nadie } [Subj]. [Subj].

{ "I didn't realize / "I didn't see } that { a. anything had happened." / b. anyone had gone in." }

The sentences in (22) are ungrammatical because in Spanish no negative particle other than *no* can be postverbal unless there is another negative particle in preverbal position. Thence, for instance, the relative grammaticality of the sentences in (24):

(24) a. *Dijo nada.
 b. Nunca dijo nada.
   "He never said anything."
 c. *Dijo nada nunca.
 d. No dijo nada nunca.
   "He didn't say anything ever."

But then, why are the sentences in (23) not ungrammatical? The answer is that there must be an abstract preverbal negative (neg.) particle in the underlying structure of the complements in (23) which allows for *nada* and *nadie* to appear postverbally. Moreover, I would like to suggest that this particle negates whatever appears on the surface as the complement. For example, in (23a) the semantic content of the underlying complement is "[neg.] Nothing happened"; this is equivalent to some positive proposition which "Nothing happened" would deny or negate. Such a proposition can have many forms, e.g. "something happened," "many things happened," "a few things happened" and, in general, "X happened" or some semantic equivalent of it – X being any situation. And it is this positive counterpart of the surface complement that the speaker denies having perceived.

To illustrate this analysis further, in (23b) the underlying representation of the complement *entrara nadie* is semantically the negation of "no one went in," which is equivalent to the positive statement that the speaker uses to deny perceiving or having perceived someone's entry which another speaker has previously asserted. Thus, for instance, *No vi que entrara nadie* "I didn't see anyone going in" can be the rejoinder to any of the sentences in (25):

(25) a. Entró el ejército entero.
  "The whole army went in."
 b. Entró alguien.
  "Someone went in."
 c. Entraron dos personas.
  "Two people went in."

My analysis provides a pragmatic explanation for a phenomenon noticed by Rivero (1971) regarding certain idiomatic expressions that are used only in negative sentences. One is *palabra de* "word of" and the other is *gota de* "drop of." Their use is illustrated in (26):

(26) a. No sabe palabra de francés.
  "He doesn't know a word of French."
 b. *Sabe palabra de francés.
 c. No bebió gota de vino.
  "He didn't drink a drop of wine."
 d. *Bebió gota de vino.

But, as Rivero notices, both sentences in (27) are ungrammatical:

(27) a. *No me di cuenta de que supiera palabra de francés.
  *No me di cuenta de que bebiera gota de vino.
  "I didn't realize that he knew a word of French/drank a drop of wine."

These sentences do not exist for the simple reason that (26b, d) do not exist, and no one could have asserted them. As positive statements they have no semantic interpretations and therefore no semantic equivalents.

7. A NOTE ON STYLE

AK complements in the subjunctive can be used ironically (facetiously, sarcastically) to hint that the speaker believes or actually has noticed that the situation described in the complement did not take place. For instance, if I ask a piano player to play a certain song for me and he fails to do so while I am present, I could say (28) to him:

(28) No noté/oi que tocara lo que le pedí.
  "I didn't notice/hear your playing what I asked you to [Subj]."

In (28) the speaker may be assuming a real or imaginary assertion made previously by the piano player to the effect that he would play the song in question.

8. INTERROGATION AND MOOD IN SPANISH AK PREDICATE SENTENCES

The ambiguity noticed by Kartunnen (1971) for complements of English semifactives in interrogative sentences does not exist in Spanish: if the complement is in the indicative, it is semantically presupposed, but if it is in the subjunctive, it is not presupposed at all. For instance, in (29) I am asking the hearer whether he noticed/saw what I have already noticed/seen, which I take to be true:

(29) ¿Notaste/viste que mi ponencia tenía muchos errores?
 "Did you notice/see that my paper had many errors [Ind]?"

(There is also of course the echoic sense in which I am asking the hearer to confirm what he said, with the question in (29) being somewhat equivalent to saying, "Did I hear you right? My paper did have many errors?") But in (30) I take no position regarding the truth of the complement:

(30) ¿Notaste/Viste que mi ponencia turiera muchos errores?
 "Did you notice/see if my paper had [Subj] many errors?"

As the English gloss indicates, with (30) I may be enquiring whether or not my paper has many errors. If it is an inquiry, it does not require any previous statement regarding the truth-value of the complement. In other senses it does; for instance, when it is a rhetorical reformulation of (31):

(31) No noté/vi que mi ponencia turviera muchos errores.
 "I didn't notice/see that my paper had many errors [Subj non-presupposed]."

In addition, (30) may be used ironically to imply that my paper really doesn't have that many errors.

If the interrogation is negated and the complement is in the indicative, the speaker's attitude toward the truth status of the complement remains constant. In (32) I still hold that my paper had many errors:

(32) ¿No notaste/No viste que mi ponencia tenía muchos errores?
 "Didn't you notice/see that my paper had many errors [Ind]?"

However, when the interrogation is negated and the complement is in the subjunctive, the speaker takes no position regarding the truth-value of the complement. Furthermore, such a syntactic combination appears only in sentences uttered to verify what one's interlocutor said, as the gloss in (33) indicates:

(33) ¿No notaste que mi ponencia tuviera muchos errores?
"You didn't notice that my paper had [Subj] many errors? (Is that what you said?)"

A sentence like (33) can only be a response to (34):

(34) No noté que tu ponencia tuviera muchos errores.
"I didn't notice that your paper had [Subj] many errors."

9. KNOWLEDGE PREDICATES

Knowledge predicates (henceforth K predicates) are those which express that the speaker knows or doesn't know the information contained in their complements, as in example (35).

(35) { Sé
      Me doy cuenta (de)
      Estoy consciente (de) }   que ella está muy deprimida.

{ "I know
  "I realize (I'm aware)
  "I am aware }   that she is very depressed."

Like AK predicates, K predicates in the indicative always presuppose their complements semantically. The test of negation cannot be applied in the present tense because, obviously, negated first-person singular present-tense cognitive predicates do not exist,[2] since they are contradictory, e.g. (36):

(36) *No sé que ella está deprimida.
    *"I don't know that she is depressed [presupposed]."

But such a test can be applied in the past tense:

(37) Sí/No sabía que ella estaba deprimida.
"I did/didn't know that she was depressed [presupposed]."

When the complement of a K predicate is in the indicative it may be either asserted or presupposed pragmatically, e.g.:

(38) (Said to an audience that is not aware of developments in pragmatics:)
Se sabe ahora que hay dos tipos de presuposiciones.
"It is now known that there are two types of presupposition [complement asserted pragmatically]."

When a complement of a K predicate is asserted pragmatically, the speaker's intention is of course to inform; when it is presupposed pragmatically the intention can be described as announcing that the information is not unshared.

As in the case of AK predicate sentences, there is no contrast in mood in the complement of an affirmative K predicate sentence: only the indicative occurs. In negation, however, the subjunctive occurs too, in which case the complement is no longer presupposed semantically, and the sentences have pragmatic characteristics identical to those of AK predicate sentences with subjunctive in their complements. For instance, in (39) I cast doubt on the likelihood of the bar being closed:

(39) No sé que el bar esté cerrado.
"I don't know that the bar is closed [Subj complement not presupposed]."

There is also an ironic or facetious use of these predicates, as in (40):

(40) No sabía que tocaras el piano tan bien.
"I didn't know that you played the piano so well [Subj complement not presupposed]."

This hints that, since the speaker was not aware before of the hearer's piano-playing expertise, the latter does not play the piano so well after all. In contrast, (41) praises the performer:

(41) No sabía que tocabas el piano tan bien.
"I didn't know that you played the piano so well [Ind complement presupposed]."

Parenthetically, the pragmatic function of (41) can be described as announcing that the information was unshared in the past but is no longer unshared.

In interrogation, too, the pragmatic characteristics of K predicate sentences are identical to those of AK predicate sentences, e.g. in (42a) the speaker informs of the complement and in (42b) inquires about it:

(42) ¿Sabes que { a. ha llegado Julio?
                 b. haya llegado Julio? }

"Do you know { a. that Julio has come? (For he has.)"
               b. that Julio has [Subj] come?
                  (Whether or not he has come.)" }

In general, in interrogative K predicate sentences, a complement in the subjunctive is never presupposed semantically whereas a complement in the indicative is always presupposed semantically and may be either asserted or presupposed pragmatically. In this they do not differ from interrogative AK predicate sentences. The similarities between K predicates and AK predicates regarding the mood of their complements is then quite obvious. Therefore, we can speak of a broader class of knowledge-and-acquisition-of-knowledge (henceforth KAK) predicates.

10. SUMMARY AND CONCLUSIONS

I have presented an analysis of mood selection in the complements of KAK predicates in Spanish. In my description I have distinguished – as many do – between two types of presupposition: semantic, which is independent of speaker and hearer relationships; and pragmatic, which is equivalent to an assumption on the part of the speaker that the information in the sentential complement is shared by the hearer. Following Kempson (1975) I have remarked that it is pragmatic presupposition that is mutually exclusive with assertion, which in turn is equivalent to an assumption on the part of the speaker that the information is not shared and has to be offered to the hearer. In KAK predicates mood selection is not for distinguishing between pragmatic presupposition and assertion but between semantic presupposition and non-presupposition. I have attempted to show that my analysis provides a pragmatic explanation for certain phenomena in the syntax of Spanish negation.

In conclusion I would like to point out with Rivero (1971) that in Spanish there are no invariable correlations between semantic notions like presupposition and the use of one or the other mood. The complements of certain predicates are semantically presupposed even though the verb is in the subjunctive,[3] as in (43):

(43) Siento que se haya muerto tan joven.
 "I am sorry he died so young [Subj]."

It of course meets the test of negation.

It should be clear then that if our interest is to correlate mood choice both with meaning and with sentence use, we should analyze separately the different types of matrices that take sentential complements.

NOTES

1 This chapter is a revised version of Guitart (1980). I thank Mireya Camurati and Pablo Golibart for complementing my intuition with theirs. All errors are mine.
2 Unless they are in the historical present.
3 A few years ago I conducted an empirical investigation on the use of subjunctive and indicative in the complements of so-called emotive verbs. As part of one experiment (see Guitart 1982) I gave native speakers the context: *Una cosa que me molestaba de niño era que* "One thing that bothered me as a child was that" and asked them to fill it out with what they would tell a biographer who did not know them personally. Both the subjunctive and the indicative occurred. Results suggest that the following correlation might be posited: the indicative is used when the speaker assumes that the information in the complement would be new to the hearer (and thus unexpected), and the subjunctive when in the speaker's estimation the information would be old to the hearer or expected though new. In another experiment (Guitart 1987) the informants were asked to complete two imaginary dialogues between man and wife. In the first dialogue they were asked to fill in which of two previously identified situations the wife would say had bothered her the most (old information in the complement); in the second dialogue they were asked to fill in what the wife would say when informing her husband of a situation unknown to him which had bothered her (new information in the complement). A strong correlation was found among educated speakers between old information and subjunctive/new information and indicative. The results must be taken with caution since the number of informants was small (N = 18 for the largest dialect group tested).

REFERENCES

Fillmore, C.J. (1971) "Verbs of judging: an exercise in semantic descriptions," in C.J. Fillmore and D.T. Langendoen (eds) *Studies in Linguistic Semantics*, New York: Holt, Rinehart & Winston, Inc.
Fillmore, C.J. and Langendoen, D.T. (1971) *Studies in Linguistic Semantics*, New York: Holt, Rinehart & Winston, Inc.
Guitart, J.M. (1980) "On the pragmatics of Spanish mood in so-called semifactive predicates," in Frank H. Nuessel, Jr (ed.) *Contemporary Studies in romance Languages*, Bloomington: Indiana University Linguistics Club.
—— (1982) "On the use of the Spanish subjunctive among Spanish-English bilinguals," *Word* 33: 59–67.
—— (1987) "Sobre el uso del subjuntivo español en dos dialectos caribeños," *Thesaurus* 62: 141–8.
Hooper, J.B. (1974) "On assertive predicates," mimeo, Indiana University Linguistics Club.
Hooper, J.B. and Thompson, S.A. (1973) "On the applicability of root transformations," *Linguistic Inquiry* 4: 465–98.
Kartunnen, L. (1971) "Some observations on factivity," *Papers in Linguistics* 4: 55–69.

—— (1973) "Presuppositions of compound sentences," *Linguistic Inquiry* 4: 169–93.
Keenan, E.L. (1971) "Two kinds of presupposition in natural language," in C.J. Fillmore and D.T. Langendoen (eds) *Studies in Linguistic Semantics*, New York: Holt, Rinehart & Winston, Inc.
Kempson, R.M. (1975) *Presupposition and the Delimitation of Semantics*, London and New York: Cambridge University Press.
Kiparsky, P. and Kiparsky, C. (1970) "Fact," in M. Bierswich and K.E. Heidolph (eds) *Progress in Linguistics*, The Hague: Mouton.
Klein, P.W. (1977) "Semantic factors in Spanish mood," *Glossa* 11: 3–19.
Rivero, M.L. (1971) "Mood and presupposition in Spanish," *Foundations of Language* 7: 305–36.
Terrell, T. (1976) "Assertion and presupposition in Spanish," in M. Lujan and F. Hensey (eds) *Current Studies in Romance Linguistics*, Washington, DC: Georgetown University Press.
Terrell, T. and Hooper, J.B. (1974) "A semantically based analysis of mood in Spanish," *Hispania* 57: 484–94.

10 Verbs of cognition in spoken Spanish: a discourse profile[1]

Elizabeth G. Weber and Paola Bentivoglio

1. INTRODUCTION

In this chapter we will present a discourse profile of two verbs of cognition: *creer* "believe" and *pensar* "think." In addition to these, the class of "think" type verbs includes *saber* "know," *entender* "understand," *esperar* "hope," *imaginar* "imagine," *suponer* "suppose," etc.

Justification of this class of verbs rests on semantic grounds. Verbs of cognition all refer to mental activities or cognitive states. They have been called private verbs because they refer to activities available for perception by the speaker only (Palmer 1965).

The syntactic properties characteristic of this verb class will be related to the syntagmatic patterns which are associated with these verbs in discourse. The factors we will examine include transitive vs. intransitive clauses, complement types, tense and aspect, lexical choice, relative order of matrix and subordinate clauses, and intonation contours. This approach is motivated by the idea that some kind of explanation for the emergence of grammar – or syntactic types – might be forthcoming if the demands which discourse use places on verbs can be shown (Du Bois 1985, 1987a, 1987b). In the following section, we will discuss the relation between discourse and grammar.

2. DISCOURSE AND GRAMMAR

The emergence of syntactic types has often been discussed with regard to lexical elements (Givón 1979b: 82–97). This view of grammaticization focuses on the change which a linguistic unit can undergo from a lexical role to a grammatical role (cf. Meillet 1912: 13; Kuryłowicz 1965: 52). Some of the processes of grammaticization involving lexical elements have been the development of relative pronouns (Justus 1976a, 1976b; Langdon 1977; Sankoff and Brown 1976), tense-aspect markers (Hopper 1979a, 1979b), and genitive particles (Givón 1976). Grammaticization processes involving clauses rather than lexical elements have also been discussed. Givón (1979b: 95) cites the development of, on the one hand, subordinate structures from conjoined clauses and, on the other hand, serial verb constructions of several clauses into a single syntactic unit under one intonational contour (cf. Stahlke 1970; Hyman 1971; Li and Thompson 1973a, 1973b; Lord 1973).

There is another approach to grammaticization, however, one in which linearized text is seen as acting as a filter between semantic types and syntactic types (Du Bois 1985). According to this view, grammaticization is conceptualized as a process whereby language (*langue*) is created or shaped from its source material, discourse (*parole*). Discourse becomes "the pattern model for grammar" (Du Bois forthcoming). Benveniste articulated this view of grammaticization in his dictum: "Nihil est in *lingua* quod non prius fuerit in *oratione*" (1966: 3, cited in Laberge and Sankoff 1979: 419). In other words, syntactic types are motivated by the patterns of the token aggregate, i.e. *parole*. Du Bois (forthcoming) articulates this view of the relation between discourse and grammar as follows.

> Once we see that the grammaticization of new structure *depends* on variability, it becomes clear that this need cannot be fully satisfied by the lexicon, which after all is a collection of types in language. In speaking, new combinations are produced (as tokens) in variable profusion. But this variability is ordered, in accordance with the general consistency of speakers' goals, plus the requirements of the current language system.... Since the production of discourse is driven by speaker goals, the new patterns are suffused with functional implications from the outset.... Discourse is thus capable of providing patterns already imbued with functional significance as models for potential grammar.

It is this view of grammaticization which motivates the use of discourse profiles. Since discourse is motivated by speakers' goals, the syntactic patterns which emerge from an examination of tokens found in discourse are explainable in terms of the uses of these tokens. Discourse use involves factors of both information flow and interactional goals.

3. DATA

The data[2] upon which this chapter is based are drawn from a corpus of Venezuelan spoken Spanish collected from twenty-four speakers from three socio-economic levels – twelve men and twelve women between the ages of 30 and 45. The data were collected in 1977 by two interviewers in a situation designed to obtain samples of "careful" speech (Labov 1972: 79–109).

4. TRANSITIVE VS. INTRANSITIVE FORMS

Verbs were classified as transitive or intransitive. If the cognitive verb takes a second argument which is a lexical (vs. sentential) direct object, it was classified as transitive, regardless of whether the object follows or precedes the cognitive verb. Examples (1) and (2) were both classified as transitive clauses.

(1) Ellas creen eso.... (20725.77: 18)[3]
    "They do believe that...."
(2) Eso $\emptyset_i$ lo pienso, cuando $\emptyset_i$ estoy en el carro. (20725.77: 11)
    "I think about it when I'm in the car."

If the cognitive verb is followed by a sentential complement, it was also classified as transitive. Sentential complements include finite verbs (as in (3)) and non-finite verbs, i.e. infinitives (as in (4)).

(3) Yo creo que la gente maneja mal. (20725.77: 5)
    "I believe that people drive badly."
(4) $\emptyset$ pensé hasta ofrecer dinero a todo el mundo. (21925.77: 14)
    "I thought of offering money to everybody."

The following example is the single case in the data in which a sentential complement clause marked by a conjunction precedes the verb of cognition clause. This case was also classified as transitive.

(5) Que se podría planificar mejor [el tráfico en Caracas] crees tú.
    (20725.77: 4)
    "That traffic in Caracas could be planned better is what you think."

If the cognitive verb takes an oblique or takes no direct argument, it was classified as intransitive, as in examples (6) and (7).

(6) $\emptyset$ no piensan en los demás.... (21014.77: 7)
    "They don't think about others...."
(7) *Interviewer.*   ¿Y con eso le rinde para treinta personas?
    (21114.77:4)
    "And with that would you have enough for thirty persons?"
    Speaker.   Yo creo....
    "I believe so...."

If the cognitive verb is preceded by a sentential clause with which it is interpretively associated, it was also coded as intransitive, as in

(8) Debe ser que yo soy burguesa... a lo mejor, Ø creo....
(22725.77: 24)
"Maybe I am bourgeois...."

The intransitive form of *creer* is functioning as a hedge on the immediately prior clause. It serves to limit the speaker's responsibility for the truth of the previous statement.

Table 10.1 exhibits the distribution of verbs in the data according to the classification transitive vs. intransitive. Three utterances with the verb *pensar* were aborted and could not be classified.

Table 10.1 Transitive vs. intransitive clauses

	Creer	Pensar	%
Transitive	159	72	87
Intransitive	18	13	12
Aborted	0	3	1
Total	177	88	100

Table 10.1 shows that fully 87 per cent of cognitive verbs appear as transitives, i.e. they take a direct lexical object or are followed by a sentential or infinitival complement (with the exception of example (5), in which the complement precedes the verb of cognition clause). The *Diccionario de la lengua española* of the Real Academia Española lists only transitive meanings for *creer* and *pensar*. The data confirm that these verbs are most frequently used as transitives, though intransitive uses do occur.

4.1. Transitive verbs

Table 10.2 shows the distribution of sentential complements (with

Table 10.2 Complements of transitive clauses

	Creer	Pensar	%
Sentential	153	51	88
Non-sentential	6	21	12
Total	159	72	100

finite verbs and infinitives) vs. non-sentential complements among the transitive clauses in the data.

Sentential clauses (with finite verbs and infinitives) account for 88 per cent of transitive complements. *This distribution demonstrates that verbs of cognition serve to report complex chunks of information which the speaker holds, with more or less conviction, to be factual.* Non-sentential objects constitute 12 per cent of all transitive complements.

Table 10.3 shows the distribution of sentential complements with regard to verb form. Sentential complements with finite verbs are classified according to their introductory element, e.g. *que*, an interrogative or conjunction, or lo *que* as a marker of a pseudo-cleft.

Table 10.3 Complement types of sentential transitive complements

	Creer	Pensar	%
Finite verb clauses			
Que-S	146	41	92
Ø-S	2	3	2.5
Interrogative element	0	2	1
Pseudo-cleft	1	0	0.5
Non-finite verb clauses			
Infinitive	3	4	3
Ø verb	1	1	1
Total	153	51	100

4.2. Finite verb clauses

Table 10.3 shows that fully 96 per cent of all sentential clauses are realized by finite verbs. Hadlich (1971) states that *creer* prefers finite verb constructions to those constructed with an infinitive. Our data support this observation. The conjunction *que* is used by speakers to introduce 92 per cent of all sentential complements which appear with *creer* and *pensar*. Example (9) is the most frequent complement type found in the data: *que* + a finite clause.

(9) pero sí Ø pienso que todas las personas de un signo tienen afinidad.... (21925.77: 10)
"But yes I think that everybody with the same sign has some affinity...."

4.3. Infinitive verb clauses

Example (10) is a case of a cognitive verb followed by an infinitive clause.

(10) Bueno, yo$_i$ más o menos creo Ø$_i$ interpretar tu pregunta acerca del libro.... (23013.77: 12)
"Well, I more or less think I understand your question about the book...."

Aguilar (1981: 185) states that *creer* can take an infinitive complement if the subjects of the two clauses are co-referential. The variation between complement clauses with finite verbs vs. infinitives will be discussed below in section 10 with reference to the appearance of coreferential subjects in the matrix and complement clauses.

4.4. No verb clauses

Example (11) is a case in which the complement clause has no verb; *que* is followed by an adverb.

(11) Yo creo que sí. (21623.77: 18)
"I believe so."

This form is possible with other adverbs, e.g. *no* "no."

We have seen in Table 10.2 that *creer* and *pensar* take non-sentential complements 12 per cent of the time. Table 10.4 shows the distribution of these complements.

Table 10.4 Complement types of non-sentential transitive complements

	Creer	Pensar	%
Clitic	3	5	29
Eso	1	3	15
Demonstrative pro + clitic	0	4	15
Lo que	2	2	15
Lexical NP	0	7	26
Total	6	21	100

While both *creer* and *pensar* take non-sentential complements, they do so with an interesting difference in frequency (cf. Table 10.2). *Creer* takes non-sentential objects in 4 per cent of all cases (6/159), while *pensar* takes non-sentential objects in 29 per cent of all cases (21/72). This distributional difference will be discussed below in section 8 with reference to information flow in discourse.

4.5. Intransitive verbs

Only 12 per cent of verbs of cognition appear as intransitives, i.e. without a direct object (cf. Table 10.1). Both *creer* and *pensar* appear in the data with the oblique prepositional phrase *en* + noun phrase (NP), as exemplified in (12) and (13).

(12) pero yo no creo en ese tipo de congreso.... (20515.77: 5)
  "But I don't believe in this type of congress...."
(13) Uno$_i$ cuando Ø$_i$ va a cruzar, Ø$_i$ no piensa en las motos, Ø$_i$ piensa en los carros.... (20725.77: 9)
  "When crossing (at a light) one doesn't think of motor cycles but of cars...."

In these cases, the verb may be lexicalized as verb + *en*, even as the English verb *think of/about* can be considered a single lexical unit.

Some intransitive forms have transitive meanings which apply to a previously mentioned clause interpreted as the complement. When the cognitive verb is preceded by a sentential clause with which it is interpretively associated, it functions as a hedge, as in example (8), repeated here as (14), and as in (15).

(14) Debe ser que yo soy burguesa... a lo mejor, Ø creo. (22725.77: 24)
  "Maybe I am bourgeois...."
(15) Ø se reparten algo más, creo yo.... (21014.77: 11)
  "They share something more, I believe...."

In the following example, the speaker closes his remarks by expressing the fact that everything he has previously said on the topic was his opinion, and requests the interviewer's agreement.

(16) ...yo pienso así ¿no? (20314.77: 7)
  "...I think so, don't you agree?"

5. SUBJECTS

The distribution of subject types in the data clearly reflects the demands that these verbs place on their subjects, viz. that the speaker must have access to the mental state to which the verb refers. Thus, there is a preponderance of first-person subjects.[4] Given this condition of access to a mental state which these verbs impose on their subjects, it is also possible to question someone about their cognitive state. While speakers do report third persons' mental states, they tend to do so far less frequently than they report their own mental states. Table 10.5 shows the distribution of subjects by person.

Table 10.5 Subject distribution by person

	Creer	Pensar	%
First person	143	66	79
Second person	15	3	7
Third person	19	19	14
Total	177	88	100

Table 10.5 shows that first-person subjects constitute 79 per cent of the data. Second-person subjects constitute 7 per cent of the data. One-half of these utterances are questions. Third-person subjects constitute 14 per cent of the data. Not all of these utterances are cases in which a third person's mental state is being reported. Impersonal subjects constitute 18 per cent of all third-person subjects (7/38). The remaining twenty-eight cognitive verbs with third-person subjects function simply to report a mental state. In summary, people do not tend to talk about what others (non-participants in the speech situation) feel, think, and know. First- and second-person subjects combined account for 86 per cent of the subjects in the data.

6. TENSE/ASPECT

Cognitive verbs tend to be simple present-tense forms. Table 10.6 shows the distribution of the verbs in the corpus by tense and progressive vs. non-progressive form.

Table 10.6 Distribution of verbs by tense and progressive vs. non-progressive form

	Creer	Pensar	%
Simple present	166	58	84
Present perfect	0	6	2
Other present tenses (subjunctives, infinitives)	4	6	4
Present progressive	0	0	0
Present perfect progressive	0	1	0.3
Non-present non-progressive	7	16	9
Non-present progressive	0	1	0.3
Total	177	88	100

As it illustrates, 84 per cent of all cognitive verbs are in the simple present tense. Present perfect forms constitute 2 per cent of the data, and other non-indicative present tense forms appear in 4 per cent of all cases. There is one instance of a present perfect progressive form, constituting 0.3 per cent of all cases. Among non-present forms, non-progressives constitute 9 per cent of all instances in the data, while there is one progressive form constituting 0.3 per cent of all cases. Cognitive verbs, then, frequently appear in the simple present tense and are rarely progressive. This distribution is explicable in terms of the semantic meanings which the cognitive verbs in the data realize.[5] All instances of *creer*, and most instances of *pensar*, realize a stative meaning, i.e. they refer to a mental state which is undifferentiated and lacking in any defined limits. The two progressive cases of *pensar* realize an activity meaning, i.e. they refer to a continuing though bounded activity (Leech 1971: 19). The interpretation of a stative meaning is incompatible with a progressive form. The distribution of tense and aspect exhibited in Table 10.6 shows that cognitive verbs overwhelmingly realize stative meanings, i.e. they report unobservable mental states.

7. LEXICAL MEANING

Speakers have a choice between the verbs *creer* and *pensar* when they want to communicate opinions without taking full responsibility for the truth of those opinions. These verbs may be contrasted with the verb *saber* "I know" which commits the speaker to the truth of the information reported. The data show 177 instances of *creer* and 88 instances of *pensar*. Thus *creer* appears twice as often in the data as *pensar*. These verbs, when used in discourse, are not always interchangeable. A range of meanings for *creer* and *pensar* appear in the data, though they are not all listed in the *Diccionario de la Real Academia*. The following meanings are interpretable for the forms of *creer* and *pensar* which appear in the data.

Creer	*Pensar*
1. to hold in one's opinion	1. to hold in one's opinion
2. to expect	2. to expect
3.	3. to have an intent, intend
4.	4. to bring to mind, to recollect
5.	5. to muse, meditate, weigh mentally
6.	6. to have regard for
7.	7. to bring the intellectual faculties into play
8. to take as true	8.
9. to have trust or confidence	9.

Verbs of cognition in spoken Spanish 203

Both *creer* and *pensar* can mean "to hold in one's opinion" and "to expect." *Creer* appears in the data with two additional meanings, while *pensar* appears with five additional meanings. An examination of the data reveals that the nine meanings interpretable for *creer* and *pensar* show different correlations with subject person and number, verb mood and tense, and transitive and intransitive usage. There are twenty-four utterances with *creer* which were aborted by the speaker before their meaning was clear. These tokens were classified as unknown. There are 153 cases of *creer* whose meaning could be determined.

Table 10.7 shows the distribution of person and number of the subject, tense, and form for tokens of *creer* which have the meaning "to hold in one's opinion." Tokens with this meaning constitute 87 per cent (133/153) of all appearances of *creer* whose meaning could be classified.

Table 10.7 Creer, meaning 1: "to hold in one's opinion"

Subject	1st person	87%	Other	13%
Mood/tense	Ind Pr	92%	Other	8%
Transitive/intransitive	Transitive	90%	Intransitive	10%
Transitive complement	Finite sentential	96%	Infinitive	1.5%
			Lexical NP	3.5%

This meaning of *creer* appears most frequently in discourse. It appears overwhelmingly (1) with first-person singular subjects; (2) in the indicative present tense; and (3) with a finite sentential complement introduced by *que*. Among all tokens of *creer*, these three syntactic variables co-occur in 108 instances. Among these 108 tokens, there are nineteen cases in which the utterance is aborted by the speaker at some point after the *que*; the meaning of these aborted utterances could not be classified. In eighty-seven cases, *creer* has the first meaning "to hold in one's opinion." In the two remaining cases, *creer* has the second meaning "to expect." No tokens of *creer* with meaning 8 or meaning 9 follow this pattern. Tokens which realize this dominant pattern constitute 61 per cent of all occurrences of *creer* and 71 per cent of all sentential transitive occurrences. Those tokens of *creer* which differ from this dominant pattern stand out from the statistical norm.

Table 10.8 shows the distribution of person and number of the subject, tense, and form for tokens of *pensar* which have the meaning "to hold in one's opinion." There are ten cases of *pensar* whose meaning was classified as unknown; seventy-eight tokens were classified as to meaning. Tokens of *pensar* with this meaning constitute 59 per cent of all appearances of *pensar* whose meanings could be classified.

Table 10.8 *Pensar*, meaning 1: "to hold in one's opinion"

Subject	1st person sg.	85%	Other	15%
Mood/tense	Ind Pr	80%	Other	20%
Transitive/intransitive	Transitive	93%	Intransitive	7%
Transitive complement	Finite sentential	81%	Infinitive	0
			Lexical NP	19%

As in the case of *creer*, the first meaning of *pensar* appears most frequently in the data. When it has this meaning, *pensar* appears overwhelmingly: (1) with first person singular subjects; (2) in the indicative present tense; and (3) with a finite sentential complement introduced by *que*. Among all tokens of *pensar*, these three syntactic variables co-occur in twenty-seven instances. Among these are four cases in which the utterance was aborted by the speaker at some point after the *que*; the meaning of these aborted utterances could not be classified. In twenty-three cases, *pensar* had the first meaning "to hold in one's opinion." No tokens of *pensar* with any other meaning follow this pattern. Tokens which realize this dominant pattern constitute 31 per cent of all occurrences of *pensar* and 53 per cent of all sentential transitive occurrences. *Pensar* with the first meaning takes a lexical NP object 19 per cent of the time in contrast to *creer* with this meaning, which takes a lexical NP object only 3 per cent of the time. This difference will be discussed further in section 8 below.

Pensar with the fifth meaning "to muse, meditate, or weigh mentally" is more frequent than any meaning other than the first. It differs in its syntactic form from the first meaning of *pensar* in that it tends to take lexical objects rather than sentential complements. These objects are clitics, pronouns, or both. Rather than being used predominantly to report complex chunks of new information, then, utterances with this meaning of *pensar* refer to information already discussed in the discourse.

Tables 10.9 and 10.10 summarize the form-meaning correlations for *creer* and *pensar*.

Table 10.9 Creer: distribution by form vs. meaning

Meaning	1	2	8	9	Total	%
Trans + complement						
finite verb	115	8	4	1	128	84
infinitive	2	0	0	0	2	1
lexical NP	3	0	3	0	6	4
Intransitive						
+ en	0	0	0	4	4	3
bare	13	0	0	0	13	9
Total	133	8	7	5	153	100
%	87	5	5	3		100

Table 10.10 Pensar: distribution by form vs. meaning

Meaning	1	2	3	4	5	6	7	Total	%
Trans + complement									
finite verb	35	1	0	0	5	0	0	41	53
infinitive	0	1	3	0	0	0	0	4	5
lexical NP	8	1	0	0	9	0	2	20	26
Intransitive									
+ en	0	0	0	0	2	3	0	5	6
bare	3	0	1	1	0	0	3	8	10
Total	46	3	4	1	16	3	5	78	100
%	59	4	5	1	21	4	6		100

An examination of the distribution of person and number of the subject, tense, syntactic form, and meaning for tokens of *creer* and *pensar* reveal a dominant pattern of first-person singular present indicative verbs which take a *que* complement. This distribution is explained by the following facts: (1) the speaker must have access to the mental state of the subject of the verb, thus the first-person singular subject; (2) the speaker is reporting an unobservable mental state, thus, the indicative present tense; and (3) the speaker uses this verb to introduce complex chunks of information, thus the *que* clause.

8. SENTENTIAL AND LEXICAL COMPLEMENTS AND INFORMATION FLOW IN DISCOURSE

We have seen in Table 10.2 above that 88 per cent of transitive verbs of cognition take sentential complements, i.e. they report complex chunks of information. The remaining 12 per cent take lexical objects which are predominantly clitics, pronouns, both clitics and pronouns, and empty lexical nouns, e.g. *lo mismo* "the same thing," *tal cosa* "such things," *las cosas* "things." The nouns, as well as the clitics and pronouns, refer to complex chunks of information which have been previously mentioned in the discourse. Although both *pensar* and *creer* are used predominantly to introduce new complex information into the discourse, *pensar* is used over one-quarter of the time to refer to previously mentioned information in order to confirm or agree with it, or to disagree with it. Most cases of these clauses with lexical objects are affirmative and confirming.

9. RELATION OF COGNITIVE VERB CLAUSE TO ASSOCIATED CLAUSES

The possible syntactic relations of a cognitive verb clause to its sentential complement or another sentential clause interpreted as its complement are (i) before it; (ii) after it; or (iii) embedded within it. Only those tokens whose meaning could be determined were considered. Table 10.11 shows the relative order of the cognitive verb clause to its sentential object or interpreted complement.

Table 10.11 Relative order of verb of cognition clause to complement clause

	Creer	Pensar	%
Before	128	45	92
Embedded	1	2	2
After	11	1	6
Total	140	48	100

It shows that 92 per cent of all cognitive verbs precede their sentential objects. None of these cognitive verbs is stressed. They are bound to their complement clauses under a single intonation contour. We have found no cases in which the cognitive verb and its sentential complement have separate intonation contours.

Of these remaining verbs, 6 per cent follow their interpretable sentential complements. These cognitive verb clauses serve as hedges on the preceding statements. The verb and its complement have separate intonation contours and are separated by a pause. This is similar to their use in English (cf. Weber forthcoming). Another 1 per cent of cognitive verb clauses are embedded within their interpretable sentential complements.

Transitive cognitive verbs that take sentential complements are both unstressed and tightly bound to their complements under a single intonation contour. In discourse, we communicate opinions constantly. Speakers are not willing to take full responsibility for the truth of many of these opinions. In these cases, they can mark their opinions with the verbs *creer* or *pensar*. This usage is realized by a cognitive verb clause that has lost its stress and is bound to its complement under one intonation contour (cf. Thompson and Mulac forthcoming).

10. SUBJECTS OF COMPLEMENT CLAUSES

We have seen in Table 10.3 that infinitive clauses constitute only 3 per cent of all complement clauses. This distribution raises the question as to why infinitive complements are so infrequent. Infinitives may only appear in complement clauses when the subject of the complement clause is the same as the subject of the verb of cognition clause. Table 10.12 shows the distribution of coreferential vs. non-coreferential complement subjects with regard to the subject of the verb of cognition clause.

Table 10.12 Coreferential vs. non-coreferential complement subjects

	Creer %	Pensar %	Creer + Pensar %
Coreferential subjects	18	15	17
Non-coreferential subjects	82	85	83

It shows that fully 83 per cent of complement clause subjects are non-coreferential with the subject of the verb of cognition clause. The choice of an infinitive vs. a finite verb clause in this syntactic environment is eliminated. The speaker has the choice between an infinitive and a finite verb clause in only those 17 per cent of sentential complements in which the complement clause subject is coreferential with the subject of the verb of cognition clause. Table 10.13 shows the distribution of finite verbs and infinitives in complement clauses which have the same subject as the verb of cognition, i.e. those cases in which the syntax allows an infinitive.

Table 10.13 Finite verbs vs. infinitives in coreferential subject complement clauses

	Creer	%	Pensar	%
Finite verbs	20	87	3	43
Infinitives	3	13	4	57

This table shows that even when the syntax permits the appearance of an infinitive, speakers overwhelmingly use finite verbs with *creer*. With *pensar*, infinitives appear more frequently than finite verbs. Our data suggest that finite verb complements are grammaticizing in the complement clauses of *creer* which have subjects coreferential with the subject of *creer*. The same observation cannot be made for *pensar*. Because of the relatively small number of cases of coreferential subjects in the data, these observations should be considered preliminary. An examination of a greater number of cases of *pensar* with coreferential subjects is necessary in order to confirm these initial results. The variation between finite verbs vs. infinitives in the complement clauses of other verb classes is a subject for further research.

11. SUMMARY OF RESULTS

This discourse profile has revealed two syntactic types:

(1) the verb of cognition and the complement clause are tightly bound together under a single intonation contour for both *creer* and *pensar*;
(2) for *creer*, there is minimal variation between finite verbs and infinitives in those complement clauses which have a subject coreferential with the subject of *creer*; finite verbs constitute the dominant syntactic pattern.

Verbs of cognition appear overwhelmingly with sentential complements, i.e. they are used in discourse to introduce complex chunks of information. The cognitive verb clause has lost its stress and is bound to its complement under one intonation contour. The verb of cognition clause and the complement clause, united under a single intonation contour, constitute a syntactic type which has emerged from uses of these verbs in discourse.

The complement clauses of verbs of cognition are overwhelmingly realized by finite verbs rather than infinitives. The possibility of speaker choice between finite verbs and infinitives occurs in those cases in which the subject of the verb of cognition clause is coreferential with the subject of the complement clause. As we have also seen, the subject of the verb of cognition is overwhelmingly a first person subject. Since these verbs are used by speakers to code complex chunks of information about the world, the subject of the complement clause is overwhelmingly a third person subject. Thus, the syntactic environment which allows infinitives is limited by the discourse use of verbs of cognition.

Although the syntactic environment which allows the choice of an infinitive occurs with equal frequency for tokens of *creer* and *pensar*, our results show a difference between these verbs with regard to the distribution of finite verbs in complement clauses. In those environments in which it is possible to have an infinitive, *pensar* takes finite verbs less than half the time, while *creer* overwhelmingly takes finite verbs. Finite verbs in complement clauses of *creer* constitute a syntactic type. The explanation for the emergence of this type is based on the frequent use of *creer* in discourse to code information as an opinion held by the speaker. Tokens with the statistically most frequent discourse profile (1st person Pr tense + *que* clause realizing the meaning "to hold in one's opinion") constitute 61 per cent of all tokens of *creer* and 71 per cent of all sentential transitive tokens of *creer*. This syntactic association of *creer* and a finite verb complement generalizes to most cases where speakers, in fact, have a choice between a finite verb and an infinitive. Even in the 18 per cent of syntactic environments in which an infinitive is permitted, 43 per cent of tokens fit the most frequent discourse profile. Among the 57 per cent which do not exhibit the statistically most frequent discourse profile, finite verbs appear in 77 per cent of the cases.

Tokens of *pensar* with the statistically most frequent discourse profile (1st person Pr tense + *que* clause realizing the meaning "to hold in one's opinion") constitute 31 per cent of all tokens of *pensar* and 53 per cent of all sentential transitive tokens of *pensar*. Among those tokens which have coreferential subjects, only a single case (14 per cent) exhibits the statistically most frequent discourse profile; in this case, however, the utterance was aborted after the finite verb was produced. Among tokens which have coreferential subjects, 86 per cent do not exhibit the statistically most frequent discourse profile; among these, finite verbs appear in 33 per cent of the cases, infinitives in 67 per cent. None of these realizes the meaning "to hold in one's opinion." On the basis of so few tokens of *pensar* with infinitives, it is not clear what discourse factors are involved in the variation between finite verbs and infinitives in complement clauses. The meaning of the verb, however, appears to be a relevant factor.

12. CONCLUSION

Discourse profiles, as complexes of semantic, morphological, pragmatic, and intonational categories, illuminate the relation between discourse and grammar by showing the interaction between syntactic types and their discourse uses. A discourse profile provides an important means of uncovering both instances of grammaticization, or syntactic patterns, and the discourse uses motivating these syntactic patterns. From the perspective of those linguists who "view grammar as the name for a vaguely defined set of sedimented (i.e. grammaticized) recurrent partials whose status is constantly being renegotiated in speech and which cannot be distinguished *in principle* from strategies for building discourses" (Hopper 1988: 104), discourse profiles are "a most powerful tool for understanding why languages are the way they are" (Du Bois forthcoming).

From the perspective of those linguists who assume that syntactic structure constitutes an autonomous structural level of language, an examination of the interaction between syntactic patterns and discourse uses is theoretically relevant in so far as it serves to distinguish autonomous aspects of syntactic structure from those aspects which are the result of the way speakers use verbs in discourse. Such a distinction is extremely important for formal theoretical linguistics (García 1979: 25). Formal linguistics is the study of language structure conceived as a tool in the service of meaning and communication (García 1976, 1977). But only the structure of the tool, not the use to which the tool is put, is taken as the proper domain of linguistic study. The structure of the tool, i.e. syntactic structure, is thought to reveal the structure of the human mind. If, however, certain regularities of syntactic structure are consequences of the uses to which elements of language are put, those regularities of syntax cannot be considered autonomous or independent of anything else, as García (1979: 25) notes:

> It is indeed self-evident that if the regularities are to constitute bona fide linguistic constraints on speakers' behavior they must perforce be *ARBITRARY*, that is, they cannot follow from anything else. If the regularities did follow from something else ... they would not deserve independent description. It cannot be stressed too much that something cannot simultaneously be "independent" and "the result of larger considerations." However, if it should turn out that com-

municative considerations *DO* play a role in explaining certain facts of distribution, and we ignore them, then we clearly run the risk of postulating as independent, arbitrary facts of language structure to which a speaker must conform merely the consequences of other facts (of a communicative nature) that we have not bothered to explore.

In short, when speakers' use of language in discourse results in the creation of syntactic structure itself, those aspects of structure cannot be considered autonomous or independent.

NOTES

1 This chapter is the result of a larger ongoing project on English discourse, which is investigating the discourse bases of grammatical phenomena. The project was conceived and is being directed by Jack Du Bois, and we are indebted to him for clarifying both the methodological and theoretical concepts involved. We thank Sandy Thompson both for her helpful comments and for her most insightful discussions with us concerning the emergence of grammar from discourse. We also thank Suzanne Fleischman, Linda Waugh, Marian Shapley, and Carmen Silva-Corvalán for their comments.
2 We are indebted to Cleris Molaré of la Escuela de Letras de la UCV for her help in the preparation and organization of the data base.
3 The data are coded by six categories as follows: 2 = age group (30–45 years); 07 = speaker's code (01–36); 2 = sex: female (1 = male); 5 = social level: middle (3 = high; 4 = low); 77 = year of data collection; 3 = page number.
4 The presence or absence of the pronoun appears to be related to word order factors (cf. Bentivoglio 1980, 1987).
5 We are indebted to Suzanne Fleischman for suggesting this explanation.

REFERENCES

Aguilar, R.C. (1981) *Estructuras sintácticas transitivas en el español actual*, Madrid: Gredos.
Bentivoglio, P. (1980) "Why *canto* and not *yo canto*? The problem of first-person subject pronoun in spoken Venezuelan Spanish," MA thesis, University of California, Los Angeles.
—— (1987) *Los sujetos pronominales de primera persona en el habla de Caracas*, Caracas: Universidad Central de Venezuela.
Benveniste, Emile (1966) *Problèmes de linguistique générale*, vol. 1, Paris: Gallimard.
Chafe, W. (1982) "Integration and involvement in speaking, writing, and oral literature," in D. Tannen (ed.) *Spoken and Written Language: Exploring Orality and Literacy*, Norwood NJ: Ablex Publishing Corp.
Du Bois, J. (1985) "Competing motivations," in J. Haiman (ed.) *Iconicity in Syntax*, Amsterdam: Benjamins.

—— (1987a) "Absolutive zero: paradigm adaptivity in Sacapultec Maya," *Lingua* 71: 203–22. (Repr. in R.M.W. Dixon (ed.) *Studies in Ergativity*, Amsterdam: North Holland.)
—— (1987b) "The discourse basis of ergativity," *Language* 63: 805–55.
—— (forthcoming) "Discourse as pattern model for grammar: the possessor =ergator affiliation," in B. Heine and E. Traugott (eds) *Grammaticization*, Amsterdam and Philadelphia: John Benjamins.
García, E. (1976) "The generative approach to the Spanish reflexive," *Romance Philology* 30: 361–89.
—— (1977) "On the practical consequences of theoretical principles," *Lingua* 43: 129–70.
—— (1979) "Discourse without syntax," in T. Givón (ed.) *Discourse and Syntax*, New York: Academic Press.
Givón, T. (1976) "Topic, pronoun, and grammatical agreement," in C. Li (ed.) *Subject and Topic*, New York: Academic Press.
—— (1979a) *On Understanding Grammar*, New York: Academic Press.
—— (1979b) "From discourse to syntax: grammar as a processing strategy," in T. Givón (ed.) *Discourse and Syntax*, New York: Academic Press.
Hadlich, R. (1971) *A Transformational Grammar of Spanish*, Englewood Cliffs, NJ: Prentice Hall.
—— (1973) *Grámatica transformativa del español*, Madrid: Gredos.
Haiman, J. (1984) *Iconicity in Syntax*, Amsterdam: Benjamins.
Hopper, P. (1979a) "Observations on the typology of focus and aspect in narrative language," *Studies in Language* 3: 37–64.
—— (1979b) "Aspect and foregrounding in discourse," in T. Givón (ed.) *Discourse and Syntax*, New York: Academic Press.
—— (1988) "Emergent grammar and the a priori grammar postulate," in D. Tannen (ed.) *Linguistics in Context*, Norwood, NJ: Ablex Publishing Corp.
Hyman, L. (1971) "Consecutivization in Fe'fe'," *Journal of African Languages* 10 (2): 29–43.
Justus, C. (1976a) "Topicalization and relativization in Hittite," in C. Li (ed.) *Subject and Topic*, New York: Academic Press.
—— (1976b) "Syntactic change: Evidence for restructuring among coexistant variants," manuscript, Oswego: State University of New York.
Kuryłowicz, J. (1965) "The evolution of grammatical categories," *Esquisses linguistiques* 11: 38–54.
Laberge, S. and Sankoff, G. (1979) "Anything *you* can do," in T. Givón (ed.) *Discourse and Syntax*, New York: Academic Press.
Labov, W. (1972) *Sociolinguistic Patterns*, Philadelphia: University of Philadelphia Press.
Langdon, M. (1977) "Syntactic change and SOV structure: the Yuman case," in C. Li (ed.) *Mechanisms for Syntactic Change*, Austin: University of Texas Press.
Leech, G. (1971) *Meaning and the English Verb*, London: Longman Press.
Li, C. and Thompson, S. (1973a) "Historical change in word order: a case study in Chinese and its implications," in J. Anderson (ed.) *Proceedings of the First International Conference on Historical Linguistics*, New York: American Elsevier Publishing Co., Inc.
—— (1973b) "Serial verb constructions in Mandarin Chinese: subordination or coordination?" in C. Corum, T. Smith-Stark, and A. Weiser (eds) *Papers from the Comparative Syntax Festival*, Chicago: Chicago Linguistic Society.

Lord, C. (1973) "Serial verbs in transition," *Studies in African Linguistics* 4 (3): 269-96.
Meillet, A. (1912) *L'Évolution des formes grammaticales. Linguistique historique et linguistique générale*, vol. 1, Paris: Klincksieck.
Palmer, F.R. (1965) *A Linguistic Study of the English Verb*, London: Longman Press.
Real Academia Española, (1984) *Diccionario de la lengua española*, Madrid: Espasa-Calpe.
Sankoff, G. and Brown, P. (1976) "The origins of syntax in discourse: a case study of Tok Pisin relatives," *Language* 52: 631-66.
Stahlke, H. (1970) "Serial verbs," *Studies in African Linguistics* 1 (1): 60-9.
Thompson, S. and Mulac, A. (forthcoming) "A quantitative perspective on the grammaticization of epistemic parentheticals in English," in B. Heine and E. Traugott (eds) *Grammaticization*, Amsterdam and Philadelphia: John Benjamins.
Weber, E. (forthcoming) "Verbs of cognition: a discourse profile," in R. Fasold, D. Schiffrin, and P. Lowenberg (eds) *The Proceedings of NWAVE XIV* (1985), Amsterdam: Benjamins.
Webster's New Twentieth Century Dictionary, 2nd edn 1976, USA: Collins World.

Index of subjects

abstract (of a narrative), 59, 61–2, 66, 83–4
acquisition-of-knowledge predicates *see* knowledge predicates
actual/non-actual, 152
affirmation *see* assertive/non-assertive
Aktionsart (situation type), 2, 8, 14–16, 99, 101, 104, 106, 110–11
ambiguity 86, 91, 93, 114; *see also* multivalency
anaphora, anaphoric relation, anaphora approach, 2, 7–9, 11–13, 19–23
Arabic, 52
aspect *see* tense
assertive/non-assertive, 149–50, 157–61, 164–67, 173, 176, 179–81
autobiography, 64–7; *see also* narrator; first person
auxiliaries, 116, 124

background *see* foreground/background
basic meaning, 87, 89–90, 114
boundary signal *see* demarcative signal
Bulgarian, 46

Catalan, 147
change (of setting) *see* setting
clause: order, 5; types 3, 59
coda, 59–63, 69, 75, 83
cognition, verbs of, 194–211
comment, commentary, 14, 28, 39, 43, 70, 79, 176
commentative mode, 45, 49
communicative approach, 194–95, 210–11
communicative competence, 121, 143
competence, definition of, 142
complement type, 5, 206–9
complicating action, 43, 64–6, 80
compound past, 82; *see also* passato prossimo; passé composé
conceptual meaning, 123
conditional, 147, 161, 165, 175–6
conditional sentences, 165–8, 173–6
connectors, linking elements, 121–2, 124, 143
coordination, 136
current relevance *see* present relevance

degrees of focus/attention, 167–77; *see also* foreground/background
deictic zero point, 87, 89
deixis, 25, 31, 90; *see also* time adverbs
demarcative signal, 30, 78–9
detachment (and passé simple), 50, 83
diagesis, 28, 49
direct speech, 38, 45–6, 50, 105–10
discours, 43, 45
discourse: context, 1; functions, uses, 2, 45, 57, 113, 115, 210; origin of grammatical phenomena, 5; profile, 195, 208–11; relevance, 148, 160; representation structure,

9–10; saliency *see* foreground/background; signals, 4, 120–44
distance, temporal and psychological, 56, 58, 65–7, 83, 92–3, 113–15

embedding, 135
English, 9, 12, 31–3, 65, 114–15, 161, 165, 176, 180–82, 188, 200, 207
énoncé, 49; time frame of *see* story time
énonciation, 49; theories of, 120, 143
epistemic modal, 46
evaluation, 3, 59, 70–81, 83–4, 106, 108
event, 9–24
event (narrative) *see* foreground/background
expressive (functions, items) 75, 113

factives/semi-factives, 180–82
focalization, focalizer, 3, 27–30, 34–40, 42, 45–7, 49–52; *see also* narrator; point of view
focus of attention *see* foreground/background
foreground/background, 2–8, 23, 64, 80–1, 83, 104, 106, 115, 154–6, 158–60, 167–8, 170, 173–4; *see also* evaluation; degrees of focus; discourse relevance
formal linguistics, 210–11
free indirect discourse/style, 3, 30, 34, 49–50
French, 2–4, 7–24, 26–52, 65, 81, 86–117, 120–44, 188
function, functionalism, 120–3, 141–3
future, 38, 87, 114, 176; of the past, 34

Galician, 147, 154, 161
grammatical tradition, 120–1, 143
grammaticalization, 129, 194, 208, 210

hedges, 71
highlighting *see* foreground/background

histoire, 43, 45
historical present, 3, 42–3, 65–6, 69, 72–4, 78–81, 83–4, 86–117, 192
history, 64–7
homonymy, doublets, 128–30

immediacy *see* foreground/background
imparfait, 2, 7–24, 27–36, 43, 45, 50, 84, 86–7, 91, 93, 98–100, 110–12, 115–17
imperative, 4, 120–44
imperfective (aspect/past), 7, 32–3, 45, 63–4, 165, 175 (*see also* imparfait); vs. perfective 64, 98–113; *see also* simple past
implication, 15
indirect discourse/style, 50, 105–10
Indo-European, 138
informativeness, levels of *see* relevance, high-low
interior monologue, inner speech, 3, 30, 36–45, 49, 51
interjections, 124, 126–8
intonation contours, 5
inverted usage, 89–91, 113–15
irony, 6, 158, 187–8, 190
irrealis vs. realis, 152–3, 155, 165–70, 174–7
Italian, 2–4, 29–30, 49, 55–84, 95, 123, 125–8, 130–2, 143, 147
iterativity, 110–12

journalistic use/discourse, 3, 24, 83, 92–117, 148–62

knowledge predicates, 184–92

language, pragmatic definition of, 142
language change, 6
Latin, 4, 64, 147–8, 164, 195
Le Monde, 95–6
lexical choice, 5
linking elements *see* connectors
literature, literary usage, 27

markedness, 86–91, 112–13
mass-count and aspect, 50, 110–12, 117

216 Index of subjects

metanarrative *see* comment
modalization, 132–3
mood *see* subjunctive
morphological criteria, discourse signals, 130–2
multivalency, multi-semanticity, 3, 86–117

narrative (narration), 2–3, 13, 16–19, 22–4, 26, 30–1, 47, 51–2, 55–84, 92; structure of, 58–9, 83, 115; tense, 28, 65–6, 79–82, 84; *see also* narrator
narratology, 27, 47
narrator (narrative voice), 27–32, 34–9, 42–3, 45–6, 48–9, 51, 65, 106; first person, 30, 32–3, 37–40, 45–6, 49–50, 52
negation, 5, 77, 181–91; discourse signals and, 137
new/old information *see* presupposition
newspapers *see* journalistic discourse
non-specific meaning, 88–90
"now" (extended now), 30–6, 38–40, 43, 87–8, 92, 94, 99–100; *see also* deictic zero point

objectivity/subjectivity of representation, 3, 30–3, 40, 46, 48, 64–7, 75, 78, 82
Oksapmin, 46
orientation (of a narrative), 43, 51, 59, 63–4, 79

part-of-speech, word-class, 120–1, 123, 126–30
passato prossimo, remoto, 3, 55–84
passé composé, 14, 18, 26, 38, 45–6, 51, 84, 86–7, 91, 93–5, 98–100, 102–4, 110–12, 115–17
passé simple, 2, 7–24, 27–8, 31, 34–5, 45–6, 50, 83–4, 86–7, 91, 93, 98–100, 103, 110–12, 115–16; and detachment, 50, 83
perfect, 56, 102
perfective *see* imperfective
performed stories, 65
person, 141
perspective *see* point of view

pluperfect form/use, 4–5, 43, 63, 147–8, 154, 157, 160–1, 164, 166, 168, 173, 175–6
point of view, 2, 6, 8, 22–3, 26–52
polysemy, 86, 114
Portuguese, 147
pragmatic factors, 1–3, 8
pragmatic functions, 2, 4, 6, 26, 43, 45, 47, 51, 113, 123, 128, 132, 137–9, 142, 151, 154, 159
pragmatic viewpoint *see* function, functionalism
predication and discourse signals, 137–8
present relevance, 56–7, 65–6, 69, 82, 92–3, 100–4, 107–9, 113
present tense, 3, 29–30, 38, 42–3, 45, 51, 63, 65, 83, 86–117, 202; *see also* historical present
presupposition, presupposed knowledge, 5, 15, 149–51, 154–5, 158, 160–1, 173, 179, 191–2; semantic vs. pragmatic 182–3, 191
preterit, 31, 56, 62, 102
priority, high vs. low *see* relevance, high-low
pronouns, 9, 10, 124, 141; development of, 194
punctuation marks, 125, 143

-*ra* form (Spanish), 147–77
realis *see* irrealis vs. realis
recent past *see* distance
reference point, 10–13, 26, 34
referential function(s), 26, 47, 59, 74, 132, 141
register (switch), 65, 67, 83
relevance, high-low, 150–1, 154, 157, 160
reported speech *see* indirect discourse
resolution (of a narrative), 69, 75, 84
Romanian, 81, 147

self (narrative vs. experiencing), 30–3, 38, 40, 49
semantic: change, 175; coexistence, 117, *see also* multivalency; description, 124

Index of subjects

sentence, pragmatic definition of, 142
setting (change of setting), 2, 8, 16–24
Sicilian, 57–8, 62, 83
simple past (perfective aspect), 7, 12, 33, 82
situation type *see* Aktionsart
Spanish (including Castilian), 2–5, 43–5, 49, 52, 117, 125–8, 130–2, 143, 144, 147–62, 164–77, 179–92, 194–211
speaker *see* narrator
states, 9–24
story time, world, 28, 49, 84
stream-of-consciousness, 38
subjunctive mood, 4–5, 147–62, 164–77, 185; vs. indicative, 150–9, 167–8, 184–92; syntactic cues and, 153
synchrony and diachrony, 159
syntactic position, discourse signals, 138–40
syntax (syntactic function), 120–1, 124, 143; types, 194, 208, 210
system/use, 6

tense, definition of, 26; and aspect, 47; and cognition verbs, 201–2; shifts, alterations, 2–3, 6, 28, 40, 45, 55–84, 95, 102–5, 116; vs. aspect, 90, 117
time-adverbs, prepositions, 32–6, 43, 93–6, 101, 106
topic (temporal), 8, 13–14, 16–19
transitional/non-transitional events, 13–24
transitivity, 5, 196–200
truth value, 174, 180

Ute, 46

valency and discourse signals, 135
verbs of saying, verba dicendi, 50, 104–10
vividness *see* foreground/background
vocatives, 138

well-known information *see* presupposition
word-class *see* part of speech
written language vs. spoken, 109–10, 116–17, 125

Index of names

Aguilar, R. 199
Alcina Franch, J. 128
Anscombre, J. -C. 143
Auchlin, A. 123

Bal, M. 28, 48
Banfield, A. 31–3, 36, 49–50, 137
Barthes, R. 49
Bartsch, R. 17
Bazzanella, C. 123
Beauzée, N. 143
Bello, A. 165
Bellos, D. 50
Benildo Matías, H. 160
Bentivoglio, P. 5–6, 211
Benveniste, E. 43, 45, 65–7, 195
Berrendonner, A. 124
Bertinetto, P. 56, 82
Bleuca, J. 128
Blumenthal, P. 135
Blyth, C. 90
Bolinger, D. 88, 114–15, 148, 153
Boyer, H. 45–6
Brontë, C. 32–3
Bronzwaer, W. 50
Brooks, C. 48
Brown, P. 194
Bühler, K. 123
Bull, W. 165
Butor, M. 50
Bybee, J. 153, 165, 176

Calero, C. 161
Calver, E. 88, 114
Capus, A. 121
Casparis, C. 89, 109, 116

Centineo, G. 2–3, 6, 51
Cerquiglini, B. 49, 105
Chomsky, N. 143
Chung, S. 152
Chvany, C. 46
Cintas, P. 102
Cohn, D. 50–1
Comrie, B. 66, 87, 89, 98, 114–15
Cosnier, J. 143
Cravens, T. 4, 6, 117, 168, 176
Cuervo, R. 165
Culioli, A. 101

Dahl, Ö. 56, 84
Dale, G. 148
Damourette, J. 144
Danlos, L. 143
Dardano, M. 126
Deleddac, G. 29, 49
Desclés, J. -P. 102
Diver, W. 167, 176
Doležel, L. 47
Du Bois, J. 194–5, 210
Ducrot, O. 8, 13–14, 28, 143
Dujardin, E. 38

El Cid 154–6

Fillmore, C. 161, 183
Flaubert, G. 31–2, 34–5, 51
Fleischman, S. 2–3, 6–8, 23, 31, 45, 47, 49–51, 56, 58, 78–80, 83, 89–90, 113–14, 116–17, 165, 167, 175–76, 211
Fox, B. 167
Friedmann, K. 47

Index of names

García, E. 176, 210
Genette, G. 27–8, 38–40, 47–51
Givón, T. 1, 46, 164, 174, 194–5
Goosse, A. 126
Graham, M. 148
Grevisse, M. 87, 126
Gross, M. 127
Guitart, J. 5–6, 192
Gülich, E. 123–4
Gumperz, J. 143

Haberland, H. 50
Hadlich, R. 198
Hagège, C. 120, 124
Haiman, J. 166
Hamburger, K. 49–50, 89
Harris, M. 2, 6, 55–7, 81, 83, 165, 176
Harris, Z. 125
Herczeg, G. 49
Hernández Alonso, C. 151, 160
Hinrichs, E. 7, 12
Hoffmann, K. 51
Hooper, J. 153, 164, 166–7, 179–83
Hopper, P. 1–2, 7, 63–4, 167, 195, 210
Hugo, V. 2, 27–8
Hyman, L. 195
Hymes, D. 143

Jakobson, R. 113–15
James, D. 175–6
Jespersen, O. 165
Joyce, J. 32–3
Justus, C. 194

Kamp, H. 7–13, 23, 34
Kany, C. 160
Kartunnen, L. 181, 183, 188
Keenan, E. 181–3
Kempson, R. 183, 191
Kiparsky, C. 180–1
Kiparsky, P. 88, 180–1
Klein, P. 176, 182–3
Klein-Andreu, F. 2, 4, 6, 153–4, 164–5, 168, 174, 175–6
Kotschi, T. 123
Kuryłowicz, J. 194

Laberge, S. 195

Labov, W. 51, 58–9, 61, 64, 70–1, 74, 83, 196
Lamiroy, B. 4, 6, 138
Langdon, M. 194
Lanser, S. 47
Larochette, J. 87, 89
Larra, M. de 156–8
Lavandera, B. 154, 161, 167, 175
Lawrence, D. 47
Leech, G. 202
Lemon, F. 148
Lenz, R. 128, 160
Lepschy, A. 55–7
Lepschy, G. 55–7
Li, C. 195
Lo Cascio, V. 2
Longacre, R. 46
Lord, C. 195
Lundquist, L. 142
Lunn, P. 4, 6, 117, 154, 168, 176
Lyons, J. 67

Mallo, J. 148, 160
Manuel, D. 168–70
Marslen-Wilson, W. 174
Martin, R. 87, 116
Martin, W. 47
Martinez, M. 175
Matías, B. 160
Meillet, A. 194
Mendeloff, H. 174
Menendez y Pelayo, M. 51
Menendez-Pidal, P. 168
Molendijk, A. 7, 11
Montero, E. 165, 167–8, 174
Monville-Burston, M. 3, 6–8, 50, 83–4, 86–7
Morante, E. 57
Mourelatos, A. 117
Mulac, A. 207
Munro, P. 116

Nølke, M. 143
Nutting, H. 147, 166

Palmer, F. 194
Partee, B. 7–9
Pennhalurick, J. 167
Pérez Galdós, B. 157–8, 161
Pichon, E. 144

Polanyi, L. 50
Pouillon, J. 48
Pratolini, V. 56–7
Proust, M. 36–43, 50–1

Raimond, M. 38
Reid, W. 167
Ricoeur, P. 38, 48, 51–2
Rimmon-Kenan, S. 28, 50
Rivero, M. 186–7, 191
Rohlfs, G. 55–7
Rohrer, C. 7–8, 10–11, 13, 34
Rojo, G. 161, 165, 167–168, 174
Roulet, E. 124, 136
Rubattel, C. 124, 133, 136, 144

Saco Arce, J. 161
Sankoff, G. 194–5
Sartre, J.-P. 26
Schiffrin, D. 58, 78–9, 81
Scott-Moncrieff, C. 50
Searle, J. 132
Silva-Corvalán, C. 58, 78–9, 81, 148, 175
Silverstein, M. 143
Simonin, J. 95, 109, 114, 116
Sirdar-Iskandar, C. 136
Smith, C. 161
Solaún, C. 148
Solé, C. 149
Solé, Y. 149
Sperber, D. 158, 160
Spitzer, L. 50
Stahlke, H. 195
Stanzle, F. 47
Staubach, C. 148, 160

Swiggers, P. 4, 6, 120, 143

Tasmowski-De Ryck, L. 22–4
Tedeschi, P. 2
Terrell, T. 153, 164, 167, 179, 182–3
Thompson, S. 2, 167, 181, 195, 207
Timberlake, A. 152
Todorov, T. 48, 50
Trifone, P. 126

Uspensky, B. 47

Van Dijk, T. 52, 92, 97, 106, 116–17
Van Hoecke, W. 120
Vendler, Z. 12, 99
Verkuyl, H. 15
Vet, C. 2, 6–7, 11, 14–15
Vikner, C. 16
Vincent, N. 2, 6
Vitoux, P. 28, 48
Vizcaino Casas, F. 151

Waletzky, J. 51, 58–9, 61, 83, 115
Warren, R. 48
Waugh, L. 3–4, 6–8, 50, 83–4, 86–7, 91, 113
Weber, E. 5–6, 207
Weinrich, H. 7, 45, 49
Wilmet, M. 87–9, 109–10, 114, 116
Wilson, D. 158, 160
Wolf, F. 51
Wolfson, N. 58, 65, 78–9, 84, 114
Wright, L. 148, 153–7, 160, 165–6, 168, 174

Zaenen, A. 2